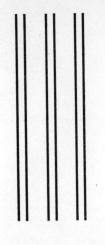

WHAT'S RIGHT
WITH
RACE RELATIONS

HARPER & BROTHERS   NEW YORK

WHAT'S RIGHT
WITH
RACE RELATIONS

Harriet Harmon Dexter

WHAT'S RIGHT WITH RACE RELATIONS

FIRST EDITION

K-H

Library of Congress catalog card number: 58-10362

To my
philosophical husband and discerning sister
—Than and Margueritte—
for whose insights and criticisms I am more
grateful than I have sometimes let them know

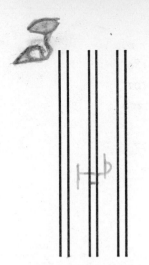

Contents

vii

Contents

1. What Date Is It?

The occasion was a dinner party in a county seat town in Missouri and the date was 1940. The hosts were a lawyer and his wife, and the guests were all friends of long standing except for a college president from another state. During a lull in the conversation the lawyer's wife announced joyfully, "Tom got Aunt Sally's case settled today."

There were comments of appreciation and then the hostess, realizing they had no meaning for the out-of-town guest, explained the reason for their rejoicing.

"For three generations Aunt Sally has cooked and cleaned for some of our families. I can remember as a child that I'd sit spellbound when she told us stories of her childhood back in the days of slavery. Her special charge was the only daughter in the master's family, a little girl only slightly younger than she was, and little Sally would stand for hours on hot summer afternoons and wave a fan over her young mistress while she read aloud. But as well as we've known Aunt Sally all these years, it was only a few months ago that we realized she wasn't drawing any kind of old age pension. Tom offered to help her fill out the application blanks. When he began asking her questions he found that she was in her nineties—she thought; and she'd been born in Missouri—she thought. But she had nothing that would be the equivalent of a birth certificate.

"What did you do?" the college president asked the lawyer.

"I started digging through old records and following one lead after another. Jim here"—he indicated the realtor—"helped me narrow the search to two plantations, only to discover that a fire had destroyed all the family records on one of them. But the great-granddaughter of the other plantation owner had a trunk full of ledgers and account books stored in the attic. There in a ledger marked 1850 was the entry of Aunt Sally's birth—among the livestock records."

"From slavery to social security in one lifetime!" exclaimed the college president.

The realtor smiled but shook his head. "I'm glad for Aunt Sally, of course, but in some ways it seems to me we're moving a little too fast."

"Too fast for whom?" asked the lawyer's wife.

"Well—sometimes Negroes aren't ready for everything we try to give them. There's no use pushing ahead of the times."

There, perhaps, is the nub of achieving equality for all races in a democracy. Who sets "the time"? All people do not live by the same calendar. When it was 1940 in Missouri it may have been 1900 in sections of Mississippi and already 2000 in some of the Quaker communities of Pennsylvania. What is meant by "ahead of the time"? "Behind the time"? "Up to date"?

Every generation has some persons who seem consistently to be ahead of their time. Such a person was Mary Church, a slender, vivacious Negro student at Oberlin College. In 1883, about to graduate, she presented a senior thesis entitled "Equal Rights for Women," and among the disfranchised she included Negro women. Mary had a good mind, the faculty agreed, but shook its composite head and bemoaned the fact that Mary Church had been born a hundred years ahead of her time. Her point of view was unrealistic, the men said. However, their evaluation did not dampen Mary's ardor; she knew that many idealists had been discounted as being unrealistic.

2

Mary Church became the first trained Negro social worker in Washington, D.C. Although concerned with the underprivileged of all races, she focused her energies on attempts to obtain clinics for undernourished Negro children and prenatal care for mothers.

After marrying Judge Robert H. Terrell, Washington's first Negro judge, she continued to plead with hospitals for beds for sick Negroes and with housing authorities for sanitary living quarters for her people. Everywhere she met the same reply, "You're moving too fast." Constantly Mary Terrell bumped her head against a social stone wall, but if she bruised her soul she kept the fact to herself and never let the wounds break her spirit. "Maybe I can reduce a hundred years to fifty," she said.

In 1951, two years before her ninetieth birthday, Mrs. Terrell, in company with white and Negro friends, was refused service in a Thompson restaurant in Washington. She was willing to be one of the complainants in a test case in the courts. The case reached the Supreme Court which ruled that under existing but long overlooked laws in the District of Columbia no person could be denied service on the basis of his color or race. This decision was the instrument which opened the eating places in Washington to Negroes. On her ninetieth birthday Mrs. Terrell was honored at a luncheon attended by seven hundred white and Negro guests, many of them distinguished persons in government services and professional fields. More than most individuals Mrs. Terrell had refused to be bound by "the times."

Just as every generation is prodded by those who act ahead of their time so is it retarded by those who act too late. In 1955, after the Supreme Court had handed down its decision that the public schools of this country were to be integrated, Senator James O. Eastland of Mississippi said to the people of his state, "You are not required to obey any court which passes such a ruling. In fact, you are obliged to defy it." Across the country many citizens said ruefully, "The senator was born a hundred years too late."

Not only individuals, but communities can be out of joint with the times. In 1950 a Milwaukee physician had offices in two buildings. In one he consulted with white patients and in the other with Negro patients. His home was in a white community and his daughter was registered in the first grade as a white student. Held in high esteem by other members of his profession and by his patients, he

3

had reached a secure status in the community when he died very suddenly. Arrangements were made for him to be buried in one of the newer cemeteries where he owned a lot.

His funeral, attended by many of his patients, both Negro and white, was in progress when an attendant of the funeral home tiptoed down the aisle to the row of seats in which were seated the members of the family—both Negro and white. The attendant quietly tapped one of the doctor's brothers on the shoulder; he rose and went out. In a few minutes the attendant returned and tapped another brother on the shoulder; he went out. A third time the attendant tiptoed down the aisle and tapped the third brother on the shoulder and he went out.

The brief service ended without the return of the brothers. When the other members of the family followed the casket out of the funeral home to form the cortege to move to the cemetery they were taken instead to a vault where the body was temporarily placed until a new lot could be bought in a different cemetery. After the funeral service had begun word had been telephoned to the cemetery officials that the doctor evidently was Negro. What if he did own a lot in the cemetery? Even dead, he was a Negro.

When in 1957 Chicago found itself with a time lag as great as that of its neighbor, Milwaukee, Chicago hastily tore a few sheets off its neglected calendar and brought itself up to date by passing an ordinance prohibiting discrimination in cemeteries.

Occasionally there are individuals or even groups of people who manage to telescope fifty years into a single year and still maintain their equilibrium, and as a result of their efforts others more easily make a social adjustment. Sometimes such action is spectacular, as in the case of the thousands of Negroes who maintained the nonviolent bus boycott in Montgomery, Alabama, in 1956. More often the action is unassuming and unpublicized, but no less effective in its impact. Such an experience came to the delegates at the Memphis convention of the Southern Baptist Women's Union in 1948. For guest soloist the program committee invited Mrs. Rosa Page Welch of Chicago, one of the nation's most moving interpreters of religious music. Her husband cautioned her that if she accepted the invitation she would have to be very careful what she said, and even more careful how she said it, because Memphis, as its citizens like to point out, is so close to Mississippi that it is often claimed as part of the Deep South. In fact, the saying goes that the Delta Country begins just outside the door of the Peabody Hotel.

However, Mrs. Welch accepted the invitation; then about two weeks later she received a letter from the chairman of accommodations apologetically explaining that she could not get a hotel reservation for Mrs. Welch but that she had secured accommodations in a pleasant Negro home. "It always puzzles me," Mrs. Welch commented later, "that white women are so taken back when they come face to face with the practices of a lifetime."

Mrs. Welch arrived in Memphis just in time to reach the convention hall for the first session at which she was to sing. The cab driver took her to the back door of the auditorium. She explained that she wanted the entrance used by the speakers—that someone was waiting to meet her just inside that door. But the cab driver could not bring himself to take her to that entrance, so they compromised on a side door.

However, Mrs. Welch located the president, who was arranging the order in which the participants on the morning program were to take their places on the platform. After their greetings Mrs. Welch, hoping to avoid any complications, suggested that since she was only to sing it might be better for her to step onto the stage just before her solo and then leave it again. But the president insisted that she wanted all the participants on the platform together, so Mrs. Welch took her place with the other women, all white. As she looked out across the room in which the women were sitting in plainly marked state delegations she wondered what might be going through the minds of some of those delegates. At the close of the session she excused herself as quickly as possible so as to avoid any embarrassment when it was time for the women to go to the dining room for lunch.

When Mrs. Welch returned for the afternoon session she was met by a committee chairman, under obvious emotional strain, who told her that the manager of the convention hall positively refused to let Mrs. Welch sit on the platform. Mrs. Welch assured her that she need not feel exercised; she would go back to her hostess' home and if the Lord wanted her to sing again He would help open the way.

"We're not through with this," the woman said as they parted. "You rest in your room until we call you."

Mrs. Welch waited for the telephone call—through the afternoon, the dinner hour, the evening session, the night. Then the next morning at half past seven she was called to the telephone and was asked to be at the auditorium at nine-thirty. When Mrs. Welch arrived she was greeted by two haggard but victorious women. "You're sitting on the platform with us," announced the president. The program chairman added, "And you're eating lunch with the rest of us."

On the surface, a simple announcement; but behind it lay the pressure of forty thousand Southern women who had insisted, through their officers, that their fellowship should transcend discrimination and that regardless of color they would worship together in the auditorium they had rented.

Commenting on that day's experience Mrs. Welch said, "I tried to imagine the courage it had taken for those women to fight for the right to have me sit on the platform with them. We all grew that day through an experience that was a victorious achievement for women who were willing to venture for the sake of the Kingdom."

Nearly ten years passed and in 1957 Mrs. Welch sang for another convention in another Southern city—Baltimore. This time she stayed with the other delegates at the Lord Baltimore Hotel, the first Negro to be received as a guest in that hotel. The privileges which she had often hoped would be enjoyed by her grandchildren had become her own. And perhaps few of the four thousand women who had been at Memphis realized how much their concerted action had contributed to bringing the dream to reality.

It is not alone Negroes and Caucasians who have been catapulted forward—or backward—with exceptional speed. Americans of Oriental background, especially the Japanese, have known similar changes in date lines. World War II, more particularly the attack on Pearl Harbor, produced a situation unprecedented in American history. Some seventy-five thousand American citizens of Japanese parentage, plus other thousands of foreign-born Japanese, were herded almost overnight into internment camps. Business and property losses to these people have been estimated at $300 million to $350 million. At the close of the war some of the internees returned to their former homes to gather up the shattered fragments of life, but many of them preferred to try a social climate more congenial than the West Coast. Approximately twenty-five thousand of them moved into Chicago where formerly there had been about four hundred Japanese. Among those who migrated to Chicago was the Hagiwara family. Today one of the sons, Abe, is director of activities at the interracial Olivet Institute. The story of his family's experiences, he feels, illustrates the time recession and succeeding time acceleration which within a ten-year span reduced the Japanese to internees in Relocation Centers—frequently referred to as "concentration camps"—and then raised them to a status which today is practically free of racial discrimination.

Abe Hagiwara's parents came from Japan about forty years ago and settled in a little colony of Swedish produce growers in Alaska, and young Abe was in his early teens before he completely realized that he was not just a black-headed Swede! His father's repeated statements that the world would never let a Japanese forget his nationality had little meaning for Abe until he came to the States to attend college. Then at the University of Washington he found Japanese graduate students selling vegetables, and engineering students employed at semiskilled labor with little hope of anything better.

Soon came Pearl Harbor and the immediate deportation of the adult Japanese males from Alaska to New Mexico, and the women, who had never become as Western as their husbands, felt very forsaken.

"At first my father was bitter," Abe Hagiwara recalls, "but basically he had a good sense of values and he realized that after all the Japanese were aliens, even if aliens from necessity and not choice, since the United States wouldn't let them become citizens. Then as soon as the Nisei were allowed to enlist my father had his two sons fighting with the American forces, and that fact pleased him."

After the war when the family moved to Chicago the elder Mr. Hagiwara was worried about looking for a job. His internment had made him sensitive to rebuffs and he feared that the sudden influx of Japanese in large numbers would create the same feeling of antagonism in Chicago which he knew existed on the West Coast. But he screwed up his courage and went job hunting and came home that first day with a good job in the cafeteria of the University of Chicago International House. He could hardly realize that such good fortune was his and what impressed him most was that nobody seemed to care that he was Japanese. Not long afterward he said contentedly, "Now at least I feel like an American citizen!" The elder Mr. Hagiwara died before the right of citizenship was granted the foreign-born Japanese. But his wife votes.

Although agreeing that discrimination against the Japanese has been nearly eliminated, a petite Nisei executive secretary of a Midwest organization added that when she returned to the West Coast to visit her family she frequently felt an undercurrent of antagonism such as she never experienced in the Midwest. While the clock differential was only two hours the attitude differential was a decade.

If the calendar for Americans of Oriental background has been brought practically up to date the same cannot be said for a large number of American Indians. Although it has long been common knowledge that some Indian tribes have forsaken the ways of their ancestors while others have clung tenaciously to their tribal customs, the passage of the Termination Act of 1953 brought into sharp focus the conditions which deter many Indians from adjusting to twentieth-century living. The act was aimed at making possible more rapid assimilation of reservation Indians into the free-moving population of the nation by terminating federal supervision and control of reservations. Such services were to be suspended on selected reservations where the Indians seemed ready to assume the total responsibilities of citizenship and competitive living; later, other Indian tribes were to be added to the list as they requested the discontinuance of federal services.

One provision of the act makes possible the relocation of an Indian wage earner and his family off the reservation, usually in an industrial city, by supplying them money for transportation, assistance in finding a job and living quarters, money for the purchase of furniture, for rent and food for the first month, and Blue Cross for a year. In 1957 approximately ten thousand people were relocated on an appropriation of $3,500,000. For those Indians who come from reservations which have an educational, social and health status equivalent to those of the surrounding communities the problem of adjustment in the city is minimized. But many Indians come to the relocation centers from backgrounds a century behind the new environment into which they are moving. The plight of these Indians is well illustrated by the experience of the Dan Crow family who had to telescope a half century into a two-day train ride.

One night in Chicago, Mr. Thomas Segundo, a New Mexico Indian recently appointed director of All Tribes Indian Center, received a frantic telephone call from a young and inexperienced social worker who had been sent to the railway station to meet the Crow family. She explained that she could not make the Crows understand her even enough to get them to move out of the corner of the waiting room. Mr. Segundo and his wife hurried down to Northwestern Station and there they found huddled together the young couple, two children clutching their mother's skirt, while strapped on her back was a beautiful cradleboard holding the youngest child.

The Segundos discovered that the Crows had not eaten a meal that day so they went together into the station restaurant. It turned out that the Crows came from a reservation only a few miles from Mr. Segundo's home in New Mexico, but the two men spoke entirely different languages so they could not talk together in their native tongues. Mr. Crow knew very little English and Mrs. Crow could neither speak nor understand a word of English.

Mrs. Crow represents a large number of Indians who are handicapped by having no knowledge of the English language. Only very recently have enough schools been provided the Florida Seminole Indians to make possible the enrollment of all their children. And for the Navajos that goal has not yet been reached. Throughout the country approximately 130,000 Indian children are in school; one-third of them are in federal schools—special Indian schools as opposed to public schools; and four-fifths of these children entered school unable to speak English. This situation means that the great majority of children in federal schools come from homes in which the adults speak no English. Educationally speaking, what is the date for American Indians?

In July, 1958, the Census Bureau estimated the population of the United States to be 174,000,000; roughly, 15,000,000 are Negroes, 450,000 are American Indians, 200,000 are of Asian background, the remainder are Caucasians; but the majority of Americans speak and understand a common language. In the United States an individual in a remote village can reach another person in an isolated town or a teeming metropolis by telephone in a matter of seconds. In the United States a person can fly from one coast to the other in a few hours. In the United States millions of people can simultaneously watch a political revolution in South America one minute and the next follow a safari in the heart of Africa. Yet, within this tightly knit nation there is an attitudinal spread of a hundred years or more.

Moving out from this nation, the problem becomes magnified. It is reported that many individuals when crossing the international date line in the Pacific are disconcerted because they lose or gain a day. If the loss of one day is frustrating, little wonder that the time difference of a millennium between racial groups in various parts of the world results in confusion and even suspicion in the minds of many people—people in Tunisia, Algeria, Ghana, Union of South Africa, Republic of Indonesia, Cuba, Pakistan, Egypt, France, Great Britain, the United States. For each of these nations "the time" means something different even in this day when time and space are being minimized.

Today the world is struggling to establish a date line—not Anno Domini but Anno Attitudinal. Many of the nations look questioningly at the United States, where, they say, are to be found the most ideal conditions for realizing good relations between the races: if they cannot be achieved in that country, why expect brotherhood any place in the world? For the people of the United States it may indeed be that establishing a nation-wide human relations date line which is synchronized with the nation's calendar year has taken on the urgency of meeting a deadline.

2. Search for a Culprit

Who can be blamed for the present-day tensions between the Negro and the white races in the United States? Most people, human nature being what it is, experience a sense of relief if they can pin onto someone else the responsibility for a bad situation, whether or not anything is done to remedy the evil. Or, if they must tackle the job, they do it with greater relish if they can convince themselves that the sin was not theirs. /

For a century the North has magnanimously tried to forgive the South for her part in the racial conflict, thereby imputing the South's original guilt; while the South has stanchly argued its inherent States' rights, thereby shifting the issue. Americans generally continue to blame the carpetbaggers, the Civil War, the cotton industry, the plantation system—far less often the colonial shipping industry of New England—the early aristocrats of Virginia, the economic system of the mother country, even the influence of Portugal. No one today is to blame! Everyone is grateful to Jeremiah for discovering that the children's teeth are set on edge by the sour grapes their parents have eaten. Obviously all this generation needs is a proficient painless dentist to work on its edgy political, economic and social teeth. But if one person had to be singled out for blame, some might select Queen Elizabeth I, because in 1562 during the first decade of her reign, the first African slaves were imported into England, mother of the colonies. By that time, however, Portugal had been dealing in African slavery for a century, having brought the first of them to the Spanish New World as early as 1503.

Actually the Queen had serious scruples about slavery. When Captain Hawkins arrived in England with the first African slaves, the Queen sent for him and made it clear that no Africans should be carried to England without their free consent. "It would be detestable and call down Heaven's vengeance upon the undertakers," she said. The captain promised to respect the Queen's wishes but did not keep his word. However, the Queen was evidently kept ignorant of the methods practiced for a contemporary records, "Here began the horrid practice of forcing the Africans into slavery, an injustice and barbarity which, so sure as there is justice in Heaven for the worst of crimes, will sometime be the destruction of all who encourage it." Once established, the lucrative slave trade was shared by the Portuguese, Spanish, Danes, French, Hollanders, British, and the American colonists.

Apparently the English Parliament never officially legalized the slave traffic. With the passage of time the government merely assumed the continuation of the trade while scrupulously avoiding the use of the word *slave*. Various acts covered the treatment of natives from Africa and the methods of obtaining them. While conscience tempered terminology, human chattelhood flourished. The demoralizing effects of the trade extended even to some of the African tribal chiefs themselves who, desiring their share of the profits, set their own villages on fire and then captured the fleeing inhabitants.

The slave trade flourished best in those countries whose economic development demanded a large supply of cheap labor. In the West Indies, African slaves were used to work the mines. In the American colonies they filled the needs of the early plantation owners, men poorly equipped by nature or training to do the manual labor required to develop large plantings. According to an early account, of the one hundred and five first permanent inhabitants in Virginia there were no men with families, few mechanics, and only twelve laborers. The others were men of fortune who hoped to increase their fortunes in this fabulous new country; or persons with dissolute habits and no occupation.

When in 1619 a Dutch man-of-war sailed up the James River and delivered twenty African Negroes for sale, Virginia's labor problem was on the way to being solved. At approximately the same time another ship unloaded ninety women "of good character" who had been sent from England to be sold as wives to the men in this woman-less colony; and Virginia's domestic situation began to improve. In the seventeenth century the purchase of a human being did not necessarily make him a slave; purchase was merely one way of obtaining a needed commodity. In all early colonies the practice of buying indentured servants for a period of time, many of them English, was a common procedure. However, before long the practice of buying and selling Africans became organized into a slave traffic.

In Virginia the slave-worked plantations had thrived for more than a hundred years when in 1733 Oglethorpe arrived in the New World with a group of poor and persecuted Protestant Europeans, plus a few Portuguese Jews, to found the colony of Georgia. Oglethorpe prohibited slavery in the colony on the grounds that the practice was both immoral and contrary to the laws of England. He also tried to maintain some standard of honesty in dealing with the Indians, in which effort he had the help of John Wesley for a year or two; but within twenty years Oglethorpe's high idealism was thwarted by practicalities. The nature of the settlers, many of them the riffraff of England and unaccustomed to work; plus the unyielding nature of the soil; plus the practice of slaveholding in neighboring Virginia and Carolina—all these factors combined to bring about the recognition of slavery in Georgia.

That slavery did not flourish in the Northern colonies cannot be explained, as many have tried to make it appear, solely on the ground that the Puritans had a higher ethical standard than did the other colonists. An added reason was that slavery was not compatible with the mode of life and the economic practices of the Northern colonists. New York and New England, with their smaller farms, needed no large supply of cheap labor. Besides, the sturdy New Englanders were a different breed from many of the early settlers. Coming from lower and middle class artisans they were extreme individualists who magnified the merits of hard work and austerity. They would till

their own soil with the help of a few "hired hands" who were usually white laborers. Therefore, although the consciences of both the
North and the South were troubled by the practice of slaveholding,
the North, because it depended less on slave labor, was in a better
position to be objective and to detect the moral evils of the system.

If the Calvinistic morality of New England had been strong
enough to put an early end to all connection with slavery the pages
of American history would be whiter. But the Yankees saw good
profit in supplying the ships in which the slaves were carried. By
the latter part of the eighteenth century Northern vessels, plying the
Atlantic with their reeking cargoes of human beings chained in the
holds, almost monopolized the transportation of slaves to America.
Moreover, many men in important government positions, including
a senator from Rhode Island, and many families in high social circles
owed their positions to the wealth they made from the slave traffic.
For several generations this source of income made Northern mer-
chants very touchy on the matter of ending the slave trade.

Yet even while slavery was developing into an extensive business
there were individuals and organizations in the colonies which strenuously opposed it. As early as 1696 the Society of Friends (Quakers)
had an organized opposition force and in 1776 they officially announced that action would be taken against any of their members
who held slaves. Many local congregations of various other religious
bodies also attacked slavery as an institution, but frequently kept
silent on the question of slaveholding, or else advocated that the
practice be eliminated gradually. To a Congregational church in
Rhode Island, whose pastor was Dr. Samuel Hopkins, goes credit
for being the first local congregation absolutely to end the practice
of slaveholding among all its members. There was no indication of
temporizing in the action taken by this congregation in 1769:

> Resolved, that the slave trade and the slavery of the Africans, as it has
> existed among us, is a gross violation of the righteousness and benevo-
> lence which are so much inculcated in the gospel, and therefore we will
> not tolerate it in this Church.

And they didn't.

By the latter quarter of the eighteenth century general revolt
against slavery was developing in the Western world. In 1792 Den-
mark became the first nation to end the traffic in Africans. At the

same time a strenuous campaign against the practice was being waged in England. Although many men were prominent in the struggle the name of William Wilberforce leads them all. A man of wealth and a member of the House of Commons, Wilberforce was converted to Evangelical Christianity and immediately organized his interests around reform measures, becoming especially devoted to the cause of stopping the slave trade. In 1788, in conjunction with reformer Clarkson and statesman Pitt, Wilberforce succeeded in getting a measure introduced into Parliament which called for an inquiry into the traffic, but the bill was lost. Between this date and 1799 Wilberforce brought onto the floor of the House seven bills calling for the end of the slave trade, but each was lost before passing both houses. Three times during the following five years he introduced bills and finally in 1807 he obtained passage of a measure stipulating that after May 1 of that year no vessel bound for slave cargo should clear any port within the entire British Dominion; further, that no slave should be landed in any British colony after May 1, 1808. By that time the American colonists were of course independent of Britain and were already fighting their own slavery issues on their own soil.

Even while the colonists were facing the possibility of war with the mother country they were gravely concerned with the slavery question. In September, 1774, the fall before the first shot of the Revolution was fired, a Congress of the Colonies was called in Philadelphia to consider a course of action. In preparation each colony held its convention to elect delegates and to draw up resolutions to be presented to the national assembly.

The Virginia Convention went on record: "Resolved, We will neither ourselves import nor purchase any slave imported by any other person after the first day of November next. . . ." Similar resolutions came from other Southern states. Such unanimity prevailed that the General Congress went on record: "That we will neither import nor purchase any slave imported after the first day of December next; after which time we will wholly discontinue the slave trade. . . ." Thus, two years before the Declaration of Independence announced to the world "that all men are created equal, that they are endowed by their Creator with certain unalienable Rights," the colonists had gone on record as opposing slavery.

However, they were still a little sketchy and inconsistent as to who was a slave. For instance, sixty-nine years after the introduction of slavery into South Carolina a statute was passed declaring that all Negroes, Indians, mulattoes, and mestizoes, except those who were then free, should be slaves. But no previous law had established who were free!

In Maryland a curious state of affairs resulted from a law which held that a free woman (even an English woman) married to a slave became the property of the master during the lifetime of the husband, and that the children of the marriage were slaves after the condition of the father.

When it came to drafting the Declaration of Independence the Founding Fathers tried to discredit the practice of slavery in this new nation. Their troubled thinking is apparent in the reworking of their Declaration, thinking frequently overlooked in the flag-flying, oratorical pronouncements of subsequent Fourth of July celebrations. But beside the desire of many of them to eliminate slavery they also had to keep in mind the frayed nerves and diverse points of view of the thirteen colonies. Thomas Jefferson wrote in his diary, "As the sentiments of men are known not only by what they receive, but by what they reject also, I will state the form of the declaration as originally reported." Following the original wording he then indicated the changes in the final draft necessitated by two pressure groups. The first group consisted of those Americans who wanted to give as little offense as possible to England; the second was composed of those who were loath to forego slavery. Jefferson's diary then states:

The clause, too, reprobating the enslaving of the inhabitants of Africa, was struck out in complaisance to South Carolina and Georgia, who had never attempted to restrain the importation of slaves, and who on the contrary still wished it to continue. Our northern brethren also I believe felt a little tender under those censures; for though their people had very few slaves themselves yet they had been pretty considerable carriers of them to others.

The deleted section on slavery reads:

He [the King of England] has waged cruel war against human nature itself, violating its most sacred rights of life and liberty in the persons of a distant people who never offended him, captivating and carrying them into slavery in another hemisphere, or to incur miserable death in their transportation thither. . . . Determined to keep open a market where

MEN shall be bought and sold, he has prostituted his negative for sup-
pressing every legislative attempt to prohibit or restrain this execrable
commerce.

From the vantage point of 1848, Horace Mann looking back upon
this earlier colonial period said:

The New England colonies, New Jersey, Pennsylvania, Virginia, presented to the throne the most humble and suppliant petitions, praying
for the abolition of the trade. The colonial legislatures passed laws
against it. But their petitions were spurned from the throne. Their laws
were vetoed by their Governors.

So the institution of slavery was carried over into the new United
States of America. During the thirteen years which elapsed between
the writing of the Declaration of Independence and the ratification
of the Constitution, the young republic experienced a new urge for
the freedom of all peoples. Personal letters and public speeches were
filled with unequivocal statements that slavery should immediately be abolished. Such a general wave of slave-freeing swept the
country that even while the drafting Convention was in session the
Old Congress passed the Northwest Ordinance of 1787 whereby
slavery was excluded forever from the territory that later became the
states of Iowa, Illinois, Indiana, Ohio, Michigan and Wisconsin.

Nevertheless there was an undercurrent of proslavery sentiment
among some of the men who drafted the Constitution, especially
those who came from slaveholding states. So in its final form the
Constitution contained three clauses usually referred to as the "great
compromises," one of which dealt with slavery. This latter provision
gave Congress power to pass navigation acts, an advantage to the
shipbuilding North; and for the South it guaranteed that the slave
trade could be continued for a period of twenty years.

That the people generally considered this clause to mean that
slavery would be abolished at the end of this twenty-year noninter-
ference period is clear, for at their ratification conventions state after
state expressed its sentiments. In the Pennsylvania convention James
Wilson said, "I consider this clause as laying the foundation for ban-
ishing slavery out of this country; and though the period is more distant than I could wish it, it will produce the same kind, gradual
change as was produced in Pennsylvania," where slavery had been
eliminated on a twenty-eight-year plan. "If there was no other feature

in the Constitution but this one, it would diffuse a beauty over its whole countenance. Yet the labor of a few years, and Congress will have power to exterminate slavery from within our borders."

In the North Carolina convention James Iredell, later an associate justice of the United States Supreme Court, expressed the opinion, "When the entire abolition of slavery takes place, it will be an event which must be pleasing to every generous mind, and every friend of human nature."

By 1840 when the slavery issue had come to dominate the thinking of the country—political, economic, religious—many states had virtually eliminated slavery within their borders. Connecticut had reduced the number of her slaves from 2,759 to 17; Rhode Island counted five among her population; and New York had freed 10,000 slaves in a single day. The total number of slaves in the states commonly considered nonslaveholding had fallen from 46,009 to 1,129. At the same time, in the so-called slaveholding states a reverse trend had developed. In South Carolina alone the slaves numbered 327,038; and the total slave population in these states had grown to 2,386,126.

During this era, 1790–1840, abolition societies sprang up in many states, not only in the North but in some Southern states as well. The Maryland and Virginia abolitionists had especially active organizations, and all the abolition societies kept a stream of petitions pouring into Congress requesting that it assume its rightful role in bringing about the abolition of slavery. From Virginia came a memorial reading, "Your memorialists . . . lament that a practice so inconsistent with true policy and the inalienable rights of men should subsist in so enlightened an age, and among people professing that all men are by nature equally entitled to freedom."

Over the signature of Benjamin Franklin, Pennsylvania petitioned ". . . that you will be pleased to countenance the restoration to liberty of those unhappy men, who, alone in this land of freedom, are degraded into perpetual bondage. . . ."

From the debate on this stream of petitions it is also clear that both the North and the South expected Congress to regulate slavery. There is no indication that any state considered Congress a meddlesome body if it assumed this power, or considered that the control of slavery was a state's right.

What happened to turn a nation once united in its desire for freedom for all people into two embittered camps that would eventually settle their differences on the battlefield? Out of the many events and movements which help explain the change four trends stand out clearly.

First of all, that fervor for freedom which had carried the Revolution to victory, which had spoken to the world in the Declaration of Independence, and which had later been formulated into the Constitution of the United States—that fervor had cooled. With freedom guaranteed to themselves and their posterity the original proponents of the cause had settled back in the lethargy that often follows extended effort and the exhilaration of success; while the second and third generation citizens had never experienced the passionate urgency for the guarantees of freedom which their fathers once knew.

A second trend that affected the thinking of the people lay in the changes which had taken place in religious thought. The terrific God-centered morality of the preaching of Jonathan Edwards and other leading divines had become watered down by their successors. When Edwards pictured "sinners in the hands of an angry God" men shuddered at the thought of God's holding them over the fiery pit of hell as a man might hold a spider over some burning coals. Thus when Edwards said that slaveholding was "a greater crime than fornication, theft or robbery," it was looked upon as a sin. But by 1849, when Professor Moses Stuart of Andover Theological Seminary had become the leader of religious thought, the interest of the theologians had shifted from the wages of sin to more intellectual matters. Proudly hailed as "the father of the science of biblical criticism in America," Stuart's academic arguments occasioned little soul searching on the part of the average person. Although many individual preachers were passionate and eloquent in their pulpits the religious thinking of the day reflected the impersonal impact of the scientific method, and conviction of sin was no longer the motivating factor in men's lives that it once had been.

Another explanation for the decline of fervor for freedom is to be found in the development of a certain kind of aristocracy which had always existed in this country. In 1852 William Goodell, journalist and student of constitutional law, wrote of an "aristocracy of intellect, combined to a great extent . . . with high moral worth . . . a conscious superiority of intelligence and character and a distrust in the capacities of the mass of people for self-government." For a century exponents of this aristocracy had played important roles in American life: John Adams of New England, Alexander Hamilton, one of the writers for the *Federalist* and first Secretary of the Treasury, and other men who had put the interests of the nation before their own interests. On grounds of morality and humanity many of these men had freed their own slaves. However, never having had complete faith in the ability of the common man such intellectuals did not suffer mental anguish when the most inferior group of people in the nation, the Negro slaves, were deprived of equality in civil rights.

A fourth factor contributing to the entrenchment of slavery was found in developments which today would be termed technological advances. The invention of the cotton gin in 1793 by Eli Whitney was the first step in the mechanization of the cotton industry. Where formerly the bolls had to be cleaned by hand, a slow process of separating the seeds from the cotton, with one of Whitney's hand-worked gins one man could do the work of ten; with a horse-operated gin one man could replace fifty. So fast did the cotton industry grow that in a single year twenty thousand slaves were imported into Georgia and South Carolina to work the cotton fields. By 1850 the South was supplying three-fourths of the world's cotton, and if she was to hold this lead she had to have slave labor.

During all this development the North remained economically tied to the South through the developing textile industry in New England. But after the importation of slaves had been discontinued and the North had lost its lucrative slave-transporting business it began to look with increasing abhorrence at the institution of slavery.

A final factor in the cooling devotion to freedom during these decades was that the slaveholders of the South, although a minority of the total population, were men of wealth, of political power, of social prestige; they were The South for all practical purposes.

Hardly is there an American who does not know the course of events and the growing tensions in the decade before the Civil War. Regional recriminations, bitter hatreds between formerly close friends, families split over the issues of States' rights and slavery; political compromises and other expedients; territorial fights over slave or free populations; a nation torn in two.

Then Civil War.

A united nation emerged but a divided people survived. Nor did the days immediately following the war tend to unite them. These were the days of the corrupt carpetbaggers; of freed slaves with no place to go; of plantations with no one to work them; of uneducated and inexperienced ex-slaves facing a world of political and economic competition; of people in general trying to piece together a nation from material of unequal tensile strength, with no pattern to guide them.

But out of the confusion emerged several new patterns. And one of them was segregation.

3. *Segregation—A State of Mind*

Segregation as practiced in the United States has not been an attempt to keep people apart. Nor is it today. It is an attempt to keep them separate in those relationships where togetherness would suggest equality. In a segregated society members of two races may work together as long as one does labor subservient to the other. Two races may live in adjoining neighborhoods with equanimity as long as their houses are separated by an alley rather than facing each other across an avenue. Members of two races may prepare a meal together but one of them must eat in the kitchen. The races may worship the same God if they do so in separate buildings; or even perhaps in the same sanctuary if an invisible line separates their seating.

This particular concept of segregation is of course a carry-over from slavery, an institution which developed a state of mind as well as a state of society. The steps by which the mental attitudes of white Americans were formed are as discernible as the steps by which political and economic policies were formulated. By the fourth decade of the nineteenth century the thought processes which had made possible a society based upon the superiority of one segment of the population had been incorporated into laws. A volume entitled *A Practical Treatise of the Laws of Slavery*, published in 1837, contains "all the decisions made on that subject in the several courts of the United States and the state courts." One section of the table of contents reads: "Of Slaves Considered as Property; when considered as real property; when considered as personal property." Another section deals with: "The Incapacity of Slaves; to make a contract; to take by devise, descent or purchase; to be a witness; to be a party to a suit; to contract matrimony." For many decades before the war life in the South had been regulated by such legal considerations.

As early as 1812 a South Carolina court ruled that slaves "are generally considered not as persons, but as things." In 1819 a Louisiana court contended that slaves have no legal right to marry; that with the consent of their master they may enter into such a contract but "it cannot produce any civil effect because slaves are deprived of all civil rights."

In Kentucky a case was tried in 1823 involving the right of a slave owner to will to his son a female slave, Pen, but to will to his daughter the increase of the slave from the date of making the will. The court upheld the will on the basis that "he who is the absolute owner of a thing owns all its faculties for profits or increase."

On the question of the status of children born to a free mother and a slave father a New York court in 1822 handed down the decision that policy and humanity would dictate that the children follow the condition of their mother and that "she should have exclusive custody and control of them as though their father was dead."

Ideas are seldom changed overnight, and the basic philosophies of a group are not eradicated by the signing of a treaty. The concerted thinking of a people is modified slowly and in the meantime life goes on with many philosophies and attitudes running at cross purposes. After the war belief persisted that slaves were actually the "things" the courts had ruled them to be. Even the Thirteenth Amendment which abolished slavery in the United States in 1865 could not abolish the deeply entrenched attitudes of many toward those who had been slaves.

Some of the Southern states hardly knew what to do with the suddenly emancipated slaves. North Carolina extended to them the same status held by former free persons of color, which was something higher than a slave but lower than equality with white men; Louisiana required that every Negro be attached in regular service to some white person who became responsible for his conduct; and Mississippi required every Negro to carry on his person written evidence that he had a home and an occupation.

Although between 1866 and 1875 a special series of civil rights acts was passed by Congress to safeguard the rights of this anomalous new group of citizens, it remained for the Fourteenth and Fifteenth Amendments to the Constitution in 1868 and 1870 to stipulate that no person should be deprived of life, liberty or property without due process of law; and that no citizen's right to vote should be abridged because of race or color. Further, the Fifteenth Amendment delegated to Congress power to punish any state abridging this right to vote. But even the ratification of these amendments failed to raise the Negroes to the same status before the law as was enjoyed by white citizens.

Then in 1896 the Supreme Court settled the now-famous Plessy *vs.* Ferguson case and the "separate but equal" principle was firmly established. Although this decision legally upheld segregation only on trains the principle involved was accepted as covering all contacts between the races. The result was separate schools, separate jail accommodations, separate playgrounds and parks, separate doors to public buildings, separate stairways, drinking fountains, pay windows and ticket windows. In some places separate Bibles were required in courts for use in administering oaths to Negroes and white people. Separation became the trademark of a large part of a nation which a century earlier had stated in its Declaration of Independence, "with a firm reliance on the protection of Divine Providence, we mutually pledge to each other our Lives, our Fortunes, and our sacred Honor."

Today many people who are outspoken against segregation nevertheless realize that at the close of the Civil War some demarcation between the races may have been the only framework within which they could have operated; also that within that framework all relations between the races were not antagonistic. Countless Southern families continued to care for their former slaves until they could maintain themselves. That same kind of protection an adult gives to an insecure child many Southern families gave to the inexperienced Negroes around them.

Had relations between Negroes and whites been the only racial concern of America during the first two hundred seventy-five years of her existence, life would have been more simple for the citizens of those decades—as well as for those that followed. But simultaneous with the problems resulting from Negro-white contacts there were the complications that arose from Indian-white contacts. For these tensions also segregation was the hoped-for solution, but segregation according to a different pattern from that accorded the Negroes.

Early in their colonization of the New World the English discovered that the American Indians could not easily be enslaved; and that the few who were reduced to slavery were most unsatisfactory in that capacity. It seemed equally impossible to create a co-operative society out of peoples whose cultures were centuries apart in their development. However, the white settlers needed the land which the Indians possessed; and to a people who considered themselves superior, the logical way of obtaining that land was to dispossess the inferior owners.

The conflict between the red man and the white man which began in Virginia during the days of John Smith and in New England during the first month of the Pilgrims' sojourn on the continent, followed the westward trek of the white settlers. When after a century and a half of colonial life the thirteen colonies pooled their problems and their fortunes to form a new nation, the republic assumed the warfare with the Indians which the colonies had previously carried as their separate concerns. Almost immediately the new federal government tried to regulate Indian-white relationships by treaties with the result that between 1795 and 1809, forty-eight million acres of land were taken from the Indians.

In 1824, in order to better handle the mounting troubles with the Indians, Congress created a Bureau of Indian Affairs within the War Department. Since the purpose of the bureau was to promote peaceful relations it was often embarrassed to be part of the department that was carrying on war with the Indians. In 1849, when the Department of the Interior was created, common sense suggested that the Indian services be transferred to this department.

Two centuries of conquest and several decades of treaty making and breaking lay behind the United States when in 1835 President Andrew Jackson referred to the Indian situation in his annual message: "The pledge of the United States has been given by Congress that the country destined for the residence of this people shall be forever 'secured and guaranteed to them.' " Nevertheless as the lands guaranteed to the Indians became important to the white men in their continuous and often frenzied push to the West, the security promised the Indians was overlooked. They continued to be obstacles to be removed, not human beings to be respected.

The first important change in relations between the United States government and the Indians came in 1871 when Congress put an end to treaty making and declared that it would legislate for the tribes as it did for the rest of the inhabitants of the country. There would be no more dealing with the Indians as separate nations. However, the new policy did not obviate the old hazards; there continued to be no uniformity in the cultural and economic development of the tribes; some were partially self-supporting while others depended on poorly organized governmental or charitable sources for subsistence; some were rebellious, some apathetic; and apparently all faced eventual extinction. With the introduction of the new system of supervision by Congress the Indians faced a new hazard —regulation of their tribal affairs, and often their personal affairs, by a body of lawmakers far removed from the people whom they were to supervise; removed in space, in time, and in interest. But for the time being, at least, the Indians were segregated on their reservations and either overlooked by the white population or given mere token consideration by the white fathers in Washington.

With the Indians thus unhappily contained on scattered locations and the Negroes unwillingly confined to a position of inferiority the rest of the citizens of the United States might have enjoyed a few years free of harassment in which to think out an interracial philosophy; but already Chinese coolies were beginning to trickle into California. The trickle rapidly became a stream and by 1852 the stream had become a torrent. That year—three years after the gold rush—eighteen thousand Chinese arrived in San Francisco, a city of only thirty-seven thousand population. Then almost as suddenly the demand for Chinese laborers ceased. With the completion of the transcontinental railroad in 1869, men from all parts of the United States swarmed into California and soon San Francisco had three men for every available job. In this situation the feeling of paternalistic kindliness which Californians had once felt toward the "little yellow man" turned to hatred as competition for jobs became more keen. Once hailed by the mayor of San Francisco as "the best immigrants in California," the Chinese became the "Yellow Peril." By 1871, according to the governor of California, the Chinese were "avaricious, ignorant of moral obligations . . . and dangerous to the welfare of the state." In the same period a special report to the supervisors of San Francisco contained the sentence: "The beasts of the field, the vagrant dogs that the poundmaster gathers upon the streets to put to death by drowning, are vastly better worthy of our commiseration than the whole Mongolian race when they seek to overrun our country and blast American welfare and progress with their miserable, contaminating presence."

The Chinese, forced to withdraw from as many contacts with white people as possible, holed up in Chinatowns where crowded tenements, lack of sanitation and police protection won for them the reputation of being "centers of filth and dens of iniquity." The people were blamed for the conditions under which they lived, rather than the conditions being blamed for the diseases, physical and moral, which would have been bred in any people. As far as the white Americans were concerned, the Chinese were effectively segregated.

But already the Japanese were quietly immigrating to the West Coast and as the newest emigrants automatically fell heir to the lowest and most menial jobs. Arriving first in 1884, within six years they were coming in sufficient numbers to draw attacks equal to those which the Chinese had previously received. Oddly enough, the Japanese were hated for traits which Americans had always considered virtues. They were industrious, skillful, intelligent, ambitious; and instead of being willing to live in ghettos, they wanted homes in good parts of the cities. They incorporated too many traits that made people successful, and thus became a threat to Americans. Gradually the emigration of the Chinese and Japanese was restricted until in 1924 the passage of the Exclusion Act providing that "no alien ineligible to citizenship shall be admitted to the United States" virtually stopped it altogether, since the privilege of becoming citizens had never been granted the Orientals.

At the same time that the United States was closing its west door it was throwing wide open its east door so that the latter half of the nineteenth century saw the beginning of an emigration unparalleled in history. The invitation inscribed on the pedestal of the Statue of

Liberty became a personal message from this country to the discouraged of Europe:

> . . . *Give me your tired, your poor,*
> *Your huddled masses yearning to breathe free,* . . .
> *Send these, the homeless, tempest-tost to me,*
> *I lift my lamp beside the golden door!*

In the twenty-five-year period, 1870–95, the British Isles alone sent three million immigrants to this country; the Germanic peoples another three million; the Scandinavian states, more than a million; the Slavic peoples, slightly under a million; and the Latin countries about the same number. More than ten million people entered the United States during those twenty-five years. For another quarter of a century immigration continued, although at decreasing rates. These people found work, homes, a new lease of energy, and they became an accepted part of American life. Today a person rarely says, "I am a Norwegian," or "I am an Italian"; rather he remarks, "My grandparents were Norwegian," or "My folks came from Italy"; the generation born in this country is merely American. So completely have European peoples been fused into Americans that nationality tags are commonly used only for purposes of identification, not separation. However, the use of racial origins as labels is a different matter; discrimination is implied. In most minds "American Negro" does not suggest an American who happens to be of Negro, or partly Negro, origin. It means a Negro—who happens to live in the United States.

Today as a nation we are in a position which demands a considered choice between being tossed about by conflicting currents of thought or steering a purposeful course. The Constitution as interpreted by the Supreme Court has set a course; as the populace accepts it this country will move into a society commonly described as integrated. Like many words that come into popular use during periods of strain, *integration* has come to have unhappy connotations. "We don't use the word *integration* here in North Carolina," said a schoolteacher. "It makes people see red—or black." And a Louisianan commented, "We prefer *mongrelization* to *integration*." The Rev. Robert B. McNeill of Columbus, Georgia, suggests that since 1955 the word *integration* has become so weighted with emotion that it has lost its true significance. He offers the term *creative contact* as best suggesting the present desired objective.

28

Whatever word may be the best to use, the idea inherent in integration can stand scrutiny. Coming from a Latin word meaning "to make whole" *integration* denotes a one-ness of parts. An integrated society is one in which the parts fit together in a well-ordered whole. But society is not an abstract term; society is people. So the aim of an integrated social order is to make possible the experience of one-ness for all its members—equal opportunity to contribute to society and receive the benefits from society on the basis of co-operation and mutual respect. Such a union of interests does not mean a one-level society. Men vary in their capacities and abilities, just as they vary in their willingness to contribute to the common good. However, it does mean a society in which every man has the opportunity to achieve all that he can achieve. Therefore the first step in integration is to eliminate discrimination.

The Commission on Human Rights of the United Nations defines discrimination as "a detrimental distinction based on grounds which may not be attributed to the individual and which have no justified consequences in social, political or legal relations (color, race, sex, etc.), or on ground of membership in social categories (cultural, language, religious, political or other opinion, national circle, social origin, class, property, birth or other status)."

Removal of discrimination, of which segregation is one form, is only the first step in creating an integrated society. If all discriminatory practices were thrown on the junk heap tomorrow an integrated society would not result. In housing, for example, ordinances may direct that a project be open to members of every race. Ordinances might even require that families of different races be located alternately in checkerboard fashion. By this order discrimination and segregation would be abolished and in a loose use of the word the building might be said to be an integrated housing unit. But if there resulted no community of interest, no desire for mutual helpfulness, there would be no true integration. The same criteria apply to other relationships—in churches, labor unions, schools and public facilities. Any group can know when it has achieved the goal because the final mark of an integrated society is that it is no longer conscious of its integration.

4. *The Right to Civil Rights*

When it was announced that the Negro vote in the 1956 National elections was estimated at 3,000,000 there was rejoicing in many quarters. This number represented a large increase over the 1,200,000 vote in 1952 and the 500,000 vote in 1944. Also the fact that the number had to be an estimate encouraged many people, for it suggested that at least on registration blanks citizens were just citizens and color or nationality no longer mattered. But although the total number of Negro voters was increasing, in many communities fewer Negroes were seen at the polls.

For instance, the 1955 report of the National Association for the Advancement of Colored People (NAACP) indicates that during the twelve-month period which it covers the registered Negro vote in the Southeast states was reduced from 22,000 to 8,000. Early that year the Negro leaders in Humphreys County, Mississippi, had felt encouraged when the registered Negro vote reached a new high—400 out of the county's 16,012 Negroes. But by the end of the year one lone Negro voter, Mr. Gus Courts, remained on the registration lists with 7,013 white voters. The other names had been withdrawn because of economic pressures and threats of violence.

One of Mr. Courts's associates who refused to take his own name off the list after several warnings from white groups was killed by a shotgun blast. At the inquest lead bullets were found in his mouth, but the sheriff thought they might have been fillings from his teeth. When the FBI identified the lead as having come from a shotgun, the sheriff conceded the case looked like murder; but he made no arrests. Still Mr. Courts hung tough, and the going got tougher. The rent on the building in which he operated a grocery store was raised from $25 to $75 a month. His credit was cut off, and when wholesalers refused to sell to him he was left with almost empty shelves. On the night of November 25, he was shot, but in time recovered from the wounds.

the This denial of the right to vote is an extension through ninety years of a form of protection established by the white South during Reconstruction days. These were the days when scalawags and carpetbaggers threatened the political and social integrity of many communities. The scalawags, who were Southern white opportunists, most of them Republicans, used the newly liberated slaves as a "front" to gain political power for themselves. They teamed up with the equally unscrupulous carpetbaggers—Northern politicians who rushed in to fill the vacuum created by the economic and political collapse of the South. In many sections the frauds perpetrated by this postwar leadership produced intolerable conditions: more Negro voters were registered than there were Negroes in an area's population; Negro voters were escorted by white leaders from one precinct to another to cast a ballot at each voting place; ballots were inspected before being cast into the ballot box; Negroes voted as told to vote without even knowing the names of the men running for office.

In the first post-Civil War elections in seven Southern states carpetbaggers put into office four governors, ten out of fourteen United States senators and thirty-five members of the House. Northern Negroes were placed in some of these offices but others were held by recently liberated slaves, men with no education, training or experience in government. In Issaquena County, Mississippi, all five county supervisors were illiterate Negroes.

Misappropriation of funds was common. One governor who had been put into office by the carpetbaggers was later found guilty of confiscating and selling the food sent into his state by the Freedmen's Bureau for the relief of former slaves. Another governor received $15,000 for approving a certain printing bill. Salaries of state officials were doubled, trebled, and sometimes multiplied many times over. In Alabama, before the war a circuit judge received $13,500 but during the Reconstruction period his salary soared to $36,000; while the salaries of the governor's clerks jumped from $500 to $5,400. In 1868, among the delegates to the South Carolina reconstituting convention seventy-six were Negroes whose only qualification was amenability as pawns of white politicians. Other conventions were madhouses of noisy Negro ruffians and scheming white politicos.

However, when occasionally competent Negroes, such as Frank Cardozo of South Carolina, were put into office they brought credit to their constituency. Cardozo was a free-born Negro with some Jewish and Indian ancestry who had been educated in Glasgow and London and had served as a Presbyterian minister in New England before coming to Charleston. As secretary of state for South Carolina and later as its secretary of the treasury he served ably. Mississippi also found in Robert Gleed a capable leader and an honest senator. Although a slave until liberated at the end of the war, he had some education, was a good speaker, financially stable, and tactful.

During this period the South frequently pointed out that the North, which boasted of its free and economically independent Negroes, had never elected one of them to office. Instead, Southerners commented, in helping to saddle the South with untrained Negro officials, Northerners forced the Negroes to bear the brunt of the tensions and hatreds that developed while the irresponsible politicians took the loot of office and high-tailed out of the country. One Negro editor summed up the matter: "When the smoke and fighting is over the Negroes have nothing gained and the whites have nothing left, while the jackals have all the booty."

The intellectual South, once it regained control of its politics, reasoned that the surest way to prevent a repetition of Negro office-holding was to strip the Negroes of all political power. Toward this end the Negroes had to be disfranchised; if none could vote none would ever be elected to office. But how could the Fifteenth Amendment which guaranteed them the right to vote be by-passed? The answer was found in the amendment itself which granted to Congress the power to pass legislation to enforce the provisions of the amendment. Since such legislation had never been enacted, the South could act first.

Some states took their stand on the theory that exercise of the franchise was a privilege which should be enjoyed only by those capable of exercising it intelligently. Thus in 1890, Governor Benjamin R. Tillman, upon assuming his duties in South Carolina, said, "The whites have absolute control of the government and we intend at any hazard to retain it. The intelligent exercise of the right of suffrage is as yet beyond the capacity of the vast majority of the colored men." However, the governor remarked further that he saw no reason why the two races should not live peaceably together—the basis for peaceful living being, of course, recognition of white supremacy.

Other states took the position that the state as such could not deny any citizen the right to vote, but organizations within the state—a club or even a political party—could set up their own standards for membership. Since at that time the South was solidly Democratic, and since there was no opposition from a second party, the candidate who won the Democratic nomination was as good as elected to office. The Democratic party, so the argument went, was a private organization and could set its rules for membership. It simply admitted no Negroes. Therefore no Negroes could vote.

Still other states required every voter to pay a poll tax, including payment in full for all years he might be in arrears. A three, two, or even one dollar per annum tax became an insurmountable obstacle to the man, Negro or white, whose annual cash income was well under $500. If he was unable to pay the tax for two years he was practically disfranchised for life. In addition, payment did not guarantee voting. A would-be voter might also be required to demonstrate his ability to read or to reasonably interpret any clause in the Constitution—always to the satisfaction of white registration officials. Sometimes ability to write selected clauses was required. Obviously most Negroes were thereby disfranchised, but so were many whites who were as poor and as illiterate as the Negroes.

At length someone came up with an expedient for disfranchising Negroes only—the grandfather clause. According to this provision any citizen could vote if he had an ancestor who had possessed the right to vote in 1867—the year before Negroes were given that right —or if he had an ancestor who had fought in the army or navy of

33

the Union or Confederacy. If in spite of these legal precautions a Negro tried to register to vote he still faced the process of elimination by discriminating treatment. Registering boards kept Negroes in line for hours only to close the doors on them, with the suggestion that they come again, at which time the treatment was repeated. Also, registering officers found it a simple matter to discover technical mistakes in Negroes' application blanks. Then if by chance a Negro still qualified on any grounds he could always be eliminated by intimidation or violence. The fact that these restrictions proved effective is a matter of historical record. That some of them are still used as deterrents to voting is a matter of contemporary record.

It is a puzzling situation that a state may restrict voting privileges guaranteed by the Constitution. The adoption of certain restrictive devices—such as the White Primary and the Boswell Amendment—has been facilitated by the power of the states, under the Constitution, to regulate the time, places and manner of elections for Congress. Further, considerable time and money are required in order to obtain a Supreme Court ruling invalidating state laws which disenfranchise Negroes. First the rights of someone who is willing to sue must be violated, since the courts will pass only on a particular controversy—not on a state law as such. Then there is the slow process of carrying the case up the ladder from the trial court to the Supreme Court, and for various technical reasons a given case may never reach that Court. Although a Supreme Court ruling counter to a state law is authoritative and final, a recalcitrant state may always invent a new device whose validity must again be tested through the courts.

Since such a court process is very involved and very expensive, most persons of any color will endure a large amount of injustice before going to court. In addition, if it is known that public opinion, and hence probably jurors, is against the desired decision, proponents of the case are likely to be doubly cautious in taking a losing chance.

Late in 1956 many people, both Negro and white, wanted to precipitate a test case on segregation of public buses in Atlanta, Georgia. But in order to make a case someone had to ride a bus, sit in the wrong section, be publicly arrested, and from there on take the consequences. Six Negro ministers took the risk. The case is still in the courts.

Occasionally white citizens disobey a segregation law, using this act as a means of expressing their disapproval of discrimination. After the Civil War Mary Curtis Lee, the daughter of Robert E. Lee, was known to ride in the back seats of the streetcars running between Washington, D.C., and points in Virginia. On crossing the state line into Virginia she would refuse to move forward. On at least one occasion she was arrested. But because white persons who break a segregation law seldom receive more than a reprimand or token punishment, little is accomplished in making a legal case out of their action.

If a federal court rules that a state law or an action of a state is unconstitutional there still remains the problem of enforcing the court's decision. Usually a state abides by the decision of the federal court and declares its state law null and void. But if a state does not accept the decision of the federal court and will not enforce its decree, the use of federal force is the last resort to accomplish this end. Nowhere has the series of possible court actions been as clear as in the Little Rock school integration case. First there was a federal court order to desegregate the schools in compliance with the Supreme Court decisions. When the school board delayed, a group of parents brought an injunction against the board's procrastination; and a federal court ordered the school board to proceed with integration. When this federal court order was then flouted by the governor, for the first time in decades American citizens saw the federal government resort to its final action—use of federal troops to enforce federal mandate. In explaining his action President Eisenhower said:

Our personal opinions have no bearing on the matter of enforcement. . . . We are a nation in which laws, not men, are supreme. . . . The very basis of our individual rights and freedoms rests upon the certainty that the President and the executive branch of the government will support and insure the carrying out of the decisions of the federal courts, even, when necessary, with all the means at the President's command.

Events moved rapidly in the Little Rock case, but frequently a case may be in the various courts for years before a final decision is reached. However, slow as is the process of court decisions, it is nevertheless by this method that people of color in the United States have been gradually winning the right to exercise the privileges of citizenship. The courtroom has become the setting for the drama of civil rights.

5. The Road to Civil Rights

In 1915 the Supreme Court struck down the first of the legal devices which for half a century had prevented Negroes from voting. It declared the grandfather clause to be unconstitutional.

Next in 1923 the constitutionality of the white primary came into question. A mild-mannered Negro of deep conviction, Dr. L. A. Nixon of El Paso, Texas, assumed the responsibility of attempting to vote in order to make a test case in the courts. He was refused the ballot. Four years later the Supreme Court upheld his right to exercise the franchise, but Texas immediately tried to circumvent the Court ruling by passing legislation which technically changed eligibility for voters in the primary election. Dr. Nixon's case went back into the courts and five years later the Supreme Court again ruled in his favor. By this decision the Negroes' right to vote was reaffirmed, but states still held the power to enforce or defy the Court ruling as they willed. Negroes continued to be disfranchised. Then in 1935 another Court case testing the white primary was lost by the Negro contestants. But in 1941 the Supreme Court reversed its ruling of 1935 in two important decisions. In a case originating in Louisiana it ruled that since the only way a voter in that state—a one-party Democratic state—could help to choose a political candidate was to vote in the primary, then to withhold that privilege was equal to disfranchisement. Therefore the law was unconstitutional.

Another case originated in Houston, Texas, on behalf of Dr. Lonnie E. Smith, a Negro dentist who had been denied the right to vote. So important was this case to other Negro voters that hundreds of them contributed to a fund to defray costs. In 1944 after three years in the various courts, the Supreme Court in an 8-to-1 decision declared: "The United States is a constitutional democracy. Its organic law grants to all citizens a right to participate in the choice of elected officials without restriction by any state because of race. This grant . . . is not to be nullified by a state through casting its electoral processes in a form which permits a private organization to practice racial discrimination in the election."

Then began the next round in the cat-and-mouse game of politics. South Carolina, taking note that the Court had said that a primary was a function of government because it was regulated by state law, simply wiped out all state laws which governed her primaries, making a primary election no longer a state concern. However, Federal District Judge J. Waties Waring, whose name was to become associated with a series of liberal civil rights decisions, scorned the idea that a state could thus dodge its responsibilities and ruled ". . . private clubs and business organizations do not vote and elect a President of the United States, and the Senators and members of the House of Representatives of our national Congress; and under the law of our land, all citizens are entitled to a voice in such elections."

The game took on new zest as South Carolina hunted another loophole through which to run. She found it by requiring separate procedures for registering white and Negro citizens and by requiring *all* citizens, before voting, to take an oath declaring themselves in favor of separation of the races and of States' rights. Another trial case to test the constitutionality of this action utterly defeated the state's efforts.

Meanwhile Alabama was trying a different course. In 1946 that state passed the Boswell Amendment which required that any person in order to qualify as a voter had to be able to read, write, understand, and explain any article in the United States Constitution. Two years later an all-Southern panel of judges rendered a decision against this law. For one thing, they said, since the most distinguished justices of the Supreme Court frequently disagree on the interpretation of the Constitution, how can untrained boards of registrars be competent to ascertain correct interpretations? And further, they pointed out, the fact that the amendment makes no reference to race or color does not keep it from being discriminating. "We cannot ignore the impact of the Boswell Amendment upon Negro citizens because it avoids mention of race or color; to do this would be to shut our eyes to what all others than we can see and understand."

Thus by a series of court decisions through the years the legal obstructions to Negro voting were removed; but in many communities by common consent of the majority of white people "our way of doing things" remained the established way. Congress alone, by virtue of the authority given it in the Fifteenth Amendment, had the power to pass punitive legislation to enforce compliance with court orders, but all attempts to establish penalties had consistently been defeated.

Then about 1940, as the result of many forces, sentiment in the United States began to shift in favor of enforcement and penalties. One determining factor was the New Deal emphasis on social reform during the administrations of President Franklin D. Roosevelt. Another was the tremendous impact which World War II gave to the demand for more comprehensive democracy in this country. Both white and Negro service men and officers discovered the inconsistency of fighting for democracy on foreign battlefields while continuing undemocratic practices of segregation in their own ranks. When they tried to explain to the people of other nations, or to themselves, why the United States segregated its fighting men, they were often embarrassed; even confused.

A third pressure upon the nation was the publication in 1947 of the report, "To Secure These Rights," the official findings and recommendations of the Committee on Civil Rights appointed by President Truman to make a comprehensive evaluation of the status of civil rights in this country. The report was given wide publicity and made the basis of study by women's organizations, schools, churches, civic and labor groups many of whom prepared special study guides for use by their members. Although the recommendations contained in the report were never officially adopted, the widespread study of the document had a far-reaching influence on the thinking of the American people.

Another pressure upon the nation to reconsider its civil rights practices came from the police action in Korea where for the first time desegregation of the fighting forces was tried and found effective. The inconsistency of then sending service men, many of them beribboned and bemedaled, back to home communities in which they could not vote made many Americans stop and think, and prompted President Truman to issue an executive order calling for desegregation of all the armed services.

Further, the presence of the headquarters of the United Nations on our soil became a constant reminder that our professions of democracy exceeded our practice of it. As a signatory to the Universal Declaration of Human Rights of the United Nations we were on record before the world as agreeing to the principle: "All are equal before the law and are entitled without discrimination to equal protection of the law. All are entitled to equal protection against any discrimination in violation of this Declaration and against any incitement to such discrimination."

Representatives of the eighty-one nations which comprise the United Nations are sensitive to discriminations against people of color whether they are from foreign lands or are citizens of this country. When visitors to our country opened their copies of the *New York Times* for May 14, 1948, they read the story of a group of fifty-one New York school children who had won a trip to Washington as a prize in a safety patrol contest, only to have the trip canceled because the four Negro children were barred from the hotels and restaurants where the group was scheduled to be entertained.

Foreign guests read also of the young couple from India who, at a lunch counter in an Eastern ten-cent store, were told to stand up while they ate—Negroes were not allowed to sit at the counter. Persuading the waitress that they were from Asia and were not Negroes, they were allowed to sit down again.

Foreign guests read also of the young Negro mother in Washington, D.C., who gave birth to her baby on the sidewalk outside a hospital because the institution accepted only white patients.

As Americans saw the reactions of foreign diplomats and UN delegates to scenes such as these they began to look closely at themselves as seen by others. The mirror was more boldly held up in April, 1955, when delegates from twenty-nine African and Asian countries met at Bandung, Indonesia, to discuss their mutual problems. The delegates, representing 1,300,000,000 people, also represented a contrast of geographic, cultural and ideological backgrounds; a contrast in almost everything except color. Together they discussed their grievances against colonialism and racial discrimination as practiced by Western nations. Unanimously they admitted that although the racial practices of South Africa were the worst in the world, the United States ran a close second.

However, if other nations and their representatives on our shores spotted, eagle-eyed, our many discriminations against people of color, they also began to be aware of our increasing accomplishments in abolishing discriminations. The whole world watched the progress of desegregation in Washington, D.C., where as late as 1950 civic leaders had openly stated that Washington was a Southern city, that segregation was so entrenched in its way of life that the people would never accept any change in the status of Negroes. Yet by 1955 the schools in Washington were integrated, another step in a long series of desegregation procedures which have made our capital city the best racially integrated Southern city in the United States.

Moreover as Americans became increasingly aware that integration *could* take place they became more insistent that it *should* take place. The responsibility for appropriate legislation to protect the civil rights of all citizens was laid on the doorstep of the 85th Congress. Although the legislators stepped over the awkward bundle as long as they could, before the end of their 1957 session they carried it into the legislative chambers, unwrapped it, took a good look at the contents and finally acted to remedy some of the deformities with which they were faced.

Because Negroes made up the largest group whose civil rights were at stake the legislative controversy centered around correcting injustices experienced by Negroes. And finally, instead of trying to correct all injustices in one bill the legislators agreed to deal only with voting privileges. The main provisions of the bill which came up for consideration called for the creation of a Civil Rights Division in the Department of Justice which would review all cases of alleged obstruction to voting that were brought to its attention by federal agents. It further provided direct access to federal courts for any citizen whose voting privilege had been denied because of his racial origins. By a third provision, if individuals or groups were found guilty of obstructing another citizen from voting, the federal courts could issue an injunction, or restraining order, enjoining them to stop their interference. If the injunction was not obeyed, the person or group against whom it was issued could be brought into federal court, tried for contempt of court, and if found guilty could be fined or imprisoned without trial by jury. These provisions were included in the bill that passed the House.

In the Senate controversy developed over the issue which had previously killed all civil rights bills—the question of state *vs.* federal authority in the matter of voting. Opponents of the bill pointed out that all states set up certain voting requirements: nineteen of them have educational requirements; seven require loyalty oaths; forty-one disfranchise criminals and an equal number disqualify the insane. Historically and currently, they contended, qualification for voting and supervision of voting have been and still are a state's right.

Proponents of the bill pointed out that in two amendments, the Fifteenth and Nineteenth, the federal authority stipulates that no person may be disqualified from voting because of race, color or sex. Violation of these guarantees becomes a federal offense. If other requirements are desired by any state, and these requirements do not conflict with the federal guarantees, the state has the right to legislate them.

The hottest fight came over the question of trial by jury. The opponents argued that trial by jury is as much a guarantee of the Constitution as is the right to vote; that to protect one right by forfeiting another is poor logic.

The supporters of the bill cited many instances in which cases of contempt of court have been considered civil cases and have been tried without a jury. They contended further that any state that would curtail the voting privileges of Negroes would also make sure of the selection of juries prejudiced against Negroes.

Throughout the debate the country waited for a promised filibuster in the Senate, because some Southern senators had threatened to hold the floor with continuous talk until the Senate would have to adjourn without acting upon the bill. Since 1922 successful filibusters had defeated nine civil rights bills: three of them antilynching bills, four antipoll tax bills, and two fair employment practices bills. As the weeks passed and debate continued it became clear that the bill's opponents could not count on enough votes to defeat it, but the filibuster developed nevertheless, this time a one-man performance, with Senator J. Strom Thurmond from South Carolina setting a new record by holding the floor for twenty-four hours and eighteen minutes. But as his final words died out the filibuster died with them. A compromise on the trial by jury issue saved the bill. In its final form it provided that only cases involving the right to vote would be considered under the provision for criminal contempt of court, and that if the penalty in a contempt of court case exceeded forty-five days in jail or a $300 fine the defendant could demand a new trial, this time before a jury.

During the first week in September President Eisenhower signed the bill and in November appointed W. Wilson White, then Assistant Attorney General, to head a Civil Rights Division in the Department of Justice. In January, 1958, a Commission on Civil Rights under the chairmanship of Dr. John Hannah, president of Michigan State University, was empowered to make a two-year investigation of federal laws and policies governing equal protection of the law and to consider alleged denials of voting rights.

Thus the machinery for the protection of civil rights has been manned but the wheels have not started to turn at any great speed. Organizations for and against granting voting privileges to Negroes have each promised continued effort on behalf of whichever cause they champion, but at least the question of equal protection of the law for all citizens is out in the open with federal support on record in its favor.

The controversy over civil rights for the Negro minority has always generated more interest in this country than have abridgments of the rights of the lesser minorities. Historically, the theoretical citizenship granted by the Fourteenth and Fifteenth Amendments was never applied to the American Indians. Long considered wards of the government, their status differed from that of any other group in the United States. By the Citizenship Act of 1924 Congress conferred citizenship to all American Indians born in this country not hitherto made citizens, but many of them were excluded from the polls by state laws, the same device which kept the Negroes disfranchised. As late as 1938 seven states still had voting restrictions for their Indians; but by 1956 Utah alone continued to disfranchise some of her reservation Indians. The following year these bars were removed and in 1957, all Indians qualified for citizenship on the same basis as did other Americans.

Unlike the Negroes and Indians who lived in this country as disfranchised Americans, foreign-born Orientals living in this country retained the status of aliens. Rights of citizenship were never extended to them as they were to peoples of European background. However, immediately following World War II an all-out effort was made to secure citizenship for the older generation of foreign-born Orientals. Many bills were proposed in Congress before the Omnibus Bill was finally passed in 1952. This bill provided that immigration from Asian countries should be put on the same quota system that covered other nations; that Asian husbands, wives and children of American citizens could enter the country without counting in the quota assignment; and that the English language requirement be waived for Asians over fifty years of age who had resided in the United States for twenty years or more.

In 1953 the first naturalized Orientals cast their ballots. An issue of *Pacific Citizen* carried the headline, "Best Story in 50 Years: The Issei Votes," and under the headline a picture of Hirosaburo Yokozeki, seventy, and his wife Tsuru, sixty, holding their marked ballots in their hands. Mr. Yokozeki, a 1913 graduate of Stanford University, had at one time been executive secretary of the Southern California Japanese Fisherman's Association and active in civic affairs. The newspaper concluded:

As pioneers who converted the deserts and swamps into lush farm lands, and who trolled the shores for fish to increase the wealth of this nation; then raising their American born children, the Nisei, to be upright citizens in spite of the "worst wartime mistake" of evacuation and relocation camp life, the simple but solemn gesture of marking their ballot on Election Days is most significant in the history of persons of Japanese ancestry in America.

The following year, 1954, fifteen thousand people gathered at the Hollywood Rose Bowl to watch seventy-five hundred applicants, most of them Asians, receive their citizenship. In the history of the nation this was the largest group ever to be naturalized at one time.

With all racial groups within the United States now holding voting privileges in common, they also hold a voting problem in common—the simple matter of using the franchise they possess. *Newsweek,* July 15, 1957, published a state-by-state study of the estimated number of Negroes going to the polls. The percentage of eligible voters who cast their ballots ranged from 60 per cent in Illinois, New York, and Michigan, to 25 per cent in Georgia, 19 per cent in North Carolina, and 10 per cent in Alabama. Long-standing obstacles in the way of voting explain the low percentage in many Southern states. But for the nation as a whole, general apathy accounts for the poor showing. Since 1920, including voters of all races, no more than 65 per cent of eligible voters have ever cast their ballots in a national election. In the 1957 Wisconsin special election for a United States senator approximately 33 per cent of the voters voted, a percentage which approximates the proportion of eligible Negroes voting in Louisiana.

For that large group of American Negroes and Indians who are uneducated, a lack of concern about voting is a heritage from preceding generations who had found it well to leave good enough alone. With no understanding of political issues but with full understanding that to get involved in politics was socially unhealthy, many of them held to a philosophy that it was better "to take what you got from the government than to take what you got at the polls." During a campaign to get out the Negro vote one mother of six children, living on the top floor of a crowded tenement in the steel district of Gary, Indiana, said, "Us has always been this way. Us gets along all right. We don't want to stir up nothin'."

On several New Mexico pueblos which had no registered voters in 1952 it was discovered that there was a general belief that if they voted they would also have to pay taxes on their land; and that if they made a mistake in marking a ballot they would be fined. A voter education program was undertaken in these pueblos and by 1956 some of them could boast 100 per cent registration. Although this number is above the average for reservation Indians, Helen L. Peterson, executive director of the National Congress of American Indians, speaks of the "startling increase in the registering and voting" of Indians today.

44

With the increased number of Negro and Indian voters political parties are wooing their votes. Although racial origins are no longer recorded on voters' registration blanks, general methods of voter analysis reveal that the balloting of these minority groups is not unduly influenced by racial factors excepting in issues which involve discrimination.

Corollary to the privilege of voting is the privilege of holding public office. Today Negroes in the United States hold scores of high offices in government, some appointive and some elective. Doubtless most white Americans think first of Ralph Bunche, winner of the Nobel Peace Prize, who has been under-secretary of the United Nations, and mediator in the dispute in Palestine in 1949. Also it is well known that New York, Michigan, and Illinois have Negro representatives in Congress. If beyond that most Americans become a little hazy it may well be because the sensational aspect of placing a Negro in office no longer attracts the attention it once did. But the list includes a judge of the United States Circuit Court, an alternate delegate to the United Nations Assembly, an assistant director to the U.S. Office of Education, a consul general and a first secretary to foreign embassies, an assistant secretary of labor, and state and municipal posts too numerous to be counted.

Beginning about 1940 several communities experimented with Negroes on their police forces, the theory being that qualified Negroes deserved the right to serve there and that the total community would profit from a bi-racial force. Winston-Salem, Raleigh and Charlotte, North Carolina, had found the plan very satisfactory when their neighboring city, Greensboro, decided to try it. For fifteen years Greensboro, a community of sixty thousand, about one-third of them Negroes, had shied away from the idea because "it just wouldn't work here." A bank teller was sure that the white police force would never accept Negroes. A housewife wasn't going to have her children protected by any but a white officer. A store-keeper in the heart of one of the largest Negro sections in the city when asked his opinion thought a long time while he carefully measured and cut the proper-sized square off the end of a piece of chewing tobacco. "Well," he said, "when they've all had such a hard time just livin', it's too much to expect one of them to crack down on another one."

According to *New South,* in 1947 several factors combined to bring the question to a point. For one thing, the number of Negro voters was increasing rapidly, and their vote was proving to be an honest and well-considered ballot—they had become a political force to be reckoned with. Also there were qualified men among the Negro citizens who were desirous of joining the police force. And of real consequence was the fact that the city manager, Henry A. Yancey, was a man of integrity whom the people respected, and in addition, he had had previous experience with Negroes on Southern police forces in other cities.

"I'm not really sure we're ready for it," Yancey commented, but he placed the proposal before the city council. The council accepted it and the chief of police backed up the acceptance. Later Yancey reported, "The white population received the action with scarcely a comment; it is certainly true to say that there was no protest. The Negroes received it with great acclaim, and the press, both local and in surrounding states, hailed it as 'a step forward.'"

Care was taken in choosing the first two Negroes assigned to the force, and they were given intensive training before they reported for regular duty. Before long people began to change their minds about Negro policemen and two more were added. The dubious storekeeper became as enthusiastic over the policeman on his street as he was about his tobacco. "The people are so proud of their policeman that they'd all give their necks to help him—if he ever needed help."

Reports have been equally encouraging from other cities. In the South the number of Negroes on police forces has increased steadily. In 1945 there were 131 policemen and three policewomen in 29 cities in nine states. By 1954, 700 men and 112 women were employed in 148 cities and 22 counties in 13 states.

The acceptance of Negroes for jury service in the South is growing although not so fast as their acceptance on police forces. In 1949 the state supreme court of Georgia ruled that in counties with a substantial Negro population Negroes should be added to jury lists. In 1954 the United States Supreme Court set a precedent when it ruled that to exclude Mexicans from juries in Texas was unconstitutional. Because Mexicans suffer the same discriminations as nonwhite peoples this decision is significant.

When progress in all areas of integration was accelerated after the Supreme Court ruling on integration in public schools, the

Fund for the Republic financed a survey of the progress in integration, both North and South, in the two-year period, 1954–56. So frequently is the word *first* used in this report that one wonders the printer's supply of these five letters was not exhausted. A sampling from many illustrations shows that in Southern states for the first time a Negro was:

—nominated as justice of the peace in Jacksonville, Florida
—appointed by a Kentucky congressman to the U.S. Military Academy at West Point
—appointed an aide to the governor of Kentucky
—appointed executive supervisor of Louisville's division of recreation. This appointment went to a woman who supervises both Negro and white personnel.
—appointed special assistant in the Office of Veterans Administration in New Orleans
—elected to the state senate of Maryland
—elected to a municipal judgeship in Kansas City, Missouri
—named to a housing authority board in North Carolina
—elected to the city council in Southern Pines, North Carolina
—placed on the city planning commission, Knoxville, Tennessee
—elected to the county board of supervisors, Kent County, Virginia
—made assistant state superintendent of schools in West Virginia, serving schools of both races.

The names of some states are missing in the list of communities in which public offices are opening in any numbers to Negroes. Some of these states are accounted for by the fact that they contain no appreciable Negro population; but in other states, although in some towns Negroes outnumber white people, voting practices effectively keep the majority from the polls and therefore out of office.

No one in Atlanta, Georgia, thought a Negro could be elected to the school board—until he was. In 1953, Dr. Rufus E. Clement, president of Atlanta University, carried forty out of fifty-eight precincts. He carried a majority of the white wards in a 2-to-1 victory over his white opponent. The only disgruntled folk were a hard core of the Ku Klux Klan, while most of the other citizens of Atlanta agreed that the city's twenty-five thousand Negro children would be ably represented by Dr. Clement. Again in 1957, during the heat of the controversy over integration in the schools, Dr. Clement was re-elected to the board.

Walter White, long-time executive secretary of the National Association for the Advancement of Colored People, once asked, "Will 1963, the one hundredth anniversary of the signing of the Emancipation Proclamation, find the Negro truly emancipated?" Part of the answer was afforded by the election of Dr. Clement to the Atlanta school board: the qualified Negro is coming to earn election to office on his own merits. Not in every state, but in enough of them so that there are unmistakable indications which way the tide is running. Also, today for the first time in history Negro citizens have the full force of federal law behind their right to vote. Today the Negro vote is already large enough to be a major balance of power in national elections. Today mixed election boards, mixed school boards, mixed legislatures, mixed juries are becoming common occurrences. Today the increasing number of people, Negro and white, who are working together to insure the civil rights of all citizens gives the best indication of what may be achieved by 1963.

6. Liberating Labor

On an unseasonably warm morning in September, 1957, the streams
of commuters pouring into Union Station at St. Louis were thin-
ning out when suddenly the waiting room again became a scene of
commotion as a train from the Deep South unloaded its passengers.
In the stream of people surging through one gate came a husky,
heavy-muscled Negro, sweaty shirt open at the neck, his face ex-
pectant but anxious. In each hand he carried a battered suitcase and
under each arm a large carton, all tied with assorted pieces of rope.
Behind him trudged his wife carrying two children, one perhaps a
year old and the other no more than a few weeks. In succession
behind her came five other children, ranging from about ten to
three years, each holding the hand of the youngster before and
behind him. Flimsy, poorly fitting dresses on the three girls; tattered
and patched jeans on the boys; no shoes on any of the dusty feet;
but as the procession of passengers slowed down three of the children
broke into a little jig—making no confusion and taking up no space;
just little feet that had to express the excitement of "goin' North."

Through another gateway came a white-collared Negro, his suit wrinkled from an all-night trip; his wife in high heels and silk stockings; their three little girls with their pink crinolined skirts still bravely billowing, even after having been slept in on a coach seat during the night. Black patent leather shoes, slightly cracked but intact, added to the effect of being dressed up for an important occasion.

Hundreds of families like these two daily pour through the gates of the St. Louis station to take trains to San Francisco, Detroit, Cleveland, or that mecca of all meccas today—Chicago. It is estimated that some months as many as three thousand Negroes arrive in that city from the South to try to find jobs and homes.

Chicago, the nation's second largest city, is shrinking in white population, the result of the trend to the suburbs, and at the same time is gaining in nonwhite population. By the summer of 1956 the white population numbered about 3,039,000 and the Negro population 682,000, or slightly over 20 per cent. In view of the increasing influx of unskilled, noncity Negroes into Chicago, all of whom compete not only for jobs but for housing in a city where there is already an acute shortage of low-income housing, Sheriff Joseph D. Lohman of Cook County has said, "The situation is enormously explosive. One incident, given proper publicity and exciting white and Negro emotions, could blow the city up."

One factor which has helped prevent the explosion has been the good labor market which has been able to absorb the new laborers. Whether a continuing recession will drastically change the picture depends upon the degree of unemployment, the amount of unemployment insurance made available and the number of public works or other "made" jobs. In 1957 it was estimated that within the next three years Chicago would need to fill 513,000 newly created jobs in addition to those which would open because of normal retirement of present workers, normal migration of workers and job changes. The development of the St. Lawrence Seaway is responsible for part of the expected increase; lesser new developments and industries account for the rest. Here, as in other cities, the greatest labor problem arises from the fact that the incoming laborers are almost entirely unskilled, while many of the jobs call for skilled workers.

In addition to the large number of Southern Negroes moving into

Chicago, unskilled Puerto Ricans from the overpopulated island are pushing into the Midwest metropolis. Also reservation Indians, lured by the free transportation, financial assistance and promise of work under the Termination Act of 1953, are adding their numbers to the unskilled labor pool.

The Chinese and Japanese are practically no part of today's labor conflict. Because they are few in numbers, are dispersed across the continent, and as a group are more highly educated than other non-whites, they are no longer primary targets for ill will, although in their earlier days they experienced all the discriminations being directed at other nonwhites today.

Since Negroes make up 95 per cent of the nonwhites in this country, the forces which have determined their rejection or acceptance in American labor are of major importance. For half a century following the Civil War the pattern of labor for freed slaves and their descendants remained practically unchanged. Having worked the land for two hundred years they continued to work the land. In 1900 the South was home for 90 per cent of all Negro Americans, and 74 per cent of this number lived in rural areas. Women and children often worked in the fields since the only other occupation open to women was household service. Then World War I started a movement of unskilled workers into Northern manufacturing cities, and once there they did not return home after the labor shortage temporarily eased. Soon after the war the new immigration policy restricted the number of European workers entering this country so that the demand for Negro workers continued and they found a permanent place in Northern industry. Almost every Northern city came to rely upon the Southern Negro for its supply of cheap labor. Then came World War II and pressure to speed up industry made factories tap every available source of labor. Negroes immediately swarmed into industrial centers with the result that by 1950 one-third of all the Negroes in the United States were living outside the South, whereas previously only one-tenth had lived beyond the borders of Dixieland. This migration accounts for the more than 200 per cent increase in the Negro population on the West Coast and the 52 per cent increase in the North.

At the same time, this exodus out of the South accounts for the decrease in the Negro population of seven Southern states. Some counties in Mississippi have lost as much as one-fifth of their Negro population. A social case worker in the small communities in the northern part of that state studied one town in which during the last fifteen years only one boy has remained in the community; every other young man of working age has gone away to work or else has gone into the service, not one of them to return to his home town to live. The one exception is a boy who has been excused from army duty to work the farm for his sick parents. "I do not have accurate figures for other communities," reported the case worker, "but I feel sure that this town is not exceptional."

Arriving in the North, the Negro worker does not find a utopia. Yet, living conditions and wages, even at their worst, are enough better than he has previously known that he remains. Discrimination he finds, but with it he finds more immediate hope for its dissolution. But also in whatever city he settles he is likely to find the same industrial pattern: he starts at the bottom and his chances of rising are frequently very slim. One reason he does not rise is, of course, prejudice. Another is his own inefficiency; not that he is incapable of doing more skilled work but because he lacks training or experience.

In the shifting of the Negro population not all the migration has been out of the South. There has also been a movement from the Southern farm to the Southern city, principally because the economic status of Southern Negro farmers is the lowest of any group of Negro workers. In 1954 the median money income of all white workers, skilled and unskilled, in the United States was approximately $4,400; of all Negro workers, $2,500. The median money income of Southern white farm workers was $1,500; of Negro workers, $750. The future seems to hold no promise of better conditions because Southern farming is moving into large-scale operation with the increased per farm acreage necessitating the use of heavy, costly machinery. The farmer with no capital, which is the average Negro farmer, is naturally squeezed out.

Accompanying this change in agricultural methods has been a movement to strengthen the economy of the South with an underpinning of industry, and so the search for factories for the South got under way. The favor with which industry looked upon the invitation to move South was heightened by developments in many Northern states where high taxes, high wages and high operating costs were consuming profits. Also the tendency toward decentralization of industry made feasible placing plants in varied locations instead of extending the mile-long factories characteristic of Detroit and other cities. The solution to problems of both the North and the South seemed to lie in the establishment of industrial plants in Southern states. So fast did the movement progress that by 1950 one-third of the Negro population of the South had moved into Southern cities.

However, simultaneously Southern white farmers from submarginal farms were moving into the newly developing industrial centers and the age-old practice of giving the white worker priority continued. Mr. Herbert Hill, labor secretary of the NAACP, reported that in 1957 the Lockheed Aircraft Corporation in Marietta, Georgia, employed 18,000 workers, of whom 1,350 were Negroes. Of the total number of workers 2,400 were women, but only seven were Negro women, all employed in custodial jobs. Of 450 job classifications, only thirty were open to Negro workers, and these on a segregated basis. Another study revealed that the employees of one large factory commuted from thirty counties although there was a labor supply near at home which—except for the matter of color—could immediately qualify for many of the jobs, and with training could qualify for many more.

Several factors account for the long record of discrimination against Negroes in industry. Unions have feared loss of prestige if they opened membership to nonwhites; employers have feared walkouts and loss of production if nonwhites were hired and especially if a nonwhite was put into a supervisory position. Stores have feared the reaction of the public if they employed colored saleswomen. White employees have feared for their own jobs, and at times nonwhite employees have feared for their lives. However, one factor emerges from many experiments in integration: most fears never materialize. A study conducted by the National Conference of Christians and Jews indicates that this is the testimony of many industries which have inaugurated policies of nondiscrimination.

One of these industries is the Radio Corporation of America which has had a voluntary policy of nondiscrimination for many years. In 1954, Frank M. Folsom, then president of RCA, stated that nondiscrimination is plain good business. Minority groups in the United States are a large consumer market, Negroes alone spending about $12 billion annually. The company figures that good jobs for Negroes will increase their dollar potential and thereby help expand business. As part of its nondiscriminatory practices RCA has eliminated from its employment blanks any reference to race, color, or religion. Individual skills and talents alone are criteria for hiring workers. A continuous public relations program keeps workers, management and community informed of company practices and also notes the reactions of each group to new developments in integration.

RCA does not hesitate to select the best man for foreman regardless of his race or the color of the group over which he is placed. Television technicians, whatever their color, service sets in any homes where they are needed. Clerical work is open to any qualified person. In recent years college students qualifying for high-grade engineering training have been selected from senior classes of many colleges, including Negro schools. About thirty Negro engineers, including one woman graduate of Howard University, are employed at the highest professional level.

Mr. Folsom concluded: "We have found that it takes courage to be the first to bring races and nationalities together in certain areas under the proper conditions. But in each instance, we have found that reluctance on the part of the employers to initiate such a policy has been based not so much on prejudice as upon fear of the unknown. RCA feels that its experience has shown that there is little basis for such fear."

In the field of retail merchandising is the experience of Carson Pirie Scott & Co., one of Chicago's largest department stores. In 1950 when the store inaugurated a new policy, president S. P. Carson, Sr., said: "Since Carson Pirie Scott & Co. is strictly a business institution we have no right to adopt any policy that would hurt business, but we believe that employment on merit is the right thing to do and we are proud that our store has the courage and character to lead State Street in this program."

Mr. Carson was not wrong in his guess that in Chicago's 600,000 Negroes there would be some who could qualify on merit. He began his program with the practice of putting the first Negro workers in skilled jobs and also putting them where they would circulate among the other employees. No dark cubbyhole job for a tryout. The first Negro trainee hired was a young college graduate who by the end of a few months had worked at several jobs in the adjusting bureau and in the employment office, during which time he had circulated in every department and had come in contact with every department manager and every floor service manager. Before long, having heard via the grapevine that the store was now employing Negroes, applicants began coming for interviews.

Company officials had wondered about the reaction of the white employees. A few were dubious; the older workers more than the younger ones who had grown up attending integrated schools; but no matter what their personal opinions, all the employees made an honest effort to facilitate the new setup. As each new nonwhite was employed he was put under the sponsorship of one of the older white employees whose responsibility it was to see that the new employee became acquainted with other workers and generally learned the store customs.

General manager Martin recalls: "Well I remember short Italian Charlie, sponsor of the porter force, greeting a six-foot Negro porter with a welcoming smile and a cordial handshake. Such friendliness warmed the heart of everyone. In the beginning we avoided placing Negroes in departments where there were already large minority groups. It so happens that our porter force is largely Italian—so we were hesitant about hiring Negroes for this work. One day the Italian supervisor of porters went to the general superintendent's office to inquire why we were discriminating against his department —why could he not have Negroes too? Word had spread that they were good workers!"

In this store there is no arbitrary ceiling on jobs for Negroes or other nonwhites. They are employed as secretaries, comptometer operators, detectives, window and display arrangers. A nonwhite woman heads the wage administration department and a Negro certified public accountant is an administrative assistant in the controller's division. A Japanese American is an assistant manager in the merchandising division.

In Minneapolis, Dayton's, one of the oldest and largest department stores in the city, has had a policy of hiring on merit from its founding. "The Dayton family," said a high executive in the employment offices, "had high ideals which they built into the business. I doubt if you could find a period in the history of the store when several races were not represented in many departments—

and not mere token representation. Today there are Negro girls in the stenographic pool, on the sales floor and in specialized services. A Japanese man holds a high staff position and we're looking for a Japanese girl for artificial flowers and decorations, a department that demands special artistic ability. We've had American Indians, Asian Indians and Chinese. We're interested in people who can qualify for the job, not in the national origins of the applicants."

Many retail stores have been deterred from employing nonwhite personnel because they feared the reaction of the public with the resultant loss of patronage. To test shopper reaction to Negro clerks a New York department store placed several Negro girls in various departments and then followed the shopping course of several hundred women during the first day of the experiment. As these women left the store each was asked how she would feel if Negro clerks were added to the sales force. A few customers said they would never again trade at the store; others said they would not make a purchase from a colored clerk; some approved the idea. However, each woman interviewed that day had been waited upon by a Negro clerk and three-fourths of them were unaware of the fact.

The experience of International Harvester Company indicates that a well-planned policy of nondiscrimination can be carried out in Southern industries. In its Northern plants International Harvester had a nineteen-year record of nondiscrimination before it opened two plants in the South; one in Louisville, Kentucky, the other in Memphis, Tennessee. When it was announced that the established policy of nondiscrimination would govern these plants, all industry watched to see what would happen. The company carried on an educational program for all employees and for the general public. From the first, applications from both whites and nonwhites were received so there was never any question of workers of one race taking jobs away from the other race. Each applicant was carefully interviewed and had the policy of the company explained to him.

Also from the start, workers were hired on merit. Approximately one-fifth of the workers were Negro, 900 out of 4,500. Seniority rights and the rights of job transfer were guaranteed to all employees, which meant a guarantee that a Negro could work toward the top as fast as he qualified to fill job vacancies.

Since output determined individual pay, teamwork benefited all workers and the record of the company was better than the average for other companies operating under the same bargaining agency but under a policy of racial discrimination. In the Memphis plant three wildcat strikes caused some work stoppage for short periods, but by the third strike the workers realized that the company intended to stand by its principles and the sporadic opposition turned into co-operation.

Following a visit to the Southern plants in 1953, vice-president Ivan L. Willis said: "Without exception the managers of these operations reported that Negroes are as efficient and in some cases more productive than other employees. They reported no appreciable difference between Negro and white employees as to turnover, tardiness or absenteeism. The Negro employees generally show a keen desire to make good on the opportunities afforded them. The most notable difference lies in our inability to upgrade some Negro employees because of their lack of education and skills which has often been due to the limited educational and training opportunities available to them."

From the experiences of these four companies and scores of others whose experiences parallel them come statements of four working principles. The first is that among nonwhite citizens there are individuals qualified for practically every type of work the nation demands. Second, that the customary practice of starting or keeping nonwhite workers at the bottom is unsound; they should be geared into the working force at the highest level for which they are qualified. Third, that if the same placement and promotion policies apply to all employees and are scrupulously carried out by management a minimum of friction arises. Fourth, that the proportion of nonwhite employees to rise to higher level jobs is lower than for whites because nonwhites usually come to their jobs with poorer preparation and frequently have fewer opportunities for improving themselves on the job.

Although many unions and industries have explored the possibilities of integration and have come up with strong recommendations for its effectiveness, it is not by voluntary action that most integration has been achieved. Governmental action of various kinds has been needed to mold public opinion, to bring reactionary industries into line and to insist that democratic practices are both essential and possible in business and industry.

7. *Labor Leads Out*

With the outbreak of World War II and the accompanying shortage in man power an abnormal labor situation developed in the United States. Although an economic boom was in progress the country faced the contradiction of strategic jobs calling for men and unemployed men calling for jobs—color alone keeping the demand and the supply apart.

Into the bitter tensions which this condition was generating stepped Mr. A. Philip Randolph, militant Negro president of the Sleeping Car Porters. In 1941 Mr. Randolph was no amateur in either labor troubles or race relations. He had first come into national prominence in 1925 when he led the fight of the porters against the Pullman company. At that time approximately half the country's nine thousand Pullman porters lived in Chicago. With bus and air travel still in their infancy, the Pullman company had a practical monopoly on overnight travel and bitterly fought any unionization of the porters so essential to Pullman service. The company conducted a carefully organized campaign against Mr. Randolph to discredit him in the eyes of the public. Public reaction made his job more difficult but did not weaken his determination nor his leadership. Time and again the porters' attempts to rent a hall to use for a meeting place were thwarted; so finally they met in an outdoor field and there achieved their initial organization. Not long afterward, as the Brotherhood of Sleeping Car Porters and Maids, they affiliated with the American Federation of Labor.

The Brotherhood was originally an all-Negro union because almost 100 per cent of the porters were Negroes, and it remained so for many years. By the end of ten years the Brotherhood had achieved a living wage for porters, a wage based upon salary contract so that they no longer had to rely almost entirely upon tips. From this protracted fight Mr. Randolph emerged a leader who figured in every ensuing national convention of labor organizations with his pleas for nondiscriminatory practices in all labor unions.

It was natural that again in 1941 Mr. Randolph should become the champion of the whole body of unemployed or poorly employed Negro workers, 50,000 of whom threatened a march on the Capital to dramatize their condition. The march was averted by the issuance of President Roosevelt's executive order banning all discrimination in defense industries because of race, creed or national origin.

To carry out the provisions of the executive order the Fair Employment Practices Commission was established. Immediately the labor situation for nonwhites changed. Whereas in 1941 there was only token representation of Negroes in defense work, three years later there were 420,000 Negro workers scattered throughout aircraft, shipbuilding and ordnance plants, and many more in allied industries. Moreover, a process of upgrading had already raised half a million Negro workers above the level of their traditional menial tasks. Although at times the work of the commission was weakened because it lacked adequate power to enforce its orders, still it provided a focal point for public opinion and radically changed the job prospects for nonwhite workers.

In 1945, with the war emergency over, the federal Fair Employment Practices Commission was discontinued, but since that time fair employment practice laws or ordinances have been passed by states and municipalities. The first such state legislation was enacted in 1945 when New York set up a five-man commission composed of well-trained and well-paid specialists. The commission was empowered to investigate complaints brought before it, to try to adjust difficulties by conciliatory means, and as a last resort to issue cease and desist orders. But the commission has no power to inflict penalties if firms fail to comply with the orders. Only court action can accomplish this end.

The New York program became the model after which other states patterned their legislation, with minor changes suggested by time and experience. Then Connecticut came up with quite a different plan which called for a larger number of commissioners who work on a voluntary basis. Added strength in the Connecticut plans lies in the power given to the commission to initiate action against a person or firm that violates the provisions of the state antidiscrimination laws, and also to impose penalties for noncompliance with its orders.

The degree of authority vested in such commissions varies. The Toledo, Ohio, plan allows the commission to order fine or imprisonment for convicted violators, while the authority of the Kansas commission is so limited that its 1957 report notes: "the lack of enforcement provisions, particularly the specific prohibition which makes it impossible for the commission to hold public hearings and publicize its findings when exhaustive efforts of mediation and persuasion fail."

To illustrate its difficulties, the Kansas commission cites one experience with a railway company. Two Negro employees complained to the commission that they were refused promotion from janitor to janitor foremen, and that the company consistently refused to hire Negroes for any work outside janitorial and maintenance crews. An investigation by the commission revealed that after refusing to promote either of the Negro janitors, one of whom had fifteen years of service to his credit, the company had finally hired a white foreman with no previous experience in the building. Several attempts on the part of the commission to discuss the charges with the general manager of the railway company failed. The commission then sent a registered letter to the manager requesting him to appear before the body on a given date. Although the letter was received no representative of the railway company appeared. A telephone call to the general manager brought this reply: "We don't intend to come over there and discuss this thing." And there the matter had to be dropped. Although according to filed reports the majority of the cases have a happier ending, such defiance is possible.

Today in twelve states and sixty-one additional municipalities some sixty million workers are protected by FEP regulations. These states and cities agree that although at times the laws are broken, nevertheless they do deter many industries from carrying on discriminatory practices; and that the existence of machinery for speedy and fair hearings of grievances prevents discrimination from festering within an individual or smoldering in a racial group.

States which have not passed fair employment practices legislation frequently use as their excuse the argument that voluntary acceptance of good standards is preferable to legislated requirements. This was the theory upon which Cincinnati operated when in 1948 its Chamber of Commerce called twelve of its leading industrialists into conference to discuss methods of facilitating fair practices. During repeated meetings the group worked out a statement of policies which was acceptable to the Chamber of Commerce and to the labor unions, including both white and nonwhite workers. Then a sixteen-man committee representing these groups was charged with getting the newly formulated policies incorporated into the practices of business and industry through an educational campaign for which a budget of $31,500 was provided. At the end of fifteen months there was little progress to show for the investment of brains, time and money.

Then the sponsoring committee asked themselves, "Why should legislation be feared?" Checking through the usual excuses and finding none factually substantiated, the committee suggested that the Chamber recommend a city ordinance. It was recommended and passed, whereupon Cincinnati discovered that the ordinance was more readily accepted than the voluntary plan had been. Hence Cincinnati came to the conclusion, as have many other communities, that personal prejudice will make people argue long and inveigh loudly, but that when the social conscience is solidified into law, objections are reduced to a whisper and finally die out.

In addition to the number of workers covered by FEP laws other large segments of the nation's working force have come under other nondiscriminatory regulations. For many years government contracts have carried a clause forbidding discrimination because of race. When in 1951 President Truman found this clause being disregarded on a wholesale scale, by executive order he created the Committee on Government Contracts Compliance. In 1953 this committee was superseded by President Eisenhower's President's Committee on Government Contracts, whose responsibility it is to see that firms holding government contracts comply with the nondiscriminatory provisions in them.

To date the committee has not eliminated all discrimination on federal jobs; contractors have found ways of circumventing the non-discriminatory requirements by hiring workers for federal government projects through labor unions that have ironclad rules against employment of Negroes. Under these circumstances the contractors claim they are not responsible for hiring procedures. The result is illustrated in Cleveland where the NAACP reports the construction of six NIKE launching and control sites and the construction of a Veterans Administration hospital, all with federal funds but utilizing the services of the International Brotherhood of Electrical Workers which excludes Negroes from membership, even in defiance of the Community Relations Board of Cleveland.

Until 1957 Milwaukee Local 8 of the Masons and Bricklayers' Union had kept its membership all white. The previous year two qualified Negroes sought membership in the union and were refused admission as all Negroes before them had been. They took their case to the Wisconsin Industrial Commission, but it had power only to recommend to unions that they cease discriminatory practices. When Local 8 refused to comply with the recommendation of the commission the two Negroes took their case into court, hoping that a court order could force the union to open its membership to all qualified workers. But the court ruled that "the measures already taken by the Commission provide the entire remedy given by the state law. . . . We grant it is cold comfort to the appellants. . . ." Since the weakness obviously lay in Wisconsin's inadequate fair employment practices law, the only hope for remedy was in a new law. During the following session of the state legislature a new code was formulated which put teeth into the power of the Industrial Commission. The new bill provided that any employer, employment agency or union that did not comply with the orders of the commission to end discrimination could be fined from $10 to $100 a day for each day it delayed. Proponents of such a bill had carried on a constant fight for its passage for twelve years, meeting repeated defeats, but the 1957 legislators passed it with scarcely any discussion and no disagreement. Almost immediately four Negroes were admitted to Local 8, among them the two men who had initiated the case which opened the union.

By barring Negroes from union membership many unions have successfully kept them from entering a given trade or industry. In some cases where membership in a union is not openly denied to Negroes the desired end is achieved by refusing to accept them in apprenticeship training programs, which in turn are required before an individual may be hired. For instance, in many of the metal working, printing, craft and building trades, workers can become qualified for employment only by completing apprenticeships. Hence to exclude applicants at this point effectively eliminates them altogether.

Major court decisions have helped to bring recalcitrant unions into line. One such decision declared it illegal for unions to claim to represent all employees while barring Negroes from union membership. Another decision awarded wages to Negro employees for the total amount they would have received had the union not discriminated against them; another required railroads to rank Negro employees on the basis of work performed rather than on the basis of work for which they were originally hired, thus preventing porters from doing the work of brakemen while retaining the status of porters; and an injunction against the Brotherhood of Locomotive Firemen and Enginemen restrained it from discrimination against Negroes.

Outnumbering the list of unions which are still trying to maintain all-white membership are those which are opening their membership to nonwhite workers. The United Mine Workers, Amalgamated Clothing Workers, and International Ladies' Garment Workers have a long and consistent record of nondiscrimination. Traditionally the CIO has had a better record of minority integration than the AFL. Union members express confidence that the merged organization will carry on the best nondiscriminatory policies of each.

Walter White, long-time national executive secretary of the NAACP, once said, "It is both safe and just to say that, in the fight for civil rights and human equality, the organized-labor movement has advanced faster and farther during the past twenty-five years than has any other major segment in the American population."

The United Packinghouse Workers of America holds a record for open membership, including its many Southern locals. It is to this persistent tradition of inclusive membership that the president, Mr. Ralph Helstein, attributes its ability to stand up under pressure from White Citizens Councils. In the North it has also carried on a long fight for nondiscrimination.

In 1955 a study was made of a Chicago meat-packing plant in which more than half the employees were Negroes. During World War II the man-power shortage made it necessary to fill jobs with any qualified workers who were available and a few Negroes were put into the Paint Shop for the first time. When fifteen white workers objected to the move the foreman answered their objections: "All right, there's a war on and the Negroes are fighting the war. We got to get the production out . . . if you don't want to work with them, then get the hell out!" Three got out. Today in the Paint Shop workers of the two races work together in teams, eat together, take their coffee breaks together and entertain each other in their homes.

Nearly ten years after this initial desegregation in the packing plant the Sliced Bacon Department still had no Negro workers. This department was considered one of the show places through which the company conducted visitors, and management contended that the public would resent seeing Negro women handling food. The union, however, pushed its demands for the desegregation of this department. The test of union power came when a few Negro women were laid off in another department and because of their seniority rights had to be placed in Sliced Bacon. The older white workers in the department quickly formulated what they called a "dexterity test" so rigid that no new Negro worker could pass it. In protest, about half the workers in the plant, Negro and white, called a wildcat strike. Management dispensed with the dexterity test and hired six Negro women.

The next department in which the union tried to break segregation offered tougher resistance than had the other two. This department was the Gas House of the plant where gas for refrigeration was produced. White employees claimed that Negroes were not skilled enough to work in this department and the first Negroes assigned there were immediately frightened away with simulated explosions and stories of violent experiences suffered by various workers.

Then a Negro who happened to be the chairman of the union Anti-Discrimination Committee was assigned to the Gas House. "When I went over there," he related later, "the foreman took me up to where the gas comes in. While I was there, there was some popping out of the gas that looked like little explosions and the foreman figured I would be scared away. But I wasn't. The men tried to scare me, too. They would jump up and get all excited and run around like there was going to be a big explosion. But I just watched them carefully because I figured as long as they were inside there, it was safe. As soon as they headed for the door, I was going out after them. But they never did, so I stayed there too."

Before long resentment against him died down and the foreman asked him to suggest a few other men from among the Negro employees who would like to work in the same department. From this series of experiences management at the meat packing plant concluded, as have many other firms, that although first contacts between the races may produce resentment, continued contacts tend to reduce prejudice.

In a case investigated by John Hope, Jr. of the race relations department of Fisk University, the trouble revolved around a Negro worker on a construction job. The Negro was upgraded to the classification of crane operator, a job traditionally held by white workers only, and when he reported for work the white workers walked out. For two days the strike continued, during which time management remained firm and so did the union, working ceaselessly to persuade its members to honor their contracts which included a nondiscriminatory clause. At the end of the two days the men went back to work and the Negro continued to operate the crane.

When the small National Agricultural Workers AFL-CIO Union met in convention in 1957 their problem was the tension between Mexican and Negro workers in the cotton fields. A delegate from Arkansas reported that in his state and in Missouri local farm wages were as low as $2 per day for Negro workers; that a tractor driver and an operator of a cotton-picking machine frequently received as little as $3 for a ten-hour day. But Mexican nationals, working under foreign labor contracts, were guaranteed fifty cents an hour, or $5 for a ten-hour day.

One Negro delegate reported that during cotton-picking time as many as twenty-five thousand Mexicans were brought into one section of Arkansas, and that the same situation prevailed in the rice-growing area of the state. The union went on record demanding of the government the discontinuance of all programs for importing Mexican or other foreign contract labor by December 31, 1959, the expiration date of the present law authorizing such imports.

Although Negro workers frequently become discouraged at the slow pace with which they are being accorded merit employment they nevertheless are conscious of the gains made in the last twenty-five years.

"Things are sure better for us now than they were for my Dad," said a puddler in a South Chicago steel mill. "He was in the Memorial Day Picnic in '37."

The picnic to which this worker referred was the occasion for an incident which took place during the Republic Steel strike in May, 1937, when following unmet demands for wage increases and recognition of the union twenty thousand men walked out of the plant, approximately a third of them Negroes. Some of the Negro employees did not strike, and for this they were despised by the striking men. But many of those who stayed on the job did so because they did not understand what the strike was about—they were too illiterate to read the fliers, too frightened to ask questions; indeed, many could not sign their own names and were afraid to have the fact discovered by other workers. But one thing they knew—their wives and children had to eat, and to feed them the men had to stay on the job.

To the bitterness created by the division in the ranks of the Negroes was added the hatred engendered when many of the strike-breakers proved to be Negroes. So tense did interracial feeling become that women in their homes were afraid to answer knocks at the door not knowing whether the caller might be a company official, a policeman, a striker, or someone bringing news that another Negro had been shot. When on May 30, a Memorial Day picnic of several thousand steel strikers' families was fired upon by the police, panic resulted. One Negro striker characterized the occasion, "I can't find words to express the horror of it. In the World War, both sides at least had an equal chance."

Following the settlement of the Republic Steel strike the CIO moved in with a strong organizational program, and also a strong educational program; classes on union membership, and also in reading, writing and arithmetic; and for the women classes in sewing, child care and cooking. From these elementary educational beginnings the unions, often with the help of management, have developed workers who can carry their share of responsibility for good race relations.

Such a person is Mr. Sylvester Perryman, a fine-featured Negro of about forty who is a member of the grievance board at the Argo corn products plant in Chicago.

"The way we're organized today," explained Mr. Perryman, "we don't let tensions develop to the blowing up point. If any man has a grievance he brings it to the grievance board for a hearing. For instance, there was a Negro in Dry Starch who had been in the plant for thirty years; he was a good operator but not well educated. A new regulation came along that everybody at a certain level had to take a test to qualify for their jobs. This man rated low in the test and was going to be demoted. So he brought his case to the grievance department and we found that the company hadn't posted a copy of the test as they're required to do, so he really hadn't had a fair chance. After he had an opportunity to study the test he took it again and this time came along okay."

Until about a year and a half ago the railroad department at Argo had consistently held to its slogan "No nigger on the railroads!" Then, based upon test results and seniority, a Negro was assigned to railroad. A miniature tempest of resentment blew up but soon died down and today there are three Negroes in this department.

"Sometimes trouble comes because we Negroes get a little too sensitive," philosophized Mr. Perryman. "We often think it's our color that makes trouble for us when it's really our inefficiency or some personality defect that is the true cause."

At the Argo plant one hotheaded young Negro got into a wrangle with a sixty-two-year-old white woman and the case came to the grievance department. The man accused the woman of having hit him, and she accused him of having pushed her in the back. Investigation proved that the young Negro had sworn rather heartily and the woman had pushed him away—perhaps not too gently. They were each given a five-day lay-off which was equivalent to an automatic discharge. The young Negro made a point of the fact that if he were not a Negro he would be treated better. To remove any taint of discrimination the lay-off for both the troublemakers was reduced to three days.

"It's experiences like these," concluded Mr. Perryman, "that demonstrate the worth of catching your troubles early and ironing them out before they get too tangled."

The fact that in one four-year period, 1949–53, union membership increased by nearly a million, from 1,500,000 to 2,400,000, indicates that fair union practices and sound management policies are paying off.

Although unskilled labor still accounts for a disproportionately large number of nonwhite workers, in the ten-year period 1940–50 the percentage dropped from 66 to 55 per cent. At the same time a sharp increase was seen in jobs held in clerical, sales and skilled categories where the number of nonwhites doubled. At the top level, nonwhites in managerial and professional positions increased eight times over.

With higher level jobs available to Negro workers their salaries have also proportionately increased. In 1939 the average Negro annual wage was $364, or 40 per cent of the white worker's $956. By 1954 the figures had risen to $1,589 for the Negro or 50 per cent of the white worker's $3,174. In industrial areas the averages were higher, but the low farm income pulled down the national averages. While still far too low, the income of the Negro worker has increased faster than that of the white worker. In 1939 one-tenth of one per cent (o.1 per cent) of Negroes earned $5,000 a year. In 1950, 5.4 per cent earned that amount or more.

From another angle the status of the Negro worker has improved. In the youngest and oldest age brackets the number employed has decreased. As head-of-the-family wages have increased and pensions and social security benefits have been provided, young people have been able to stay in school longer and older workers have been able to retire.

Excepting at the professional level, Negro women in the work force have not made as much progress as have men, but the same situation holds true for women in general. However, because of the acceptance of Negro women as teachers and nurses the proportion of Negro professional women has grown faster than the proportion of Negro professional men. Nonwhite women are also less concentrated in the lowest categories of household work than they once were. In 1940, 80 per cent of them were thus employed while by 1950 the number had decreased to 65 per cent.

Although general discrimination against the skilled and white collar Negro woman is decreasing, she still finds noticeable wage discrimination. Mrs. Bernice Doyle watched the progress of this group of Negro women when as one of them she worked for ten years in a large laundry in an Illinois city. Mrs. Doyle, a native of New

Jersey and a graduate of a secretarial school in Pennsylvania, brought to her job a good brain, good training and good personality. Because of these assets she was hired as a payroll clerk, a position which gave her status among the other employees. As the first Negro ever to be employed by the laundry in a capacity above unskilled labor she encountered jealousy and resentment from both white and Negro workers. White girls talked in her presence with a mock Negro accent which, however, was completely absent from Mrs. Doyle's crisp Eastern speech; and at first they refused to touch equipment in the rest room after she had used it.

Because of her light complexion it was easier for the white girls eventually to accept Mrs. Doyle. One of them confided that she and the other workers at the laundry had always thought that the blacker a Negro was the worse would be his character. But also because Mrs. Doyle was lighter than some of the other Negro girls they felt a resentment against her. All of these antagonisms wore off before too long, but the wage discrimination remained for the ten years she held her position.

As payroll clerk she received $64 a month. At one time when the bookkeeper, a white girl, was ill for two weeks, Mrs. Doyle did all the bookkeeping, but she received no extra pay for the higher classification work, which carried a salary of $125. Twice she was offered the regular position of bookkeeper, but each time the manager refused to pay her the wage he paid white girls in that position.

"Finally," reported Mrs. Doyle, "I told him that I was not being hired for my color but for my competency," and she refused the offer and left the business to take a high classification position with the unemployment office in Chicago. However, in spite of the salary lag, Mrs. Doyle knows that today it is much easier for Negro women to get jobs than it was ten years ago and that their chances of promotion are better.

Even with pockets of conflict and with much still to be accomplished at every level of industry the overall trend toward integration and better race relations is nowhere better illustrated than in Detroit. For a quarter of a century, 1920–45, Detroit was a synonym for labor trouble and race conflict. By 1920 this city had become the automobile center of the world and also the center to which labor thronged because it was here that Henry Ford was paying even unskilled laborers a history-making $5 per day wage. Much of the steady stream of new workers was made up of Southern Negroes who found the promised jobs, to be sure, but who also found that the only housing open to them was the worst in already disreputable slums.

These living quarters were undesirable for any people, but as time went on and they continued to be the only housing for Negroes, even those with good wages or professional status, the situation became unbearable to some families. A few of the more courageous of this group tried to move into white residential areas—not because the areas were white but because they afforded decent surroundings in which to raise a family. One of the men who attempted such a move was Dr. Ossian Sweet, a Negro physician, who in 1925 precipitated mob violence when he moved into a white block. The police were ineffective in handling the crowd which gathered and threatened the lives of the Sweet family, so in self-defense the doctor fired a shot from inside his home, and a man was killed. When brought to trial Dr. Sweet was defended by Clarence Darrow who won an acquittal for his client. But race conflict did not end with the close of the trial.

The entire decade of the 1920's was marked by repeated labor troubles in Detroit. Frequent strikes interrupted work in all the heavy industries, and since Negroes accounted for part of the workers in each plant a strike aroused racial discord as well as labor unrest. Then came the crash of 1929 followed by a few years when all industry was in a slump. But by 1934 the New Deal recovery projects were providing jobs and the labor situation in general was picking up. But with the upswing in employment there came also an upswing in labor problems. One of them revolved around unionization of industry. The CIO, mindful of minority groups, was determined the automobile industry should be unionized, and by 1940 Henry Ford, the most resistant of the automobile industrialists, capitulated.

Unionization brought increased wages, but little improved housing. During this period construction of some public housing was under way, one of the projects being called Sojourner Truth Homes after a well-known abolitionist. During its construction housing authorities wavered between making it a development for Negro or white occupants. As indecision continued antagonisms grew and when the final decision was in favor of the Negroes trouble flared as the first families tried to move in. Within minutes a full-scale race riot was under way.

The following year, 1943, brought the worst racial explosion that

Detroit had yet known. The Packard plant upgraded three Negroes and in retaliation twenty thousand white workers walked out. Nerves throughout the city became so taut that practically everyone knew something would have to snap—and it did. On June 21, a hot Sunday afternoon, while thousands of people, most of them Negroes, overran Belle Isle Park, a dispute arose between a white man and a Negro. The dispute turned into a fist fight and the fight into a city-wide race riot, which resulted in a score or more deaths before the arrival of federal troops in the early hours of the following Tuesday morning restored a semblance of order in Detroit.

Upon investigation, Walter White, then secretary of the NAACP, found that the only large-scale Detroit industries which had escaped race trouble were those in which both management and the United Automobile Workers, a CIO union, had previously achieved some degree of integration.

A few months after the 1943 race clash the mayor appointed an interracial committee with George Shirmer as its able director. This committee called together representatives of churches, labor unions, industry, the NAACP, Urban League, schools, parents' organizations and other groups to pool their resources in working out plans to prevent a recurrence of the bloody days of the previous year.

The success of Detroit's efforts to achieve better race relations was attested in a 1951 check of mid-century progress in labor conditions in that city. It indicated that heavy industry was leading the way in nondiscriminatory practices: Ford, Kaiser-Frazer, Great Lakes Steel Corporation, Detroit Edison and others. But lesser industries were falling in line. A chain of supermarkets hired its first dozen Negro employees; an office machine company allowed its first Negro salesman to call upon white prospects; two of the city's largest downtown department stores hired their first Negro sales girls. In addition, there was a steady increase in clerical and sales positions for Negroes in firms already operating on an integrated basis, with many new firms being added to the list. Altogether this first year following mid-century was a year of many "firsts" for Negroes in Detroit industry.

Opening supervisory jobs to Negroes proved to be one of the highest incentives to better production. When the manufacturing company of Shwayder Bros., Inc., with one-third of its work force Negro, found production and morale both below par, a vice-president of the firm consulted the Union League. Together they studied the practices of the plant and then recommended faster upgrading of Negro personnel. The company appointed two Negro supervisors and arranged for other advancements on merit, with the result that fifteen months later production had increased 60 per cent.

In 1956 a "Negro Panorama of Progress" was presented in Detroit to point out the economic and industrial asset of the city's 340,000 Negroes who represent 30 per cent of the local market. In order to participate in this five-day show—and there were seventy-two exhibitors—a firm had to be Negro owned, or to have shown by its practices that it had constructive attitudes toward the progress of Negroes in industry, or to be practicing merit employment for Negro workers. Large-scale employers of national reputation included Ford, Plymouth, Packard and Studebaker motor companies; Carnation Milk, Canada Dry and Better Brand Food Distributors; Michigan Bell Telephone Company and Detroit Office Equipment.

By 1958 Detroit found the policies of the city's banks one of the most encouraging areas of progress in integration; while out-and-out policies of equal opportunity were also being practiced by government offices, hospitals, technical firms, offices employing territory salesmen, supermarkets and department stores.

Spot checks across the country indicate other changes which have taken place in general attitudes toward nonwhite workers during the past decade. Following wide and long-standing nondiscriminatory policies of the nation's telephone companies the New York company went a step beyond usual practices and refused to carry in its classified directory any discriminatory advertisements from employment agencies. At the same time the *Journal of The American Medical Association* dropped all designations of race and creed from "situations wanted" advertising. The New York Greyhound Bus Lines hired the first Negro drivers on any major interstate buses. The Metropolitan Opera Company signed its first Negro ballet dancer and first opera singer. A Negro girl was added to the staff of guides at Rockefeller Center; a new Wall Street firm opened with a mixed staff, both clerical and executives; and Pan American World Airways opened recruiting to Negro stewards and stewardesses.

In Illinois, the American Airlines put Negro girls on reservation desks; several banks accepted Negroes as tellers; Armour and Company opened its training program to nonwhite high school graduates and the Illinois Bell Telephone Company opened maintenance work and other job classifications. In Boston, the ban on Negro conductors and white porters was dropped. Michigan opened a previously all-Negro packing plant to white employees. In Ohio two leading newspapers employed Negro reporters.

A state constitutional amendment in California eliminated the few remaining restrictions against employment of Chinese in public works. The President's Committee on Government Contracts refused to allow the Bureau of Indian Affairs to sign a contract with Mississippi because the contract omitted nondiscrimination clauses. Ten railroad unions voluntarily eliminated discriminatory clauses from their national constitutions. Then in 1955 the merger convention of the AFL-CIO created a Civil Rights committee to further the work of integration.

Parallels to accomplishment in the North can be found in the South, and if the list is not as long each item represents a more drastic break with the past. During this present decade a Negro woman in Alabama was added to a police staff and the first Negro man was raised to the status of deputy sheriff. In Arkansas a Negro was made an investigator for the Alcoholic Beverage Control Board, the position being the highest state government job held by a Negro since Reconstruction days, in other than all-Negro agencies.

North Carolina placed a Negro technician in a prosthetic laboratory, a draftsman in an engineering firm, skilled and office workers in an electronics manufacturing plant, sales personnel in retail stores, and a Negro teacher over an all-white shorthand class in a secretarial school. Raleigh equalized Negro-white salaries in a state mental hospital.

In 1956 Baltimore and St. Louis passed the first fair employment practices ordinances south of the Mason-Dixon line. In South Carolina, in a period of one year the number of Negroes employed at the Savannah River project grew from 76 workers and one professional to 418 workers and 25 professionals. In Texas several oil companies and the Atomic Workers Union instituted one line of progression for all employees, thus guaranteeing equal opportunity for nonwhite workers. Dallas, where the American Friends Service Committee has carried on a comprehensive program through Job Opportunities Project for Minorities, reported a long list of openings and improved relations in a variety of industries throughout the city. In Georgia white and Negro sections of the International Ladies' Garment

Workers Union merged and in doing so promoted some Negro women to machine operators and elected some to the executive board of the Atlanta Local.

A professor in a Southern medical school, who is also head anesthetist for a large city hospital, accepted a Negro girl in his class for anesthetists and upon completion of her work took her into the operating room. Although no one found fault with her work several of the doctors and some of the hospital staff suggested it would be wise not to bring her again.

"I rather expected that reaction," he confessed. "I'm a Southerner, and in my childhood home if a Negro talked back to one of us boys my father was ready to 'bash in the darkey's head.' But I found I couldn't carry that attitude into a profession which needs all the good brains it can muster."

So he took his Negro anesthetist with him into the operating room again, and then again, and before long the hospital requested her services. Eight other Negro girls have been trained by him and all placed in Southern hospitals, while the medical school has a list of openings to be filled as fast as girls can be prepared for the jobs.

When one airline company in the South hired its first Negro secretary the personnel director took her to lunch the first day. Then his assistant shared a coffee break with her and by the following day the other girls, all white, had accepted her as a colleague.

These incidents are isolated experiences, but they could be multiplied many times over and their cumulative effect is salutary for a South that wants to attract industry to her states. On this point Governor LeRoy Collins of Florida has stated: "Believe me when I say Florida cannot afford an orgy of race conflict and discord. I have talked to many here and in other regions of the United States now poised preparatory to making substantial investments in Florida. Nothing will turn these investors away quicker than the prospect of finding here communities hepped up by demagoguery and seething under the tension and turmoil of race hatred."

Southern communities which come under the governor's characterization as "hepped up by demagoguery and seething with tension" are experiencing the results which he predicted. Winthrop Rockefeller, who heads the Arkansas industrial development program, has said that the trouble at Little Rock has occasioned a financial loss to the state because it has frightened away investors.

In line with these observations, it is not surprising that Mississippi, the state which claims to be the most segregated and the most peaceful state in the nation, for some reason ranks forty-eighth among the states in the number of new industries being established. Twice during the winter of 1957–58 Mississippi's Governor James Coleman visited New York and other Eastern cities to try to interest industrialists in opening plants in his state. At the same time he tried to get a new state constitution to make industrial investment more appealing, but also to tighten restrictions which would prevent school desegregation and prevent Negroes from voting.

Not only is the Negro population leaving Mississippi, but since 1950 twenty counties have lost a sixth of their white population; Kemper County has lost half of its white residents. The same fate has overtaken Lafayette County where the state university is located, a school which has lost a third of its faculty within the past two years. "Low salaries are not the chief reason," said a remaining member of the staff. "Lack of academic freedom and the stagnation that comes from holding back the normal currents of progress are occasioning the departure of our best men."

States, industries, individuals—all are affected by the new awareness that a man's color does not determine his potential, although frequently it does determine how hard it will be for him to realize that potential. Today nonwhite college graduates as a group rate lower jobs and less pay than white high school graduates, but twenty years ago they rated lower than white eighth grade graduates. However, few individuals in the minority groups are asking special favors. A young Negro musician, graduate of Northwestern University, expressed a common point of view when he said, "My people are just beginning to feel the competition for jobs on merit. No self-respecting man of any color will ask for concessions because he belongs to an underprivileged minority. He has to make good. All he can ask is that the rewards of his efforts shall not be withheld because he belongs to the minority."

Although labor is moving steadily in the direction of integration, the speed with which it continues to move will be determined by the willingness of the unions, employers and the general public to work for nondiscrimination both voluntary and under government regulation. In 1950 business analyst Elmo Roper indicated both the direction and the speed as he saw them. "If, in 1920, I had predicted that by 1950 the forty-hour week would be in effect in all major companies in the United States many people would have labeled me a hopeless visionary. And there will be some today who will say I am dreaming when I predict that by 1980 industrial concerns will no longer even think in terms of race, religion or nationality when they hire or promote their employees."

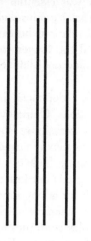

8.   *The Too Humble Homes*

For Americans, *ghetto* is an ugly word, so it has been reserved to describe concentrations of people in the old country; people who because of political, social, economic and religious reasons are forced to live in miserable surroundings and always with "their own kind." In the United States, people have found names more pleasing to the ear—Chinatown, Little Tokyo, Shantytown—but whatever the name, it stands for the same condition which the word *ghetto* signifies, people forced to live in slums with "their own kind."

Of course there has also been a natural tendency for people from foreign countries to form their own little communities in America. The ties of language, interests, relatives and friends; the need to combat loneliness; and the necessity of living in low rent areas in order to make wages cover all living necessities—all these factors encouraged Irish, German, Italian, Polish and other concentrations within the large American cities. However, there was also a general tendency for more-established Americans to help break up too-clannish groups in an effort to Americanize them as quickly as possible, frequently on the basis that Americanization was essential for the greater happiness of the children. But where racial groups were concerned a reverse process has usually controlled relations between the races; the longer they could be kept segregated the longer could be postponed the necessity for practicing democracy on Main Street—or Side Street.

Nevertheless, with the passage of time, the older racial housing patterns have broken up. As housing concentrations, Chinatowns are disappearing from the American scene. They remain as shopping centers for Oriental food and as social centers especially attractive to the older generation of Chinese Americans. Little Tokyos are also losing their housing function. As a group, Orientals are fast moving from under the shadow of discrimination which for a long time hung darkly over them. The fact that their physical characteristics make them easily distinguishable from Western peoples continues to make their complete integration slower than that of persons of European backgrounds.

American Indians, too, are moving into the main currents of American life. But all too frequently their change in locale takes them from reservations which are little better than rural slums into city tenements which are in the urban slums. The Indians by heritage do not adapt easily to city life, and the realization of this fact has led to a recent movement to locate Indian families in smaller communities within commuting distance of the larger industrial centers to which they are currently migrating. Of necessity this experiment will be slow in proving its worth and in the meantime many Indians are caught in the housing shortage which is part of the complex problem of every large city today.

American Indians find an added frustration in the fact that their status in communities differs in various parts of the country. In the East the individual with Indian blood is usually made to feel proud of his heritage. In the Midwest, especially in areas near reservations, he is generally considered inferior to white citizens; but the suburban home owner who commented, "If an Indian can meet the economic requirements of home building in our community, he's welcome," spoke a general attitude. Few can meet the requirements. In contrast, some of the Indians of the oil lands of the Southwest have accrued fortunes which make it possible for them not only to meet but to set economic standards in their communities.

Negroes carry the brunt of the tension in interracial housing. Social analysts are in general agreement that today, of all the issues arising from strained race relations, housing is the most inflammable. Morley Cassidy, veteran reporter, called attention in the November 9, 1957, issue of *Human Events*, to the situation in Philadelphia where the 500,000 Negroes give that city a colored population larger than the combined Negro population of Atlanta, New Orleans and Jackson, Mississippi. Mr. Morley pointed out that state fair employment practices laws have been accepted by business and industry with good grace, but that the housing situation has not lent itself to any graceful solution.

Sheriff Lohman of Cook County, Illinois, has stated that labor around Chicago can handle the incoming tide of Negroes, for the present at least, but that housing is a daily threat to the peace of the city. A few years ago one-half of the sections of the city which had mixed populations were no more than 50 per cent Negro. Today nine-tenths of the mixed areas are 90 per cent Negro. Also, there is a constant movement of colored population into the once all-white districts, and it is in these neighborhoods of newly mixed races that the greatest tensions exist.

Across the country housing patterns present a varied panorama of human relations. In Memphis, segregation is the general rule, but there is a section of modest single family residences where adjacent front yards will often display "FOR RENT" signs carrying the words *white* or *colored*. However, the mixed neighborhoods do not offer social equality for the renters: Negro children go to their own schools and adults observe established segregation practices.

Within the limits of segregation, Atlanta has developed an affluent Negro community not duplicated in many cities. Auburn Avenue is sometimes referred to as the Negroes' Fifth Avenue. Buildings in this area are unprepossessing when compared with those on Ponce de Leon or Peachtree, but they house business concerns of large capital —insurance companies, banks, department and specialty stores, and a radio station. Negroes may achieve a financial status that would permit a $50,000 house and a Cadillac; but Atlanta insists that the money be earned in segregated businesses and that the Negro citizens live in the parts of the city allotted them, not in those areas which would be attractive to people of wealth, education and culture. At the same time Atlanta is very willing that the Negroes spend their money in the city's unsegregated stores.

For many years the District of Columbia was the center of attack from social reformers because of the shambles in which its Negro population was forced to live. Today there are nearly two million Negroes living in the city of Washington and another million in the outlying areas of the District. With the general movement of the white population to the suburbs the ratio of Negro to white families in the city has increased. But, simultaneous with this population movement has been another social movement—a clean-up of the city's worst tenement districts.

Much of the responsibility for clearing the slums of Washington was carried by Colonel Campbell C. Johnson, appointed by President Truman in 1950 to membership on the National Capital Housing Authority, and the only Negro member of the 100-man board in a city one-third Negro. One of Colonel Johnson's first acts was to introduce a resolution to end segregation in public housing. However, since Washington is governed directly by Congress, and since many Southern Congressmen make their home in the city for a large part of every year, their attitudes affect the legislation which regulates the city life. Several times Johnson's resolution was defeated but after two years of continuous work he saw it passed and the way was then open to attack segregated housing in a practical manner.

By that time the 1952 presidential campaign was the focal point of the nation's interest. The platforms of both major political parties contained statements against racial discrimination while at the same time both vice-presidential candidates were living in houses for which they had signed restrictive covenants. However, the year following President Eisenhower's election, he declared, "I propose to use whatever authority exists in the office of President to end segregation in the District of Columbia. . . ."

Meanwhile, Colonel Johnson had been steadily working with the families about to move out of the tenements and those already in the new housing units, helping them to understand the new relationships they faced as they became part of integrated developments. At the same time, a general District-wide educational campaign to pave the way for later school integration helped to provide a climate for nonviolent desegregation of public housing—projects in which municipal or government funds are invested. By 1954, 87 per cent of the public housing had been integrated and Colonel Johnson reported that there had not been one untoward incident during the process.

Just a step from Washington lies Baltimore, a city whose persistent growth is pushing its suburbs out and concentrating its low income groups in the oldest residential areas. In contrast to Atlanta, Baltimore is rapidly integrating many aspects of its corporate life, while at the same time finding its overall program slowed down by the housing shortage which perpetuates racial neighborhoods as effectively as would a policy of segregation. Baltimore industries are desegregating and providing many jobs on merit. Since 1955 schools have been integrating. Parks, libraries and swimming pools are open to Negroes. But with the exception of the homes of a small group of wealthier business and professional Negroes, housing for Baltimore's 267,000 Negroes is antiquated—solid block-long rows of ancient brick-front houses.

Fortunately, Baltimore is aware of the plight of its Negro population and for several years the city has been trying to alleviate conditions. The frequently cited Baltimore Plan was an experiment in rehabilitating a tenement area through the co-operation of various departments of the city—law enforcement, sanitation, building, fire protection, and others. Demonstration blocks were cleaned up, buildings repaired, police protection strengthened. Nevertheless this piecemeal approach, although proving that conditions could be bettered, indicated that such a system alone could not produce satisfactory results. In residential areas whose construction dates back to Civil War days, modernization was too slow and too expensive to be continued on a large scale. So Baltimore is still struggling with its housing problem.

As space is measured today, New York City is only a step from Baltimore, but that step brings one into the most crowded section in the United States—East Harlem, the slum district of Harlem. Here in a mile by mile-and-a-half area live 300,000 people in such congestion that if all the people in the United States lived in equal congestion the entire population could be housed in half the area of New York City.

Here in one city block there are twenty-seven tenements housing four thousand people of all races and fifty nationalities. Only a few years ago one of these buildings was purchased for $6,000 and today the landlord is making an annual profit of $6.000 from the one building. Rents vary from $35 to $100 a month, depending in part upon the size of the apartment but more directly on how desperately a family needs a place to live. Then in addition to paying his rent the new tenant must "buy in"—pay cash to the outgoing tenant for the furnishings in the apartment—an expense which usually amounts to $400 or $500. But because few families in this area can pay such charges the contracted renter takes in two or three other families to share the space and the expense.

For the money invested the tenant gets broken windowpanes, sagging floors, cockroaches in all the cracks and rats running through holes in the walls and stairs. He may even be one of forty-five tenants to share a single bathroom with a broken toilet seat. An air of impending disaster pervades East Harlem—disaster that arises from cutthroat competition for jobs, from too many families living in too little space, from teenagers who must take their good times where they can make them, usually on the streets and in the alleys and involving gang warfare; from too many children who die too young because of unsanitary conditions in which they are born and must live.

How much time must elapse before these slums, and others like them, will be eliminated cannot be accurately foretold, but they are on their way out. A national slum clearance program was inaugurated a quarter of a century ago during the depression of the 1930's when the government undertook to stabilize the country's crumbling economy by partially underwriting a program of tenement clearance. Cities were given financial assistance in demolishing old tenements and replacing them with new apartment houses for low income families. The early renting practices followed the racial housing pattern of each locality which was almost invariably a pattern of segregation. Then as pressure for desegregation in American life increased people became aware of the contradiction in taking the public moneys of a democracy and investing them in segregated housing. A public conscience developed and with it a policy of nonsegregation in housing in which government funds are involved.

In East Harlem, one section of tenements has been razed and in their place has been constructed the Carver Houses, a public housing project of several units. Rents for these apartments with modern equipment and adequate conveniences depend upon the breadwinner's wages and the size of his family. For instance, a family of six with an income in the higher bracket for this community will pay about $67 for a five-room apartment. The original plan of placing on each floor two Negro families, two Puerto Rican and two families of other national or racial backgrounds could not be carried out, so in actual practice Puerto Ricans predominate and white families are a small minority. In many of the larger cities of the country public housing projects are common sights. In Chicago, Cabrini Homes, located on the Near North Side is a development which has accomplished integration in spirit as well as in renting procedures. It covers several square blocks and when completed will house thirty-two hundred families with an average of four-and-a-half members to the family. "Five would be more accurate," suggested one of the tenants, "because there is either another one on the way or some of us have relatives on extended visits."

One of the buildings in this extensive project is Lower North Center, a privately endowed neighborhood house which is the pulse of social and educational activity for the government-sponsored housing. At the heart of Lower North Center is Mr. Mark Battle, young enthusiastic Negro director who gets to the reasons behind everything that happens in the area, whether good or bad.

According to Mr. Battle, the main characteristic of this part of the city is that it has always been a transition area. Several generations ago it was predominantly Irish—back when they were the new, and therefore the looked-down-upon immigrants. The Irish still dominate the politics of this part of Chicago. Then came the Italians. Many of them are still in this area; perhaps today they are the most stable of the nationality groups. Then came the Negro, the Nisei, and most recently the Puerto Ricans. So far not many of the new Negro workers from the South have moved in, but their turn will come. At the present time the densest concentration of Puerto Ricans in the city is in this area.

Mr. Battle discounts common rumors that Negroes, Puerto Ricans and other low income minority groups are destructive, dirty and irresponsible. Occasionally, he admits, there is a slovenly family—one kept a few chickens in the bathtub, but only for a few days; the housing superintendent soon discovered the incipient poultry farm and put an end to its existence in Cabrini Homes. Many of the families that move into the units are ignorant of newfangled improvements. They may never before have lived in a house with running water, or done a washing with anything but a tub of water and a scrubboard; so the women are frightened by the automatic washers and frequently leave them unused; or as frequently jam the works. Therefore, to help make it easier for the women to learn modern methods, the Center has equipped its kitchen exactly as the units are equipped and runs several classes each week in kitchencraft.

The broad windows of Mr. Battle's office look out across the children's playground where there is no trouble with integration among the little tots on the slides, teeters and swings. And in contrast to many parts of the city, there is not much trouble at the teenage level. The director recalls that an early experience was their worst one. "Back in 1951 when we held our first teenage dance a group of rowdies from the West Side came over and tried to break it up. For a few minutes the dance turned into a free-for-all because our gang resented the intrusion and some of them broke a table over the head of a West Sider. We had to call the police and that meant dragging some of our boys through court."

However, the staff of the Center followed through on each boy's case and salvaged about three-fourths of them. The leader of the local gang took to dope for a short time but now, five years later, he is one of the best volunteer workers at the Center.

Today lesser feuds sometimes develop, usually because a member of one race taunts a member of another at some point where his pride is most easily hurt. One such feud developed between two teenage girls, a Negro and a Puerto Rican. Isabella, the Puerto Rican, was in the stage of acquiring a high school disdain for the island mannerisms of her mother. So when Mary, the Negro girl, jeered at Isabella because of the way her mother dressed and talked, Isabella flared up and the two girls had a fist and hair-pulling fight.

Shortly afterward the Center persuaded both girls to join hobby classes and then purposely put them into the same dancing class. Isabella was a whiz with the popular South American dances, and before long she was teaching them to the others, including Mary. After the girls joined these classes their mothers got up courage to join a sewing class. This group took as its project the making of a layette which they then gave to Isabella's mother. Isabella herself developed into an excellent student and became one of the junior counselors at the Center.

To be sure, everything is not sweetness and light, yet hardly a day goes by that does not bring to Mr. Battle's attention the community of interests which cross racial lines. There was the case of Mr. York, a janitor, white, with no special education but with two active little boys. One day while he was sitting in his parked car watching his children play on some park equipment he heard a loud howl and looked up in time to see a group of high school age Negro boys slug a white boy. Mr. York jumped out of his car, caught the boys and called the police. He also called Mr. Battle and asked him to help see the colored boys through the court. One of the boys had a long record of misdemeanors and it took months to get his case straightened out, but Mr. York stuck with it. When someone asked him why he wasted so much time on an apparently worthless Negro boy he replied, "I'm interested in kids—I got two of my own." So Cabrini Homes fills many more needs than the need for housing.

Public housing provides homes only for families with limited incomes. For the better paid workers and professional people there is little such integrated housing available. These are the families who today are trying to obtain homes in residential districts which until recent years were considered stable white communities. Such a community is the Woodlawn area of Chicago, a section one mile square lying south of the University of Chicago. Since 1950 this area has been the section of the city undergoing the most rapid change from white to Negro residency. At the present time more than 80 per cent of the eighty thousand people living in this area are nonwhite. For thirty years the district has had a community organization of some sort, sometimes more than one; today after changes and mergers the organization is called the United Woodlawn Conference and Miss Esther Davis is president.

In 1957 the Chicago *Sun* assigned a staff member to make a study of integrated institutions in the city. Before long another reporter asked him, "Have you met Miss Davis?"

"Who's she?" was the answer.

"Well," came the reply, "she's an institution—and she's integrated!"

A well-built, outgoing, enthusiastic individual with a thousand interests, Miss Davis seems to invite trouble to come to her for solution. Her apartment is liberally filled with gifts from the Orient, autographed pictures of diplomats and other tokens of appreciation. She earns her living in a position which bears the old-fashioned title of Christian Friendliness Missionary for the Chicago Baptist Association; but she earns her reputation from the combination of her official work with many other activities.

Interracial feeling became tense in the Woodlawn area early in this decade when the Universalist Church sold its property to a Negro congregation and for the first time Negroes moved into the area east of the Illinois Central tracks which cut through the Woodlawn community. There had been Negroes west of the tracks for several years but when the first of them crossed the tracks the residents of that part of the community were up in arms. Then when a white man was assaulted one night apprehensive rumors began to spread and there were serious threats of forming a vigilante committee of some kind. Conditions were serious enough that the Mayor's Commission called a meeting of the residents of the Woodlawn area, and especially urged Miss Davis to attend.

"I arrived late," she admits. "I came to this meeting from an observance, of all things, of World Community Day on the first Friday of November. The irate Woodlawn citizens were meeting in our branch library and the crowded room they occupied was so thick with smoke that people almost choked when they talked. But it didn't stop the talk! As I entered a lawyer was shaking a bomb-pen in the face of the local police captain and shouting, 'I know it's illegal to carry this weapon, but I've told my wife and the other women in my neighborhood to carry one every time they step out of the house.' "

The cause of the lawyer's excitement was the growing body of rumors that people were being molested on the streets by Negroes and that one man had been nearly beaten to death.

"Finally I asked for the floor," continued Miss Davis, "and I said to these men, 'Now about these rumors which our lawyer friend is so worked up over. I want to ask him if, as a lawyer trained to get facts, he ever tried to get the facts about the man who was reported to have been beaten in a Negro-white fight?' He didn't say a word. So then I asked if any of the other men had taken the trouble to call the police to get the facts; or if any of them had called the hospital to inquire about the condition of the supposedly almost-killed man; or to visit him and get the facts straight from him."

When there was no response from anyone present Miss Davis pushed them a little farther. "Most of you know who I am because I've lived in this community more than twenty years. You know I come home frequently in the middle of the night and I walk from the I.C. station to my apartment alone. And I know most of you—even to what churches you attend," and she identified several of the persons present and their church affiliations, Catholic, Protestant and Jewish. Then she quoted a verse from the Bible, "He hath not given us a spirit of fear . . . but of power, love, and a sound mind." "Anyone with a sound mind," Miss Davis added, "gets the facts."

Before the meeting closed the citizens drew up a list of complaints and demands to present to the mayor. The following Monday morning just as Miss Davis was about to leave her apartment the wife of the building superintendent came bustling up to her excitedly, "There are two awfully distinguished men looking for you. They're on their way up."

The two men proved to be Captain Enright of the city police force who had been present at the Friday meeting, and one of the city commissioners. Captain Enright explained that when he reported the meeting back at headquarters the commissioner was so impressed that he wanted to meet Miss Davis. He said to her, "We'll do all the things they asked for—give 'em more lights, more squad cars. But we're going to depend on you to tell us what this area really needs."

Of the seventy-five square blocks which comprise the United Woodlawn Conference forty now have block organizations or clubs, each with a president. If any tension arises within a block area it is immediately reported to the president of the block who in turn gets in touch with Miss Davis.

"But of course, I'm out of the city a great deal. However, there are two women I can rely on to put their heads together and act when I'm gone. One is Negro and the other is Jewish and they make a wonderful team." Recently a Conference tea was held which was attended by four thousand people, among them a liberal representation of Negroes, Puerto Ricans, Japanese, Chinese, a few American Indians, and older white families of all faiths and many nationalities.

A double transition is taking place in this Woodlawn area, not alone from white to Negro occupancy but from professional Negro families to those of lower economic strata.

"I'm caught right now in that shift," added Miss Davis. "This apartment house was opened to Negro occupancy just a year ago and is one of the most recent to be sold to a Negro owner. Negro real estate men have their share of profiteers and the new owner of this apartment house is one of them. When he bought the building last

August he gave notice to all apartment holders that their contracts were ended. He's trying to put the building on a week-to-week rental basis, leaving him free to raise rents or evict almost at will. The Conference hopes to keep him in line by insisting on better rental practices.

"So I'm moving next week," concluded Miss Davis, "but not out of the area. I've found an apartment a few blocks away. With the race tension, and with all the foreign students attending the University and living in this area, and with nationals from other countries coming here to study problems of every sort, I'm going to stay where I can be of most help. Besides," she added, "I have three porcelain Chinese statues of Lo-Han, the old gentleman who stands for good luck and long life—they ought to help me through any crisis that may develop."

This Woodlawn area, although potentially one of the most inflammable in the city, has had no violent outbreaks such as have occurred in other sections of Greater Chicago.

One of these, climaxing several scores of race riots in and around the city, was the major outbreak at Cicero in 1951, when Mr. Harvey Clark, a Negro veteran of World War II and a graduate of Fisk University, moved into an apartment in this previously all-white suburb. For three days uncontrolled rioting continued, until martial law restored order. The physical damage to the apartment house was estimated at $20,000. Sociologists have been unable to estimate the social damage to the democratic process.

Two years later an incident which overshadowed the Cicero explosion was precipitated when Mr. Donald Howard, a Negro, moved into Trumbull Park Homes, a previously unintegrated public housing development. The cost to the city in property destruction and police protection—twenty-four-hour service of hundreds of policemen for a period of several years—has called nation-wide attention to the cost, in dollars and cents, of letting interracial conflicts develop or go unchecked once they have flared up.

That such outbreaks have not occurred in the Woodlawn area is partially due to the work of the Conference in promoting mutual understanding and a meeting ground for varied political, social and religious interests.

If housing for minority groups in Baltimore, New York, Chicago and other cities presents specific difficulties, just as plainly do the experiences of each city suggest solutions. In some communities the first steps toward interracial housing have been taken by the government; in others, by some local organization, neighborhood group or solitary individual. As a result of many programs the preconceptions of the undesirable economic and social aspects of interracial housing are being exploded, and many communities are now able to report some democratic housing practices.

9. Homes for Democracy

On the theory that a problem carries within it suggestions for its solution, the housing situation for minority people in Philadelphia should indicate some of the possible means of providing more and better integrated housing, both there and elsewhere. First, there is an obvious housing shortage. Then there is the prevalent theory, perpetuated by realtors, that segregated housing is the only acceptable American pattern. Within recent years, for example, Levitt and Sons, Inc., developed Levittown, a community for sixty thousand people on the outskirts of Philadelphia, and "as a matter of good business" restricted it to white occupancy. Operating under this practice the community was unprepared for the advent of the first Negro family. In August, 1957, in a private real estate transaction a house was sold to a young Negro refrigeration technician who had previously lived in a racially integrated community. Violence in his part of Levittown lasted about a week, but tension continued after that period. Also there were threats of panic selling on the part of some of the home owners in the neighborhood but real estate men reported no early rush of property listings.

A third element in the Philadelphia housing situation is illustrated by Concord Park Homes, Inc., a privately developed community which started with a definite theory that good business is not all on the side of segregation. Instigator of the project was Morris Milgram, a junior member of a construction firm, who had entered his father-in-law's business with the understanding that he be allowed to practice nondiscrimination in his building policies; and he meant nondiscrimination at every level of the building process, planning, financing, owning. Milgram, a member of the Fellowship of Reconciliation, is also interested in the work of the American Friends Service Committee whose members and co-workers have been active in promoting sound human relations in many situations involving racial tension.

When Milgram undertook to establish Concord Park Homes he needed capital; and for this venture any capital would be "risk capital" more than for ordinary investments. Nevertheless, from individuals who shared his point of view he raised $150,000 and formed a corporation. Included in this group was George E. Otto, a Quaker builder of fine repute whose support, both financial and moral, was an asset to the corporation. Next, Negro capital was solicited in line with the concept of interracial responsibility throughout the project.

From the total group of investors a board was formed and officers were elected. Four years then went into planning and overcoming the initial obstacles. By that time a location had been secured—a fifty-acre tract on a main bus line and fifteen minutes closer to Philadelphia than was Levittown. Next came the matter of securing financing for the mortgages. The Bowery Savings Bank of New York assumed that responsibility and the way was open for construction of 140 medium-priced homes ranging from $12,000 to $13,500.

Concurrent with the development of Concord Park, Milgram undertook the development of Greenbelt Knoll, in a higher price bracket and located somewhat closer to the heart of the city.

The original plan called for opening both projects to all races, but when the first homes were put on the market there was a rush of Negro purchasers. Young Milgram was faced with a decision: if these projects were to remain interracial he had to see that they contained families of more than one race. As much as he disliked the idea of quotas such a system seemed the only way to initiate integrated housing. Finally, with the agreement of both white and Negro members of the board and to the satisfaction of the first prospective buyers, a ratio of 55–45 white-Negro residency was established.

In these early ventures Milgram discovered that achieving a balance in racial occupancy depended somewhat on the attitudes of the real estate agents who negotiated the sales. The first sales were handled by general real estate companies who seemed obsessed with the idea that a few Negro families in an area meant, before long, a Negro community, and so the agents were slow to make contacts with white families. Later when the sales personnel were selected from people with sufficient devotion to the idea of integrated housing to live in the developments themselves, sales difficulties cleared up and the communities have become the neighborly and racially balanced projects that Milgram had hoped to achieve.

Of all the types of communities on the American scene the suburbs have been the most resistant to intrusion by people of color. But encouraged by the results of Concord Homes and Greenbelt Knoll a group of Friends in the Philadelphia area organized Suburban Housing, Inc., a grass-roots movement of suburbanites who believe that "now it can be done." Membership is restricted to suburban home owners who are convinced of the feasibility of interracial communities and who desire to bring into their own community nonwhite neighbors who can contribute to the well-being of the entire group and also share in the advantages which the suburbanites themselves are enjoying. By the spring of 1958, at the end of its first eighteen months Suburban Housing, Inc., had sold nine homes to Negro families with trouble having developed in only one instance. This accomplishment is partially explained by the fact that the members of the organization are themselves home owners in the areas to which they are inviting Negro neighbors. Also most of the home owners are Friends although it is hoped that the number of people of other faiths will increase.

In other cities individuals and groups are waking to the fact that they, too, could initiate a venture in integrated housing. For example, the Beeches, a young married couple in Des Moines, Iowa, became critical of the complacency with which their city was drifting toward neighborhoods closed to Negro families. Then with a jolt the Beeches realized that mere critcism is itself a form of complacency; that to have value criticism must be translated into action. But what could one young couple with no financial reserve do about housing? The

Beeches decided that the first step was to talk over the problem with some of their friends who might be like-minded. So they invited five other couples to come to their home for an evening.

The group gathered and at the end of two hours decided that if a young man like Milgram could initiate Concord Park Homes, other people could start something in their own communities. However, no one in this group was a member of a construction company, nor did any of them have a bank account to draw on. Not even any wealthy friends. However, each couple decided it could contribute $100 to a working fund to make possible bringing in someone to counsel with them and to finance some study of projects in other communities. They further decided to work in the open, so they gave a brief story of their concern for housing to the newspapers. Although definite procedures toward an integrated neighborhood are still in the incipient stage the group feels encouraged that the press has been co-operative and that their friends and friends of their friends show an interest in the idea.

In Minneapolis, in 1944, an experiment very different from Milgram's program was undertaken by a private builder, Edward N. Tilsen, who bought up scattered lots in a twenty-square-block area which was predominantly white. Of forty-four homes which he built in the first few years forty were sold to Negro families. The first such purchase was followed by a brief wave of panic selling, some of it definitely encouraged by real estate brokers. Then when the early reaction settled down the community became stabilized with about 20 per cent of the families Negro. This scattered-lot building plan is one method that assures a reasonably slow interracial mixing in a given area; and since most large cities have but few vacant lots in any one residential section the new residents will not exceed the established racial group.

In Yellow Springs, Ohio, a well-developed policy of discrimination has never existed. Ever since Civil War days there has been free movement for the Negroes in the town and the cultural influence of Antioch College has contributed to the prevailing attitude. Yet in recent years, as the Negro population has increased, a tendency has developed for the Negroes to concentrate in certain blocks. Then two construction partners decided to open a subdivision, Westgate, on a nondiscriminatory basis. Because the Negroes were the hardest pressed for good housing, they rushed in to buy the first finished homes. The builders then decided that an interracial project should have white and nonwhite families in about the same ratio as the white and nonwhite residents in the town, so the sale of homes to Negro families was limited to approximately 30 per cent of the total number, but no effort was made to concentrate them in any part of the new division. The people of Yellow Springs have accepted the pattern of Westgate as a natural design.

In Madison, Wisconsin, it was again a builder, Mr. Jacob Sinaiko, who opened an interracial area which he expects to keep at a ratio of occupancy which will represent the ratio of whites and nonwhites in the community.

In some cities, although there are backers for integrated housing projects, the banks and mortgage companies have united in closing all doors to financial aid for such undertakings. This is the situation that prevails in Indianapolis, one of the cities which received the 1957 award from *Look* magazine for an outstanding housing program. The commendation was received for the development of Flanner Homes, Inc., a housing project for Negro families. The sponsoring corporation is an outreach of the work of Flanner House, a neighborhood institution with diversified activities ranging from a nursery school to a clinic, a food-processing program, and youth and adult activities of study and recreation. Although started as a Negro center many phases of the work at Flanner House are integrated.

Built on a former city dump the 220-home addition, with a per home valuation of approximately $12,000, this project is unusual because each family contributed a given number of hours of work in the actual construction of their home, thus reducing the necessary cash outlay. Local finance companies handled loans and mortgages.

Encouraged by the success of this venture the same corporation considered a similar project for white families. At a meeting of the corporation, composed of both Negro and white members, the project was outlined and well received, the members agreeing that such an undertaking would demonstrate their concern for the betterment of both races. But at the end of two hours of discussion one man rose to question the entire procedure. Calling attention to the fact that the public schools had recently integrated, that public works were hiring on a nondiscriminatory basis, that stores and other firms were having pressure put upon them to integrate their personnel, he asked what would be the effect on the total program of better race relations if this group should project a plan which would continue segregated housing for several generations?

"His point was well taken," commented Dr. Cleo Blackburn, director of the Flanner House project, "but the difficulty is that in Indiana we cannot get any company to finance integrated housing. We've been working on it for several years and since this meeting we've doubled our efforts. The president of a Tennessee bank and life insurance company was willing to undertake the financing but we were out of the territory in which the law allows him to invest. Several other recent attempts have each met unexpected obstructions. Our next move will be to try some Eastern banks that have helped finance other integrated housing projects. But as it stands at the present time, if Indianapolis is to have any improved housing for low income families, Negro or white, that housing is going to have to be segregated."

Part of the difficulty in getting favorable financial action on interracial housing lies in certain fixed ideas which are held by a majority of the people. One of these ideas is that the market value of property declines as soon as the first family of color moves into a community. At times and under certain conditions the statement is true. During the early influx of Negroes into Northern communities property valuations fell when the first Negro moved into an all-white neighborhood because home owners panicked and dumped their homes on the market and by that very process speeded up the decline of values.

But even in the early days of mixed neighborhoods owners who held onto their property instead of dumping it discovered that they profited by that procedure. For one thing, when good housing became available to Negro home owners the demand for it was so great that competition frequently pushed up the price beyond what it was when the area was all white.

Repeated studies have verified the fact that when families of color move into an area real estate values need not go down. Following the large influx of Negroes into California the housing situation became acute, and unsupported judgments became so damaging that a study was made and published in the *Appraisal Journal* for realtors. Realizing that too frequently comparisons are made between valuations of white and nonwhite housing units without taking into consideration the relative ages of the buildings and other pertinent data, the examiners matched neighborhoods for this study. Every aspect—distance from the heart of the city, topography, age of homes, construction costs, incomes of the owners and other factors—all were the same. The only difference was in the color of the occupants moving into the communities. The control areas remained all-white and their counterparts admitted people of color.

Two of the statistically validated conclusions were that there seemed to be no support for the assertions that nonwhites depress market values, and that the amount of nonwhite entry into the communities made little difference in values. The slight difference indicated by the total sales was in favor of sales to nonwhites. "Thus the over-all picture of comparative market prices should be reassuring to those who fear non-white entry will harm prices. . . . San Francisco's cosmopolitan attitude in racial relations may not be unique when contrasted with those apparently now prevailing in some northern cities. According to some experienced observers widespread non-white entry into formerly all-white neighborhoods is proceeding apace."

An analysis of several housing studies has been released by the race relations department of the American Missionary Association. Organized in 1846, the AMA is the oldest home missions organization in the United States. Although a department of the Congregational Christian Churches, since 1942 it has worked in conjunction with Fisk University, one of the colleges for Negro students which it established immediately after the Civil War. Some of the studies reported by the AMA deal with property valuations and all of them point to the fact that Negro buyers pay more for property than do white buyers for the same property. This fact is easily explained on the ground that a good many families from minority groups could afford to live in better homes if they were available. Taking the United States as a whole, about one in thirteen persons is a Negro, but out of every thousand vacancies only two are available for Negro occupancy while seventy-seven out of a thousand vacancies should be available.

In one community appraisers studied the facts of cost and sale value on thirty houses in a given all-white area. Market prices ranged from $2,200 to $3,500. Then the area was opened to Negro purchasers and six months later the identical houses were valued up to $5,500. According to the principle of supply and demand, if a

neighborhood does not indulge in panic selling with the first purchase by a member of a minority group, values increase. The reasons
are obvious. All large industrial cities are short on housing. In the
interests of good business landlords and real estate agencies try to
get the highest price possible for every house they sell. Because good
housing for Negroes is at a premium—and because they have to live
someplace—they are forced to pay more for property than could be
charged a white purchaser. So in practice, Negro buying frequently
increases the sales price.

In renting as well as in purchasing, Negro tenancy often raises
the income from properties. When Mr. Wesley Cobb, director of
community relations for the Urban League in Chicago, moved into
that city two years ago he made telephone inquiries concerning
apartment vacancies listed in the newspapers, and found several
desirable locations. In every case renting arrangements went smoothly
until the agency asked where he was employed. When he said he
was with the Urban League any number of reasons became apparent
why the apartment could not be rented at that time.

"I finally found one near Fifty-third Street," said Mr. Cobb. "It
was just being opened to Negro families and as each of us went into
the building we had our rent automatically raised $25 above the rent
quoted to white applicants for the same apartment. Such a difference
is general and is called the 'color rent' which proprietors feel justified
in asking of Negroes because they know they can get it."

A second idea held by most people is that Negro tenants let property deteriorate faster than do white tenants. The general fact of
greater deterioration is true; however, the reason for the deterioration usually lies in the lower maintenance provided by the owners
of the property after Negroes move into it. Commenting on this fact,
Mr. Cobb observed, "As soon as several Negro families move into
an apartment building, regardless of the higher rent they pay,
maintenance of the building decreases. The public receives the im-
pression that the Negro tenants are shiftless. Actually, many of them
are chagrined to live in deteriorating buildings and they resent the
fact that they pay first class rents and receive third class maintenance
services."

In areas composed of single family houses it has frequently happened that the first Negro owners raised the standard of home up-
keep. Delighted to have found a home of their own they take special

pleasure in making it the kind of home they have always wanted. A resident of Marion, Indiana, reported that in parts of his city the new Negro home owners paint their houses, trim up their lawns and in general set a standard that puts the white neighbors on the spot to keep up with the Negro families.

When Thomas L. Gillette made a study in Kansas City of six hundred homes purchased by Negro families over a period of years he found that 90 per cent of the new owners made substantial improvements in their properties and that many of their neighbors agreed that the Negro families raised the economic and cultural level of their neighborhoods.

A third point of view held by many people is that white residents always object to Negro residents in their midst. Exceptions, of course, would be those areas where voluntary interracial housing is the basis for a development. But even the idea that in established all-white areas the entrance of Negro families always meets with hostility has too many exceptions to be considered the current rule.

In one neighborhood in Cincinnati when it became known that a Negro family was moving in, a hastily organized citizens' committee created such strong resistance that police protection for the family was necessary. But almost immediately one home owner in the area, a man highly respected by all his neighbors, called a meeting to discuss how the new family could be made at home in the community. As a result of this gesture sentiment against the Negro family died down.

In Baltimore after the first Negro family moved into a certain block one of the neighbors reported that there were early unfavorable comments, but that was the extent of the opposition; many of the old-timers found the Negro family a greater asset to their block than the white family that moved out.

In Long Island Levittown, the first housing project undertaken by the Levitts, although Negro families are certainly not encouraged to move in, eight or ten Negro families do live in the community and no one is badly upset over the fact. One white resident strongly contends that it is the *idea* and not the *fact* of interracial housing that disturbs most people. If the Negroes had been part of the community from the beginning he felt that no white family would have hesitated to move in; but once having been an all-white community some of the people resented the intrusion of Negro families. He concluded, "I'll admit that it wouldn't have made a damn bit of difference to me originally."

Although resistance of white home owners to nonwhite neighbors has been of long standing it first received the stamp of approval from the government in 1934 when the Federal Housing Administration was established and allowed to operate by local building codes. Through the services of the FHA the federal government went into partnership with private construction by insuring loans and mortgages. To protect its funds the government charged the home owner a small insurance fee. With the builders' investments thus secured home building took a tremendous leap. For its day, the FHA was a radical social advance. However, today students of social trends find much that appears undesirable, their criticism centering on the official sanction given to the practice of segregation. For instance, one requirement for FHA insurance was that the building project be located in a stable community. "If a neighborhood is to retain stability, it is necessary that properties shall continue to be occupied by the same social and racial classes."

In his book *Forbidden Neighbors*, Charles Abrams details the successive pronouncements of the FHA in its attempt to prevent infiltration of adverse influences, which include "unharmonious racial groups." Restrictive covenants were encouraged as the best means of supporting the stable community against minority groups. The Administration prepared a model restrictive covenant for the home builder's use, reading, "no person of any other race than ——— shall use or occupy any building or other lot," and each buyer or builder signed on the dotted line that he would not sell or lease his land to any person not a member of the homogeneous group. Zoning was advocated to bar public nuisances—stables, pig pens, and occupancy by the wrong race. Care was to be taken that adverse influences such as "smoke, odors, fog" and "inharmonious racial or nationality groups" did not lower the social prestige and economic value of a community.

Then in 1948 the Supreme Court ruled that although citizens were free to enter into restrictive covenants, such covenants could not be enforced by the courts. With the removal of legal enforcement the restraining power of these covenants was broken. The following year a revision of FHA policies resulted in dropping the demand for a homogeneous community as a basic requirement for a loan. The Home Loan Bank and the Veterans Administration followed the example of the FHA and funds secured by any of these agencies could then be used for home construction in unsegregated areas.

The results of the many movements for desegregation are evident across the country. In California even with its recent 200 per cent increase in Negro population, segregation is nevertheless breaking down. In Fontana, a once-segregated town, Negroes may now live anywhere. In Milpitas a 1,000-unit project, originally planned as two separate segregated units, was opened two years ago on an integrated basis.

San Francisco, in 1954, opened six formerly all-white housing projects to Negroes. The following year twenty public housing developments were put on an integrated basis, leaving only two in the city still segregated. In 1956 the United Automobile Workers joined private businessmen in developing an unrestricted housing program. One investor, a woman strongly opposed to unsegregated housing, found herself with a new apartment building on her hands which she could not fill with tenants. To protect her investment she opened it to any renters and soon had the vacant apartments filled with Negro families. Within a short time she was reversing her previous estimate of Negro tenants and became an outspoken advocate of integrated housing. Moreover she soon found herself on boards of civic organizations, hailed as a social benefactor to San Francisco.

In Scarsdale, New York, a country estate type white community, several generations of six low income Negro families have lived for a hundred years. However, recently two homes in the $40,000–$50,000 class were built by Negroes alongside new homes for white occupants and the community was not disrupted.

In 1954 the Kennecott Copper Corporation of New Mexico agreed to open all company housing on a nonsegregated basis. The same year Nevada started its first interracial housing, and Illinois reported a long list of new projects to be added to those already operating on a multiple-race occupancy basis. In Philadelphia the Slocum Street Neighborhood formed a voluntary committee to combat panic selling when the first Negro bought a home there. So successful was the effort that twenty other neighborhood groups followed their lead. In Wisconsin the occupants of a co-operative project near Madison voted 64–30 to admit a Negro family. These samples of interracial good will can be multiplied many times over. Between 1954 and

1956, nineteen Northern states had taken specific new steps in non-segregated housing.

In May, 1954, Mr. and Mrs. Andrew Wade, Negro residents of Louisville, moved into a new home in one of the city's suburbs. The purchase had been conducted for them by a white family and a month after the Wades moved into the house it was heavily damaged by a dynamite explosion intended to intimidate the Negro family. Between the insurance company, the mortgage company and the courts the property was tied up so that not even the necessary repairs could be made. As is frequently the case with stories of racial tension the news of the Wades' plight got onto the international news wires and Mr. and Mrs. Simonson, Chicago residents temporarily in Paris, read the account. Later, having returned to the United States, the Simonsons heard a radio appeal for the Wades on a program sponsored by the Automobile Workers. The Simonsons made some inquiries and when they found that according to a court order the mortgage on the bombed property would have to be paid in full before the Wades could repair their house, the Chicagoans loaned the $12,326 to the Wades to clear all financial obstacles that were keeping them from enjoying their home.

In the South most of the movements toward a practice of non-discrimination in housing occur in the border states. Delaware, Missouri, West Virginia and Maryland offer sporadic examples of integrated housing. However, deeper in the South, at Rayne, Louisiana, a 76-unit project originally intended for Negro families opened on a bi-racial basis with the result that 13 units are occupied by Negroes and the others by white families. In Texas several projects, both publicly and privately financed, have been opened to both races.

In almost any informal group discussion of interracial housing someone is sure to inject the question, "Why do they—the Chinese, Japanese, Indians, Negroes—want to live among white people instead of with people of their own kind?" An answer can be arrived at only after there is some clarity as to what makes people "of a kind." Individuals or groups who have equivalent educational, economic and cultural interests, who share professional status and civic concern, whose ethical standards are equal and whose moral habits are similar—are they really not of a kind? Perhaps even more of a kind than if color were the only bond they had in common?

Frequently the initial shock comes in discovering the many interests held in common by members of different races; that all have similar virtues, vices, problems, ambitions, disappointments. Having discovered this fact people can become neighbors, and the color of their skin divides them no more than does the color of their eyes or the color of the ramblers climbing over their porches.

When Jackie Robinson of baseball fame first planned to build a new home at Stamford, Connecticut, there were objections from a few of the home owners in the vicinity. But when the Richard Simons, of Simon and Schuster publishing firm, shared their home with the Robinsons for several months while the new house was under construction, the action silenced most of the objections. Mr. Robinson, his wife and their three children, Jackie now eleven, Sharon eight, and David six, have found their places in the church, in Scouts, and other community organizations. And the youngsters of the neighborhood have found their places on the Jackie Robinson family baseball diamond.

A Nisei physician in Portland, Oregon, wanted to move into one of the better neighborhoods of the city but was a little hesitant about being the first Japanese American to buy a home in the section. A newspaperman who owned a home in the block made some quiet inquiries of his neighbors and found not one person who objected to having a Nisei neighbor.

In the spring of 1955 Waverly, Iowa, a town with fewer than six thousand population, received an award of $10,000 from the Fund for the Republic for giving "life and meaning to the Constitution and Bill of Rights." A few weeks earlier Captain Virgil A. Daniels, a Negro member of the air force with twelve years of service to his credit, had been assigned to a radar station at Waverly. He and his wife rented an apartment but just before moving into it they were asked by the owner if they would be willing to find another place— the occupants of three of the other apartments in the building objected to having a Negro neighbor. The Danielses quietly gave up the apartment, but other tenants in the building did not give up the Danielses. They sent an open letter to the newspaper, and then they arranged a reception for Captain and Mrs. Daniels and presented them with a framed apology. In the meantime the Danielses had rented a house, but no matter where they lived, they were deeply grateful to be in Waverly. The mayor, on receiving the award for the community, remarked that it was almost as if they were being paid for believing in God!

In charge of the Ford Foundation program for training overseas technicians at Dunwoody Industrial Institute, Minneapolis, is Dr. Nagapada Rao, a native of India who did his graduate work in the United States, later went to Korea as an economic adviser to the government, and then served for four years on an American commission as an economic adviser to the Indonesian government before coming to his present work in the United States. When some unexpected responsibilities exhausted the Raos' financial reserve and they found themselves unable to make the payments on the home they were buying, some of the neighbors quickly made arrangements for Dr. Rao to borrow money at reduced interest rates. The family had proved too valuable a community asset to allow them to move away.

Every move toward desegregated housing is at the same time a move toward desegregation in other relationships. A city may have a policy of integrated schools, but if any racial group is restricted to living in a certain part of town the school in that section is very likely to be a one-race school. And the church, however unwillingly, has a one-race parish. Shopping centers, moving picture houses, parks and playgrounds take on the color of the neighborhood. Although in many cities mortgage brokers, bankers and builders control who lives where, in thousands of communities unsegregated housing waits only the friendly gesture of two or three neighbors.

10.   *When the School Bell Rings*

In September, 1957, the eyes of the world converged upon Central High School in Little Rock, Arkansas. The cab driver in London, the president of Indonesia, the politicians in the Kremlin—all became familiar with details, true or untrue, of what was happening in that American city. In Little Rock itself reporters were everywhere mixing with the crowd made up of the curious, out to see what would happen; and the antagonistic, out to see that things did happen. Television and radio cords snarled up the efforts of their operators to reach the person in the crowd who looked as if he had a ready word. Most of those interviewed could tell how they felt about the situation, but few could explain how their city had arrived at the stalemate in which it found itself, although the condition had been two years in the making.

/ In 1955, after the ruling of the Supreme Court that integration of the public schools should proceed with "all deliberate speed," the school board of Little Rock began to plan for eventual integration with their emphasis, many observers felt, upon the term *deliberate*.

Indeed, some of the Negro parents felt that the board was playing a delaying action which was equivalent to disregard of the court ruling. After a few months the parents of thirty-five Negro students brought a case into the federal Court and the Court ordered the school board to present its plans for integration. Although members of the school board were not personally desirous of having the schools integrated, they nevertheless worked out a plan whereby integration would start in the high school in the fall of 1957.

Accordingly, a group of Negro students was screened and from them nine were selected to be the first to enter Central High School. From all reliable reports there was no apparent tension in any part of the city as schools prepared to open their doors for the fall semester on Tuesday, September 3. Then to the surprise of the entire city, including the school board and politicians close to the governor, at 9:00 P.M. on Monday night about 150 national guardsmen appeared at Central High with trucks and jeeps, tear bombs and bayonets, and took up their positions around the school. At 10:00 P.M. Governor Faubus appeared on a hastily prepared telecast and announced that because of evidence of impending violence he had taken the precaution of placing troops around the high school to preserve the peace.

The families of the nine Negro students consulted legal counsel and were advised to keep their children out of school that first day to give the lawyers an opportunity to study the situation. During that day lawyers and ministers of the Negro families arranged to have the children escorted to school the next day—many of the escorts being the ministers themselves. Plans were made for the nine students and their escorts to arrive simultaneously at the high school and to enter the building together.

The following morning the television screens of the world showed fifteen-year-old Elizabeth Eckford, one of the Negro students, arriving in her crinoline petticoated dress and her neatly cuffed bobby socks, looking very much like thousands of other girls who would enter school that day. By a stroke of chance Elizabeth arrived alone and had to run the gauntlet of the national guard by herself. The bus which should have deposited her at the site where she would have met the other Negro students arrived ten minutes ahead of schedule. "Perhaps for the first time in its history," commented one citizen. Then the watching world saw that the troops, instead of escorting Elizabeth into the school building, waved her away. When the other eight Negro students arrived they also found that the school had been declared out of bounds for them, too. Two weeks later the national guard, whose orders from the governor had been to keep Negro students out of the high school, was replaced by the local police whose orders were to proceed with integration by conducting the students into the building.

It was not surprising that by this time the disorderly crowds which collected day after day had become so unruly that the police could not cope with them. Governor Faubus failing to ease the situation in any way, an injunction was issued by the Federal District Court to restrain those people who were disrupting peaceful integration. The injunction was disregarded and the mobs continued to intimidate the Negro students and their parents. As a last resort, on September 25, President Eisenhower placed federal troops around the high school with orders to conduct the Negro students into the building, and to use whatever means were necessary to control the mob. Under troop escorts the Negro students entered school and integrated classes were conducted at Little Rock. After the first few days there was little need for troops because with the fact accomplished the need for anti-Negro demonstrations vanished. In late December, all but a small token force were withdrawn and Little Rock Central High appeared again to be a normal American high school, although during the second semester the Negro students were under continual harassment.

The whole world knows of this debacle in Arkansas, but the accomplishments of Arkansas have been buried under the debris of sensationalism and the dust of indifference. In point of time, Arkansas was actually the first Southern state to admit Negroes to its university without being forced to do so by court action. In February, 1948, the university opened to Negro students on the graduate level, and since that time five have been graduated in law, five in medicine, and more than three hundred have received master's degrees. Currently there are perhaps two hundred Negroes taking professional graduate work in various branches of the university. On the undergraduate level, in 1955, the university and all the state-supported colleges of Arkansas were opened to Negro students.

Integration on the elementary and high school levels has also been in progress since 1954 when Fayetteville became the first town in the former Old Confederacy to integrate a public school. Charleston and Hoxie integrated all grades; and Bentonville took one Negro pupil into a formerly all-white school. In the fall of 1957 four Arkansas communities, in addition to Little Rock, integrated their school systems to some degree: Van Buren, Fort Smith, Ozark and North Little Rock. However, in the latter town, after a few days, integration was postponed because of complications in their own locality and the greater tension at Little Rock. Also the Catholic parochial schools of Paris and Fort Smith enrolled Negro students without complications.

The one-sided reporting of the integration situation in Arkansas is representative of reporting over the United States generally where the multiplicity of newspaper stories, broadcasts and telecasts keep the country informed hourly of events which are considered newsworthy. But normal procedures and orderly processes are not as newsworthy as are the unusual and the spectacular; so compliance is eclipsed by complaint, peace by pandemonium.

Just as all our current race relations have their roots in the past, so the questions of *if, where* and *how* Negro students should be educated date back to the early nineteenth century. At that time the South was concerned with making good slaves, not educated slaves. The North, where the number of freed slaves was increasing yearly, provided some schools which Negroes might attend, but few communities cared to become an educational center for the Negroes.

In fact, in the early 1830's the citizens of New Haven, Connecticut, under the very shadow of Yale University, voted 760-to-4 against founding a college for Negro students in their town because such a school might be dangerous to the community. And in the same period, less than twenty-four hours before their celebration of Independence Day, the people of Canaan, New Hampshire, voted to remove a Negro academy. A month later, three hundred people assembled and with the help of a hundred yoke of oxen literally moved the school out of the community.

By the close of the Civil War, however, the North was ready to assume heavy responsibility for the education of the freed slaves. So fast did religious bodies and private organizations open schools and colleges that in 1865 Congress chartered the Freedmen's Bureau to co-operate with these educational societies.

It was to Hampton Institute, one of the early schools for Negro students, that Booker T. Washington, born in slavery, made his penniless way. It was here he first saw sheets on a bed and became acquainted with tablecloths, napkins, a toothbrush and a bath. Here he had the first regular meals of his life, and here he learned the discipline of doing a job thoroughly. As Washington became more elated over the expanding world which education opened for him he also became increasingly plagued by the thought of the large number of his people for whom no education was available. After his graduation, of several educational positions open to him Washington chose to go to Tuskegee, Alabama, where in 1881 he opened a new school for Negro students in buildings left standing on a deserted plantation after the "big house" had burned: an old dining room, a former kitchen, a stable and a hen house. From such beginnings have come other great colleges and universities for Negro students such as Tougaloo, Talladega, Fisk and Atlanta.

According to Dr. Cleo Blackburn, who in addition to being director of Flanner House is president of Jarvis Christian College, a school for Negro students at Hawkins, Texas, "The surge of mission which prompted the North to establish schools for the newly freed slaves and their children was one of the most beautiful and far reaching factors in building bridges of understanding between Northern white people and Southern Negroes. The young people who came from the North to teach in the mission schools were among the keenest and finest Northern college graduates, and the Negro students in these mission schools possessed the best minds and highest ambitions of their people. The long-range effect of the meeting of the best of both races, at a time when it was easy to think the worst of both races, cannot be overestimated."

Although desegration was the general practice in Northern schools, the South extended to its schools the same policies of segregation which it observed in other social contacts. And for this practice it soon had a sound basis—nothing less than the 1896 Supreme Court decision in the Plessy *vs.* Ferguson case which became legal protection for all forms of segregation. The lone dissenting opinion in this case was expressed by Justice John M. Harlan when he wrote, "The thin guise of 'equal' accommodations will not mislead anyone, or atone for the wrong this day done."

The educational results of the system of segregation which Justice Harlan decried are now history. In 1920, after a quarter of a century of "separate but equal," the average annual expenditure in the seventeen Southern states was $10.30 for each white child and $2.89 for each Negro child. Negro "schools" were often abandoned stores, old churches, or other dilapidated buildings. On rainy days, the children frequently had to put pails under leaking spots in the roof, move their benches to dry areas in the room and then continue their classes. High schools for graduates of these elementary schools were practically nonexistent. Atlanta, with its concentration of relatively prosperous Negroes, opened its first high school for them in 1917; in other large Southern cities the move came later.

During the next twenty years the percentage of educational funds that went to Negro schools increased. For example, by 1940 Georgia had doubled the amount she spent for each Negro child, bringing it to $14.60 a year compared to $46.70 for each white child. Another decade passed and 1950 found some of the Southern states doubling and redoubling their efforts to equalize school expenditures for the two races. Georgia multiplied her expenditures for Negro children by eight times, while increasing the amounts for white children only four times. By 1952 North Carolina had raised the salaries of Negro teachers until they were slightly above the average for white teachers, $2,910.56 to $2,807.74; and expenditures for current expenses were almost equal, the 30 per cent Negro school population receiving 27 per cent of the total. The eight states of the Deep South showed progress in raising the per pupil expenditures for Negro pupils but still out of a total of $535,030,000 spent on education, only a little over 25 per cent went for Negro schools. The per pupil allocations were $156.06 for white children and $91.43 for Negro pupils. The cost of school property was $334.94 per white child and $85.08 per Negro child.

According to a 1950 educational study, if the Southern states were to bring their annual educational expenditure for Negro children ($91.43 per child) to the level of that for white children ($156.06 per child), an estimated $134,824,000 would have been needed in addition to the amount budgeted for that year. Then if per pupil property and school facility allocations were to be equalized an estimated additional outlay of $600 million would have been required.

During this half century of "separate but equal" a growing number of citizens living in the South became convinced that "separate" would always have more emphasis than "equal." At mid-century this idea was firmly held by Mr. William Ragin, a wiry Negro farmer still on the young, hard-working side of life. In Clarendon County, South Carolina, Mr. Ragin owned a hundred acres of land which he had bought on credit in 1942 for $100 an acre, but which eight years later were free of debt. His house was not palatial, but it was clapboard with tight-fitting windows. The roof was slightly patched and a few shingles were loose but it was proof against the worst of spring rains.

In 1950 everything was going well for Mr. Ragin excepting schooling for his boy, six-year-old Glenn. Mr. Ragin talked with other Negro parents and found they shared his concern. Some of these parents were members of the National Association for the Advancement of Colored People and they felt sure that if they took the initiative in trying to get their children into better schools—which meant white schools—they would have some support from the NAACP. These parents interviewed the parents of a thousand Negro school children and obtained the names of twenty-five who were willing to take a stand against segregation. Eventually, to be sure, as threats against their property and families increased, a few of these signatories withdrew their names. But a small group stood firm and in 1951 brought a trial case into a Charleston court. They lost this case but appealed it and kept on appealing until it reached the United States Supreme Court. This suit was the first of five which were considered together for the new ruling of the Court in 1954.

The second suit originated in Prince Edward County, Virginia. When the case was first argued in federal district court the plaintiffs enumerated the many inequalities that existed between schools for white children and schools for Negro children—inequalities in facilities, in length of school terms, in teacher preparation and salary—and petitioned that segregation be discontinued. But instead of ruling on segregation, the court merely ruled that the educational facilities should be equalized. This case was also appealed.

A third case, similar to the one from Virginia, was carried from a Kansas lower court to the Supreme Court. The fourth case originated in Delaware and resulted in orders from the lower court to admit Negro students to previously all-white schools. But on a technicality the opponents of the decision appealed the case, and it also was taken to the Supreme Court.

The fifth case, originating in Washington, D.C., involved a tech-

nical question—the constitutionality of segregation in federal territory—but the principle of the case was similar to the other four
before the Supreme Court which decided to rule on all five cases at
one time.

After the plaintiffs had waited for three years, the day of decision
came—Monday, May 17, 1954. The wording of the decision, read by
Chief Justice Earl Warren, was simple, devoid of all legal jargon.
First it raised a question and answered it:

Does segregation of children in public schools solely on the basis of
race, even though the physical facilities and other "tangible" factors may
be equal, deprive the children of the minority group of equal educational opportunities?
We believe that it does.
The plaintiffs contend that segregated public schools are not "equal"
and cannot be made "equal," and that hence they are deprived of the
equal protection of the laws. . . .
In approaching this problem, we cannot turn the clock back to 1868
when the Amendment was adopted, or even to 1896 when Plessy *vs.*
Ferguson was written. We must consider public education in the light of
its present place in American life throughout the nation. . . .

It can hardly be said that this decision came as a surprise to most
of the people in the United States. Train and bus segregation were
on their way out; the armed services were already desegregated;
labor was opening its ranks on many fronts; public eating places,
parks, places of amusement, clubs, churches—an indefinite number
of movements were indicating that segregation no longer fit the
present-day concept of democracy. If the words of Alan Paton, South
African author of *Cry, the Beloved Country,* are true, that a nation
gets the Supreme Court it deserves, then the 1954 Court was reflect-
ing the national public opinion of its day.

There was also agreement from the majority of Americans with
the next point made by the Court:

In these days, it is doubtful if any child may reasonably be expected
to succeed in life if he is denied the opportunity of an education. Such an
opportunity, where the state had undertaken to provide it, is a right which
must be made available to all on equal terms. . . .
We conclude that in the field of public education the doctrine of "separate but equal" has no place. Separate educational facilities are inherently
unequal. Therefore we hold that the plaintiffs . . . are . . . deprived

of the equal protection that the laws guaranteed under the Fourteenth Amendment. . . .

This pronouncement became the official position of the federal government. Before long states began to ask how fast integration would have to be accomplished. Overnight? Twenty-five years? A year later in May, 1955, the Court ruled on what it considered a reasonable time schedule for compliance with its former order. Realizing that some communities would grasp every excuse to delay action, the Court couched its orders in courteous but firm words. "Full implementation of these constitutional principles" might vary from place to place but "disagreement with them" would be no excuse for not complying with them. "Practical flexibility" would be necessary, but so would a "prompt and reasonable start" which should be pushed to conclusion with "all deliberate speed."

During the year that elapsed between the decision against segregation and the statement covering a time schedule for its elimination, opposition to desegregation consolidated. The white robes, hoods and masks of the Ku Klux Klan of post-Civil War days were taken out of mothballs—or copied in modern wrinkle-free materials—and threatening fiery crosses burned again on public squares and private lawns to indicate the violence that awaited anyone who dared comply with integration orders.

Also a new type of organization suddenly emerged—the White Citizens Councils, whose members worked in the open, prided themselves on the names of "leading citizens" they enlisted, and published and circulated propaganda material. The Klan and the Councils had one goal in common—perpetuation of the traditional way of life in their communities and states. They had one method in common—intimidation. At times violence was added.

Many parents who joined no pressure groups nevertheless had serious doubts as to the effects of desegregation. There was widespread belief that if even one Negro pupil were admitted to an all-white school it would soon be overwhelmed with Negro children. "How do we know," asked the parents in concert, "what harm to our children may result? Negroes have a higher rate of delinquency, a higher rate of venereal diseases; they have a lower IQ and lower educational accomplishments grade for grade when compared with our white children." And from almost every corner of the South came the word *mongrelization*. Whether the fears were based upon fact or prejudice; whether in reality they were fears or defenses against change; still they did represent an emotional and intellectual hurdle which often appeared insuperable.

Many young parents who felt the logic of the new day nevertheless felt the tug of loyalty to the position taken by their home state. This divided loyalty was implied in the plea of a young mother who had recently moved North from Louisiana when she said, "Please think with love in your heart toward the people of my state. They're wonderful and they need to be understood. Of course, *I* moved North recently so that my two little girls could have a good education, but still I love my state and the parents who live there are having a mighty difficult time right now."

The answer to many of the fears about desegregation are found in an experience of a school in Delaware in 1952, two years before the Supreme Court decision. According to an article by William Peters in *Redbook* for October, 1954, "The instrument that began this revolution in the Delaware schools was the pen of a 53-year-old Negro woman." Mrs. Fred Bulah, a warmhearted, outgoing individual, was the mother of a six-year-old adopted daughter whom the Bulahs had taken into their home when she was a baby. One day Mrs. Bulah had read in the paper of a child abandoned on a doorstep. "I ran to the chicken yard, where my husband was working," she recounted, "and I told Fred I wanted that baby." As Shirley grew older her mother continued to want every possible good thing for her daughter. In the fall of 1950 Mrs. Bulah began writing letters to school authorities in an attempt to get bus transportation for Shirley, now ready for the first grade. Shirley had to walk, or be driven, two miles to the Negro school although a bus for white children passed the Bulah home twice daily.

Moreover, irregular closing hours for the Negro school created a problem. Mrs. Bulah never knew what day she might receive a call from Shirley to come get her at one o'clock, two o'clock—the mother could not anticipate the closing hour. By the time Shirley was in the third grade the Bulahs were convinced that there should be some way to have their daughter transported to school. The driver of the bus for white children told them that their only hope would be to get in touch with the supervisor of transportation at the state capital.

Mrs. Bulah then wrote several letters before she received an application to be filled out by Shirley's teacher. "Miss Beaujohn said I was just wasting my time," Mrs. Bulah later commented. "She said she had tried before to get transportation for Negro children and never could." And neither could Mrs. Bulah.

"I wrote again," she reported, "and this time I asked for Shirley to be transported on the white children's bus." But the state board of education replied that the state constitution required separate school facilities for colored and white children.

Then Mrs. Bulah went to a Negro lawyer who told her that the next step was to ask that Shirley be allowed to attend the white school. Mrs. Bulah got the expected answer. With this rebuff the Bulahs' lawyer decided that their only recourse was the courts.

For a while after applying for court action, life was not easy for the Bulahs. White neighbors talked about the "uppity Negroes"; some of the Negroes themselves thought it would be better to leave things alone than to stir up trouble—no telling where this business might end. The state immediately began improvements at the Negro school, putting in a drinking fountain, toilets, and a few other refinements. Then on April 1, 1952, the court chancery ruled that since the state required separate but equal schools, and since Shirley's school had not provided equal facilities, Negro children should therefore be admitted to the white schools.

The state appealed the decision to its Supreme Court which upheld the decision of the lower court. This action came exactly one week before the fall opening of school so there was no time to orient the four teachers or the students in the six-grade school Shirley would enter. Nevertheless, on the opening day of school, Mrs. Bulah arrived with Shirley and asked to meet the principal, Mrs. Moore.

"Mrs. Moore took the papers I had brought and she said, 'Shirley, we are so glad to have you.' I asked to meet Shirley's teacher. . . . She welcomed Shirley, too, and then she said, 'Shirley, I want you to pick out any desk you want,' and Shirley ran and picked out a desk.

"I told Mrs. Moore I had brought Shirley to school in my car and I wanted her to come home on the bus. Mrs. Moore said she'd arrange it. And that afternoon when that same bus came by my door as it always had, it stopped, and Shirley got off."

Shirley's teacher, although kindly to her, was never completely convinced that integration was the best policy. "I just believe that segregation is right," she said. "And not just in schools, but throughout."

Also Mrs. Moore, the principal and veteran of forty-three years of teaching, admitted later that her first reaction was negative. Along with most of the white parents she had expected that if the school was opened to Negro children there would be an exodus from the Negro school to the white school; the common saying had been "give 'em an inch and they'll take a mile." But, her report continued, "The biggest surprise came when Shirley Bulah was the only colored child to enroll the first day of school. . . . We've had six colored children out of a total enrollment of a little over a hundred."

Looking back after integration, Mrs. Moore felt there had been some problems of adjustment, most of them caused by the speed with which the initial integration had taken place. Parents of white children did not have time to accustom themselves to the idea of integration; some objected particularly to having their children in mixed square dancing groups and in the rhythm work in the gym classes. One mother called the principal to object to her child's sitting next to a Negro child. However, Mrs. Moore changed no seats. "I knew if I changed one I'd be through."

In evaluating the whole development Mrs. Moore concluded: "I know now after two years' experience with integration that it works. It took me a long time to see it, but I think now that integration is right." And as far as she knew only one white child had been taken out of school because of the admission of Negro children. The results of integration in this Delaware school are typical of many schools that have initiated integration.

When schools opened in the fall of 1957, the border states of the South showed varying progress in integration. Maryland, where integration had begun soon after the court order, already had 12,894 Negro children attending school with white children in nine out of twenty-four school districts. Out of twenty-three counties, nineteen were integrated, at least theoretically, although in six of the counties no Negroes had applied for admission to white schools.

Arkansas started the school year with some degree of integration in nine communities. In Missouri, 95 per cent of the school children entered integrated schools. In Oklahoma, slightly over 50 per cent of the school districts were integrated, and the state board of education had ordered that no further money be appropriated to maintain Negro schools. Delaware had made a beginning in the city of Wilmington. In West Virginia all but two counties were integrated.

In Kentucky, more than 75 per cent of the Negro students were in integrated schools. In Tennessee, Clinton had integrated its schools; and Nashville had started on a program. Farther south, Texas had made a start at integration with San Antonio its outstanding example; and North Carolina opened schools in three communities on a very restricted basis.

Because a school belongs to an integrated district it does not always follow that its student body is composed of children from both races. The school may be located in a section of the city which because of a pattern of segregated housing is entirely white or entirely Negro and the school normally follows the color of the geographic area it serves. Also, in many schools integration has been only a gesture—six, eight or a dozen selected Negro students being admitted as token compliance with integration orders. Nevertheless, in the fall of 1957, 350,000 Negro students formerly in segregated school districts were in districts practicing some degree of integration, and about one-half of them were in integrated classrooms.

Still, many Negro students are waiting their first day in an integrated school. And many white parents are working for that day, sometimes in community organizations and sometimes in lonely ostracism as Mrs. Meazles of Clay, Kentucky, well knows. In the fall of 1956 when James and Theresa Gordon enrolled as the first Negro children in the public school of Clay, white parents called a boycott of the school. One mother, Mrs. Jordan Meazles, refused to observe the boycott and sent her children to school. Members of her family protested her action, and her friends turned against her. Mrs. Meazles had no academic theories to defend her position, merely a homespun philosophy that according to her religion people weren't acting right.

As a result of the boycott the two little Negro children were removed from school, their father lost his job, and the integration issue might have died in Clay. But Mrs. Meazles has written letters to the mayor; she has talked to her friends and to the mothers of her children's friends, and she is discovering that many of them are changing their minds about letting Negro children come to the Clay public school. There are those in the community who think that the next Negro children who apply for admission may find that one white woman has eased the way for them.

Editorial comments on the school situation in 1957–58 have varied.

Depending on the point of view of the editor, the status of desegregation has been characterized as "encouraging" or minimized by "only about." Since progress can be measured from two angles—how far a movement has come or how far it has yet to go before reaching its goal—point of view is important in any evaluation of progress. But the fact remains that whereas four years ago an integrated school in the seventeen Southern states and the District of Columbia was almost unheard of, by January, 1958, 762 of 3,008 formerly segregated school districts had some degree of integration and some of them had completed desegregation in all their schools.

_11._ _By-passing or Accepting Integration_

In June, 1958, there still remained seven states in which no school bell had ever called together Negro and white children in a public school: Georgia, South Carolina, Florida, Virginia, Alabama, Mississippi and Louisiana. In these states a variety of methods is being used to circumvent the Supreme Court decision.

Virginia led in the movement to invoke a principle called interposition. The basis of this principle is that a state has the right to interpose its sovereignty when it considers the federal government to have exceeded its constitutional rights. The interpositionists insist that a special constitutional amendment is necessary before segregation in the schools can legally be abolished; and since such an amendment would be lost if thirteen states failed to ratify it, the interpositionists feel confident they could kill the amendment. But Article VI provides that the Constitution is "the Supreme Law of the Land; and the Judges in every State shall be bound thereby, any thing in the Constitution or Laws of any State to the contrary notwithstanding." The Supreme Court—not each state legislature—is the authoritative interpreter of what the Constitution requires.

Amendments to state constitutions in Georgia, South Carolina and

Mississippi permit the complete elimination of public schools and the substitution of private schools in which the tuition is paid by the state. Under these amendments, public school property can be leased or sold to become the private school property. In thus changing the school system from a public to a private institution several states have found it necessary to revise or entirely abolish their compulsory school attendance laws.

Texas provides for local option so that each community may decide on the desegregation of its own school. Under this plan, the high school at Pleasanton was the first school to become integrated. When it became apparent that the town could not maintain two systems of schools and keep either one at the level demanded for state accreditation the school board suggested integration of the systems as the best way of upholding educational standards. The proposal was put to a vote of the people and they voted 342-to-88 in favor of integration, thus opening the way for incorporating the 37 Negro students in the district into the white student body of 750, nearly one-half of whom are Latin Americans.

This decision was implemented when classes for the nine Negro students of high school age were discontinued and the students transferred to the recently constructed $550,000 high school. On the first day of integrated classes superintendent J. D. Klingman, principal D. C. Baldree, and student council president Janice Slomchinski met the new students on the steps of the high school. While newsmen, camera men, citizens and students waited in the school yard, Janice and Baldree gave short speeches of welcome, some of the new students responded, and each was then personally escorted to his first class by some member of the student council. Integration of the elementary school children is planned for a later date.

In some states control of the educational purse strings is expected to control segregation. In 1956 the Virginia legislature authorized the removal from the public school system of any school that integrated its student body; then it provided state aid to any student who could not otherwise attend a segregated school. Georgia has ordered that funds be cut off from *all* schools in a district if *any* school integrates. South Carolina cuts off the funds of the school "to which" and also "from which" a student transfers if the shift results from the integration of either school.

As each bill of resistance legislation is passed the question arises as to whether all such state legislation will not eventually be declared unconstitutional, as some of it already has been. Realizing that it may be years before all the cases involving integration can be cleared through the courts, some states are relying on this "delaying action" to postpone the necessity of integrating their schools for years or even generations. On October 15, 1957, Governor Luther H. Hodges of North Carolina suggested that his state could rely on this time-consuming process of separate court actions. The governor holds that the 1954 Supreme Court ruling was not a general order; that before a school can be forced to open its doors to a Negro student that student has to make a request for admittance and the request must be granted only after a court order specifies that that particular student has to be admitted.

A different point of view was expressed in 1956 by Georgia's attorney general, Eugene Cook, when he said, "We might as well be candid. Most of these laws will be stricken down by the Courts in due process." Also in Texas when ten segregation bills were under consideration by the 1957 legislature a triumvirate of its members were outspoken in the denouncement of the proposals. One of the men, Hubert Hudson, based his opposition on the premise that segregation practices were unchristian, that as a member of the Episcopal Church he had to stand for equality before the law. Senator Henry Gonzalez, recipient of the University of Texas award as the outstanding Latin-American of 1957, spoke for the citizens whose voices could not be raised in their own behalf—the Negroes of Texas. Gonzalez himself knew the effects of discrimination. In his youth he had at various times been refused admission to swimming pools and parks; he had been ordered to stand instead of sit in cafes; he had struggled to overcome an accent that dubbed him a "foreigner." Although a member of the unpopular desegregationists in Texas, Gonzalez is respected by his fellow legislators. The third outspoken Texan was Senator Kazen, a quiet man, son of Lebanese immigrant parents, who appealed to Texans to defend the best in the American Heritage.

Northern communities have frequently by-passed integration by the old and common practice of gerrymandering, or re-establishing school districts to conform with residential concentrations of racial groups. Thus a school may be all-white or all-Negro and still be within the law if there are no children of the other race living in the school district. A similar result is obtained by placing new school buildings in centers of one-race districts rather than in border areas which educationally might be more strategic locations but which would necessitate mixing the races in classrooms.

Because desegregation of the schools in three large cities, St. Louis, Louisville and Washington, D.C., has been carried out so uneventfully, each city has been made the subject of a special study which may indicate procedures for other cities. In each of these communities the credit for peaceful integration goes to the co-operation of the many groups involved: civic organizations, religious bodies, the school board, teachers, parents, and pupils. And in each city this co-operation has been the result of many months, or even years, of planning and orientation of each group for the changes in attitudes and practices that would have to accompany a peaceful transition.

On the other hand, the situation that developed in Little Rock was credited by many of its citizens to a lack of understanding and mutual support by the governor, the school board, and the citizens. Colbert Cartwright, local civic leader and press correspondent, lays much of the blame for the trouble in that city upon the school board which had made no wholehearted effort to prepare the community for the problems involved in integration. With demonstrations of peaceful progress in St. Louis and Louisville, and of unpeaceful progress at Clinton, North Little Rock and other places, Mr. Cartwright stated, "Preparation for so radical a change has little hope of success unless it is a community-wide program."

Because Washington, D.C., comes under such close scrutiny by Americans and other nationals the fact of the integration of its schools —five years ago declared an impossible move by one of the city's leading educators—is of especial importance. The actual steps in the desegregation process moved so smoothly that the associate superintendent in charge of the program called it "a miracle of adjustment." In reality, the accomplishment was the natural result of long-range planning and a series of previous achievements over a period of several years. School officials in the District of Columbia had for some time studied the changing ratio of white and Negro populations and the changing residential pattern of the city, because these two factors determine the racial composition of enrollment in individual schools. Largely because of the general movement of white families into the suburbs, the Negro population within the District was increasing faster than the white population. In fact during the past quarter of a century the white population has increased 47 per cent and the Negro population 113 per cent. In 1954 when desegregation was ordered, the District had a school population of 64,000 Negro children and 41,393 white children, and school officials assumed that the established trend would continue.

Although the practice of segregation in the schools had always been rigidly observed, over a period of twenty years the city had been desegregating many other of her services and activities. The trend began in 1933 when all federal picnic areas, golf courses, tennis courts and baseball diamonds were opened to Negroes. By 1943 public opinion had changed enough so that the Negro singer Marian Anderson, who in 1939 had been refused the use of Constitution Hall by the Daughters of the American Revolution, was invited by that same organization to give a concert in that same hall. Then in 1944 the YWCA set another new pattern by opening its food services to all races. Two years later the foundation for segregated housing cracked when the United States Supreme Court declared that restrictive covenants were no longer enforceable by the courts.

By 1950 the city's major hotels had opened their facilities to mixed conventions. Several department stores, the five-and-ten-cent stores, and fifty-four restaurants had opened their dining rooms or counters to Negroes. Several professional associations had integrated their memberships. Then in 1953 the District recreation department merged its two parallel divisions and opened the first desegregated public swimming pool.

All during the time that this gradual desegregation was in progress, the school board was carrying on a program of study and orientation for its own members, as well as for the teaching staff, parents and students, so that when the time came to comply with the not unexpected Court decision the schools would be ready to desegregate in a very short time. As a consequence of this thorough preparation everything was indeed ready when the time came to put the school program into operation. Their schedule of integration reflects the thoroughness of preparation.

May 17, 1954. The Supreme Court handed down its decision.
May 19, 1954. The board of education appointed a special committee to prepare a statement of principles to be presented to the whole board.

May 25. The statement of policy was presented to the board and adopted by a vote of 6-to-1. The same day the superintendent of schools presented to the board a plan for desegregation that had been in preparation since 1953.

June 2. The board approved the plan.

September 13. Schools opened for the fall semester with Negro and white pupils attending classes together in 116, or 73 per cent, of the schools, and Negro and white teachers integrated in 37, or 23 per cent, of the schools.

September to December, 1954. Period of adjustment.

February 16, 1955. The top staff reorganization was announced.

September, 1955. School desegregation was complete.

Across the nation the four questions most commonly raised regarding the effects of integration are: Does integration lower academic standards? What is the effect on the children of all races? What becomes of the Negro teachers? Will the move lead to increased intermarriage?

An answer to the first question, Does integration lower academic standards? can be found in the record of the District of Columbia. At the end of two years of integration a series of achievement tests was given on a city-wide basis. The publication of their results provided a field day for the prosegregationists. The record showed that the level of achievement had fallen, just as school officials had predicted that it would. However, the majority of both parents and teachers, instead of putting the blame on integration, put it on conditions that existed in the school system—overcrowded classrooms, underpaid teachers, and an increasing number of children whose educational, economic and cultural backgrounds were weak. The situation was the climax of a trend which had been several decades in the making, but the fact that the children were now in mixed schools made the differences in their educational and cultural backgrounds more obvious so that the results of the tests hit home to more parents. School officials began at once to attack the weaknesses which they could eliminate in the school system.

Summarizing the findings of their study the board said, "The big fear, that integration will impair the education of some children in the community, is rapidly yielding to the concentrated drive to effectuate the big solution. The prevailing spirit in the District of Columbia is positive and dynamic."

In St. Louis, observation and tests following integration revealed that in the elementary schools there was little difference in the academic level of the children of different races. But at the high school level white students as a group made better records than Negro students as a group. However, the teachers agreed that the differences "are not due to innate ability but rather to the type of environment . . . and the dual standards engendered by a bi-racial educational system and a segregated society." One teacher in the system summed up the general attitude of the teachers: "Desegregation has brought no new problems; our already present problems have simply been brought into sharper focus."

An answer to the second question, What is the effect of integration on the children of all races? can again be derived from actual situations, and also from opinions of pupils and parents connected with integrated schools. Just prior to the opening of the Louisville schools on a desegregated basis, all parents received cards carrying the name of the school to which their child had been assigned. If the parents found the assignment objectionable they were requested to state a first, second and third choice of schools and return the card. Approximately 37,000 out of 42,000 families, or 89 per cent, accepted the assigned school. A few days after the opening of school, and following the violence that resulted from the integration of the Clinton, Tennessee, schools, a few families, mostly Negro, requested transfers for their children to return to their former schools. Otherwise parents accepted the fact of the mixed student bodies.

At the end of the first year of integration in a St. Louis high school students were given a questionnaire and asked to check their opinions and reactions to certain aspects of integration. Ninety-two per cent of the white students rated the Negro students on the same level with themselves. In the section of the questionnaire where each student was to list positive and negative reactions to integration 90 per cent of all the students indicated "none" in the negative column.

In addition to the check test the students were asked to express themselves on the merits and demerits of integration. Typical replies from white students ran:

"Prejudices and superstitions have been disbanded with integration."

"We are one step closer to brotherhood. I believe the next problem that should be conquered is religious prejudice."

"I have learned that all Negroes are not rough and wisecracking; some are very nice and I like them. But then, all whites are not nice either."

From Negro students came replies such as: "Negro students study more. There is more incentive."

"I have learned to like people. I am ashamed that I hated white people simply because I thought they hated me. I have found out this is not true."

"It is teaching us all the ways of democracy; but this is especially true for the white kids who have never had a chance to practice it."

Even in those school systems where integration has proceeded without any unhappy incidents there have been a few students who have found adjustment difficult. Frequently teachers and school officials have made special efforts to help them over emotional strains, even at times suggesting that they return to their former schools.

The third question, What will become of Negro teachers in integrated systems? finds its best answer in Kentucky where 22,000 of the state's 38,000 Negro children and 200,000 of the 552,000 white children are in districts with some degree of integration. The Kentucky Council on Human Relations has made a special study of the effects of integration on the teaching staffs. The report indicates that all of the 112 Negro teachers in mixed schools are finding their teaching conditions satisfactory and their personal relationships harmonious.

In one district containing six schools with a total enrollment of eighty-seven white children and 2,963 Negro children, there were a hundred Negro teachers. The white parents in this district were given the opportunity of requesting that their children be moved out of the district, but not one asked for a transfer. In another district, in a school with 275 white students and ten white teachers there were fewer than thirty Negro students and only one Negro teacher but she commented that everything was going so well that she even forgot she was colored.

The report showed that forty-six qualified Negro teachers had lost their jobs in the process of combining classes or schools, but in practically every case these teachers had been given contracts in other schools in the state or had been retained in the schools where they had formerly taught, but reassigned to special duties in the library, office, or health-testing programs, at the same time retaining their status as teachers.

During the integration of one large district in Kentucky five Negro teachers had to be eliminated but they were immediately placed in positions equal to or better than the ones they had to give up. One went to a high school in Milwaukee; one to a Cleveland high school; one to Washington, D.C.; another to an elementary school in Columbus, Ohio; and the fifth to the department of economic security in Kentucky's capital city.

The shortage of teachers throughout the nation helps to keep all qualified Negro teachers in good positions. The South particularly needs teachers with college and advanced degrees, but generally lower salaries and segregation make the South unattractive to many well-trained teachers. Northern cities are beginning to hire Negro teachers on the same basis they hire others. Indianapolis has approximately one hundred Negro teachers in the city schools, some of them in schools where the student body is predominantly white.

In the Minnesota Twin Cities, with only about 2 per cent of the population Negro, there are around sixteen Negro teachers in St. Paul and approximately thirty in Minneapolis. In neither system do teachers' records indicate racial origins. The Fair Employment Practices Commission feels the situation in both cities is good. "It has been my observation," said the assistant director, "that Negro teachers all have been placed on the basis of subject matter which they are prepared to teach and the needs of the school to which they have been assigned. There has been no evidence that any of the Negro teachers have been assigned to schools with predominant Negro enrollments simply because of their race. In fact, just the opposite would be closer to the true situation. It is the announced policy of both St. Paul and Minneapolis public schools to hire all of their instructional staff without regard to race, color, creed or national origins, and I think that this policy carries through in all aspects of the teachers' relationships with the two systems."

The fourth question is, Will integrated schools lead to mixed marriages? The emotional complications of this question are indicated by the fact that people in the North are likely to express their fears in the question form, while people in the South more generally express themselves in the plain statement, "Integration of the schools will lead to more mixed marriages." Integration of schools in Southern states is too recent to provide any data, so the best answer comes from those states just north of the Mason-Dixon line in which practices of both segregation and integration have been carried on over a period of years. The two systems provide no perceptible difference in the rate of intermarriage.

A point of view, variously stated, is found in the comment, "If families of different races live in the same apartment houses; ride the same airplanes, buses and trains; are guests in the same hotels; worship at the same altars; read in the same libraries—then the schools should not carry the onus of responsibility for intermarriage." At best, or at worst, depending upon the point of view, integration of the public schools is only one factor in the process of complete integration, a process which does not necessitate amalgamation of the races, but which does demand that the theories of democracy which are taught within the walls of the schools shall be practiced within the entire framework of the nation.

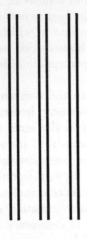

12. *Higher Education Desegregates*

The first crack in the solid wall of segregation which for generations had surrounded education in the South appeared at the university graduate level. This flaw, scarcely deeper than a scratch, was made in 1933 by Mr. Thomas Hocutt, graduate of a South Carolina college for Negroes, when he initiated an unsuccessful attempt to enroll in the college of dentistry at the University of South Carolina. In making application Mr. Hocutt was unable to present the required transcript of grades because his alma mater, fearful of losing state funds if it became a party to his attempt to enter the university, refused him a transcript. Hocutt took his case into court and lost, the court ruling that since he had not presented the proper papers with his application the university was justified in rejecting the application. Although the case was lost, it set a precedent for using the courts as a means of breaking segregation.

For the next two decades the results of court actions charted a zigzag pattern. In Maryland, when Donald G. Murray applied for entrance into the Law School at the university the court ruled that the state had to admit him to that school or supply one of equal quality for Negroes. Because of the expense involved in setting up a second law school, Murray was admitted to the state university in 1935.

But in Missouri, when Lloyd Gaines and Lucille Bluford tried to enroll in the Schools of Law and Journalism, the state decided to establish separate graduate schools for Negro students and set up a School of Journalism to accommodate Miss Bluford. A Negro law school became unnecessary at that time because during the years of waiting for his case to run the gamut of the courts Gaines either gave up the idea of entering law school or was forced to give it up; at any rate, he disappeared. Where? No one knew then and no one knows now.

In 1944, in Oklahoma, Miss Sipuel, a slender, quiet girl, daughter of an Oklahoma clergyman and an honor student from Langston University for Negroes, applied for admission to the University of Oklahoma College of Law. Although no state law required segregation there was established policy, and on the strength of this policy Miss Sipuel's application was turned down. She took the case into court, where four years later it reached the United States Supreme Court. During the arguments the assistant attorney general of Oklahoma admitted that if the Court ordered a law school for Negro students he did not know how soon one could be built up that would equal the one for white students. To which Justice William O. Douglas replied, "She might be an old lady by that time."

Oklahoma further argued that no law school for Negro students had been established for Miss Sipuel because she had not requested such action; she had asked admission into the state university, without recognizing the state's segregation policy. To which Justice Robert H. Jackson asked crisply, "Why should she?"

The result of the trial was a ruling from the Supreme Court that Oklahoma University would have to admit Ada Sipuel or provide a law school for Negro students to open the same time the university opened—a date just one week distant. The following Monday the new Law School of Langston University for Negroes opened its doors. But Ada Sipuel wanted graduate work of first quality and held out for admittance to the state university. The State of Oklahoma found technical points on which to disregard the Supreme Court ruling, and Miss Sipuel's case went back to the Supreme

Court. At length she was admitted to the university College of Law from which she was graduated in 1952—eight years after her first application to enter.

By 1950 lawsuits in many states were piling up in rapid succession. That year Mr. Gregory Swanson, a twenty-four-year-old Negro attorney, quiet, handsome, self-possessed, asked to enter the graduate school of the University of Virginia for advanced study and was refused because Virginia had a state law requiring segregation. In September, the three-judge decision was in favor of Swanson and he became the first Negro student to enter the University of Virginia since its founding by Thomas Jefferson, one hundred twenty-five years earlier.

The same year Mr. Herman Sweatt's case focused attention on Texas. In 1946 Mr. Sweatt had tried to enroll in the University of Texas, but instead of admitting him and inevitably other Negroes, the state spent $3.5 million to build a Negro university. Refusing to enter it because of its inferior work Sweatt continued on his job as mail carrier until the Supreme Court acted upon his case. At the age of thirty-seven Mr. Sweatt entered the university School of Law with four other Negro students.

Also in 1950, Mr. John S. Chase, twenty-five-year-old ex-G.I. and graduate of Hampton Institute, was enrolled in the University of Texas School of Architecture; and Horace L. Heath, dean of Paul Quinn College, Waco, Texas, with degrees from Colby College in Maine and the University of Pennsylvania, entered upon work for his doctorate in government. Also in 1950, Mr. Roy Wilson became the first Negro student to enroll in Louisiana State University.

Before the Supreme Court decision of 1954 ordering integration in public schools, Arkansas, alone of the Southern states, had opened its Graduate School to Negroes without court proceedings. In 1948, a Negro student was admitted to the School of Law; the next year a second man entered Law and a Negro girl was admitted to the School of Medicine. Today, all state-supported colleges and universities in Arkansas are open to Negro students.

Following acceptance of Negro students at the graduate level, Southern schools began to accept them for undergraduate work. By May, 1956, 164 accredited, formerly all-white colleges and universities had accepted Negro students, and thirteen formerly all-Negro institutions were open to white students. In no school had there been student rebellion or lawlessness excepting at the University of Alabama where in February of that year Miss Autherine Lucy enrolled. Four years previously she had tried to enter the university and when she was refused admittance she took her case into court where at the end of four years it was passed upon by the United States Supreme Court which ruled that the University of Alabama could not exclude a student on the basis of race. Since the university could find no other grounds to exclude her—as they had another Negro girl because they found her record and conduct unsatisfactory—there was no course left but to register Autherine Lucy.

Barred from the dormitories and eating places on the campus, Autherine knew that until she could make other arrangements she would have to commute the sixty miles between her home in Birmingham and Tuscaloosa where the university is located. On February 3, the first day of classes for the new semester, Autherine Lucy was on time for her nine o'clock class—her first class and also the first class in any white school in the State of Alabama to be attended by a Negro student. She sat through the class, the lone student in the front row. That night the first of the mob crowds visited the home of President Carmichael.

Saturday morning Autherine attended her one class for that day. Over the weekend crosses flamed, and mob demonstrations increased both on the campus and before the homes of the president and other university administrators. Monday morning at the close of her first class Autherine was escorted out the back door of the building by college officials. Target of eggs, tomatoes and rocks, and with threats to her life, she reached a car and was whisked away from the campus. That day the board of trustees met and sent Miss Lucy a telegram notifying her that for her own safety, as well as for the safety of other students and the faculty, she was suspended from school.

Almost immediately a petition, variously reported to have from twenty to two hundred signatures, was presented by a group of students, requesting the readmittance of Miss Lucy. Also the president of the university made a public statement, ". . . society could not long endure if its institutions of higher learning should array themselves at the side of lawlessness," and asked the co-operation of all connected with the school "to make certain that the University of Alabama will be on the side of law and order."

Soon the case of Autherine Lucy was again in court with the

resultant order that the suspension of plaintiff Lucy should be lifted; but immediately such charges and countercharges, suits and counter-suits developed that there was no possibility of her returning to school at that time. The twenty-six-year-old student would have to wait some time before attending the second lecture in her class in reading for children at the University of Alabama.

During the days of the demonstrations against Autherine Lucy, wherever newspapers, radio or television reached, people hung over the details of mob violence. There was no country in the world but knew of the breakdown of law and order in Alabama, U.S.A. In contrast, few people in this country or in other parts of the world knew that while one student was being thus escorted off the campus of one university there were three thousand Negro college students in twenty state-supported and twenty-seven privately endowed colleges *in the South* who were going about their everyday business of getting an education unsegregated and undisturbed.

In five Southern states—Alabama, Florida, Georgia, Mississippi, South Carolina—segregation is still enforced in state-supported institutions. However, in all but South Carolina at least one private college has opened its doors to Negroes. Many private schools have faced a rethinking of their function in American democracy. In all parts of the country some colleges have traditionally been segregated, either because of a clause in their charters specifically limiting the student body to a certain race, or because tradition has established a policy against admitting students of certain religious or racial backgrounds. Other schools have accepted token enrollments of Jewish, Negro or foreign students. However, since the movement for integration of the public schools has gained momentum, many privately endowed schools are committing themselves to serve an enlarged constituency. A growing number of institutions keep no record of racial origins of their student body, but it is estimated that on the campuses of some of the larger universities in the North there may be as many as five hundred Negro students enrolled. The list of small colleges in the United States that now receive qualified students of any race numbers over three hundred.

The trend toward integration of college campuses has also affected colleges for Negro students and many of them are enrolling white students, usually in departments in which a particular school is especially strong. In June, 1954, Miss Mary Howard received her master's degree in race relations from Fisk University, becoming the first white student in more than sixty years to receive a degree from that school. Miss Howard, although proud of her alma mater, nevertheless experienced some discrimination while attending the almost 100 per cent Negro school. She found Negro students were not free from prejudice against white students; that some of the townspeople considered her peculiar: and one evening the police thought she was drunk when they observed her going into a Negro apartment building in which she shared an apartment with a Negro faculty member. She also discovered that on occasion when traveling by car with her classmates, it was wise to eat her sandwiches in the car rather than to try to enter a restaurant with the other students, and that when passing through some Southern cities the occupants of the car felt easier when she slid down below window level.

\To the students on many campuses goes the credit for peaceful integration of the student bodies. Even in the early attempts of Negro students to enter universities, white student groups were generally sympathetic to the Negroes.\ After Miss Lucille Bluford was rejected at the University of Missouri a group of white students gave a luncheon in her honor. After the State of Oklahoma refused to accept the first ruling of the Supreme Court in the Ada Sipuel case, a group of a thousand students gathered, burned a copy of the Fourteenth Amendment and sent the ashes to the President of the United States. In one Southern college when the administration substituted free tickets for Negro students in place of the regular athletic passbooks, white students joined in a protest that changed the college practice. Following the expulsion of Autherine Lucy from the University of Alabama a group of forty students and faculty members organized a Human Relations Forum to provide opportunities for discussion and study of problems pertinent to life on the campus as it related to better human relations.

Because Greek letter organizations are social as well as academic they reflect the attitudes of students on race relations better than do organizations which are based on strictly religious, international or academic interests. In 1957 Alfred McClung Lee published the report of an extensive study of the practices of Greek letter organizations on college and university campuses. He found that campus students are more liberal in their attitudes than are the alumni who frequently control the national policies of the fraternities. This difference in attitude has resulted in withdrawal of several local chapters from national affiliation. At Amherst College, an outstanding Negro student, cross-country runner and member of the student council, was pledged to Phi Kappa Psi, a fraternity with a nonrestrictive clause in its constitution. However, the national organization ruled that although the constitution did not prohibit Negroes from becoming members, tradition was as binding as law, and tradition was against initiating Negro students. Rather than conform to the tradition of discrimination the Amherst chapter dropped its national affiliation. In Williams College the local chapter of Phi Delta Theta took similar action, as have local chapters elsewhere. Tau Kappa Epsilon, the fraternity most strenuously opposed to racial discrimination, is also the fastest growing fraternity on college campuses today.

A recent survey conducted by the National Committee on Fraternities in Education studied one hundred and twenty-five of the leading fraternity campuses to discover what definite steps were being taken to eliminate discriminatory practices. It found that thirty of the fraternities had taken some action to eliminate discrimination; ten more of them had indefinite plans for doing something; twelve others barred new chapters from practicing discrimination; and eight were taking positive steps to do something about such practices in already established chapters. Only ten of the major national fraternities had restrictive clauses, whereas forty years ago one-half of them had such clauses.

The record for sororities indicates that they have not eliminated discriminatory practices to the same extent as have fraternities. At the University of Minnesota when 70 per cent of the fraternity men thought all Greek letter organizations should drop racial and religious bars, only 56 per cent of the women were of that opinion. Even where constitutions do not prohibit discrimination the sororities have their own ways of practicing segregation. In general, the Greek letter societies of the Far West are the most liberal in their attitudes, but across the country the trend is toward eliminating discrimination.

Sometimes the experience of mixing in close social relations with people of different races is a totally new experience to students who come to a university with a mixed student body and although there may be no outward turmoil, there is frequently a battle within individual students to accept complete integration. Such an experience came to Miss Ellie Dixon, an exuberant little blonde from Pennsylvania who was attending a midwest state university. During the latter part of her first semester Ellie lost her roommate and waited eagerly for the new girls to enroll for second semester so she would again have the company of someone in her room. Then the day before the second semester opened she burst into the room of her best friend, Miss Margo Sandsten, a sleek brunette from Minnesota and the most popular girl in the hall. Ellie wept hysterically as she declared she wouldn't take the insult that had come to her, and that she knew her folks wouldn't stand for it, either. Quieting Ellie enough to get her to talk reasonably Margo found that Ellie's new roommate was to be a Negro girl.

"Ellie, you ought to feel complimented," said Margo.

The statement jarred Ellie into listening.

"Don't you mean 'insulted'?" she asked.

"I mean complimented. Someone evidently thought you were a levelheaded person. What's your roommate's name?"

"Cora. That's all I know," and Ellie buried her face in the chartreuse bedspread.

"You know, I was raised in St. Paul," went on Margo, "and I went clear through grade school and high school with two Negro girls."

"You mean you actually palled around with them?" asked Ellie doubtfully.

"Of course," Margo assured her.

"I never spoke to a Negro in my life, except waiters or someone like that," said Ellie slowly. "We didn't have any in my school back in Pennsylvania and I grew up thinking that people like us never had much to do with them. Do you think other dorms on the campus have any Negro and white girls rooming together?"

"I know they do," assured Margo. "The U admits them on the same basis it admits you and me and it treats us all alike. You go back to your room and if you decide you don't want Cora for a roommate just pretend you have a terrible headache and send for me. I'll come down and invite Cora to share my room for the night."

Ellie sat on the bed a long time, then washed her face, pushed up her hair and went back to her room. The headache never developed.

On some campuses the administration has dragged its feet in the matter of integration while on others the administration has set the pace. President John A. Hannah of Michigan State University assumed much of the responsibility for integrating the dormitories of the university soon after he came to its presidency.

At Drake University, a privately endowed college of approximately six thousand students, located at Des Moines, Iowa, it was the president who took the initial steps to end discrimination against Negro students. In 1941 when Henry G. Harmon was called to the presidency of the school Drake had no ruling on segregation but by custom the facilities of the Student Union were not available to Negro students. Nor did the eating places in the immediate university community serve them.

Not long after his arrival the new president and one of the trustees stopped at the Union to have a Coca Cola. As the men took a booth the president noticed that in a booth opposite them were four Negro freshmen, their blue and white beanies on their heads. Several other groups of students were served but no waiter approached the Negro freshmen. When one of the waiters came to take the orders from the men the president said, "I believe the boys across there came in ahead of us," and resumed his conversation with the trustee. From that time on the facilities of the Union were open to Negro students.

A few telephone conversations helped open the eating places in the university area. At various times managers called the president's office to complain that Negro students were coming into the drugstores and restaurants which had always served a white clientele only. "You've got to do something about it," was the burden of their complaint, to which the president replied, "We find at the university that the Negro students are as well behaved as other students, and that their money is just as good as the money which other students bring to the school. But if you don't feel that way, you'll have to make your own decisions and turn away any patrons whose money you don't want." The eating places remained open to the Negro students.

In the mid-forties Drake was competing in athletics against some schools which prohibited Negroes from playing on fields with white students. The result was that in about half its games Drake was crippled because some of its best players were Negroes. But when one of these schools came to Drake for a return game the visiting college played its entire first team. Finally Drake took the position that no other school should select the players that would represent Drake in any particular event.

In addition to what might be considered a selfish interest, the university felt that a moral issue was involved: that any student who was enrolled at Drake had a right to the privileges extended to other students. On this basis the school asserted that any student accepted by Drake would have to be accepted by any school which contracted to play them. Today all of the schools which were involved in this controversy of the past decade now have Negroes on their athletic teams.

The interracial relations at Drake may be better than at some universities or worse than at others. But they are typical of the problems posed on every campus where nonwhite students are being admitted on the same terms as other students. In most of these schools the movement toward complete integration must be a two-way movement because it is the common experience that such campuses have clubs or fraternities whose memberships are drawn exclusively from minority groups. This form of segregation is divisive, no matter what may be the reasons for its existence.

The breakdown of discrimination on college and university campuses is making possible a growing number of well-trained Negroes in the professions, which in turn are eliminating color bars from their organizations and fraternal societies. The trend became noticeable about 1947 and has gained momentum as Negroes have been admitted to membership not only in Northern state medical associations, but also in the medical associations of Alabama, Florida, Georgia, Missouri, Tennessee and Virginia; and to county societies in Missouri, Arkansas, South Carolina and Texas.

Approximately half the Negro doctors, dentists and nurses graduated each year have taken their work at Meharry Medical College, Nashville, Tennessee. Founded in 1876 by two Methodist missionaries and named for the five Meharry brothers who pooled their financial resources and contributed the first $20,000 to the school, Meharry has graduated five thousand professional men and women. With its first classes held in basement rooms, and using improvised equipment, the school struggled to achieve a status that would make it possible to prepare Negro doctors who could equal white doctors in professional skill. With grants for several years from the Rocke-feller Foundation the college achieved its goal; now it has a physical plant, equipment and staff that have won for it an A rating by the American Medical Association. President Harold D. West, formerly head of the department of biochemistry and one of the two Negro members of the American Society of Biological Chemists, is the first Negro to serve as president of the school.

In 1947 only eighteen hospitals in the country accepted Negro interns, and of this group ten were hospitals for Negro patients only and two were predominantly Negro. By 1952 graduates of Meharry Medical College alone were serving in forty-six different hospitals; and fewer than one-third of the fifty-eight graduates of 1953 were placed in Negro hospitals for their internships.

A further indication that professional skill alone is opening doors once closed to Negroes is found in the 1949 election of Dr. Peter Marshall to the policy-making body of the American Medical Associ-ation. Dr. Marshall became the first member of his race to hold such a position in the one hundred years the association has been in existence. Within recent years Negro doctors have been admitted to the American Board of Surgeons, the American Board of Pedi-atrics, and other specialty boards. In October, 1954, the Veterans Administration ended segregation in all its hospitals.

In 1953 the Southern Conference Educational Fund polled a sampling of 5,750 white Southern medical men. Of those queried, 71 per cent favored inclusion of Negro doctors in medical societies, and 63 per cent favored integrating Negro doctors in hospital staffs. While this degree of integration was indicated at the professional level, only 17 per cent of the doctors favored opening hospitals to patients of both races.

Integration of nursing associations has progressed so fast that in 1956 the National Association of Colored Nurses voted itself out of existence. By 1954 Georgia was the only state in which at least some associations did not include Negro nurses.

Other professional groups have been keeping step with the medi-cal profession. For some years bar associations in Ohio, Texas, Cali-fornia, Kentucky, Missouri and Washington, D.C., have been opened to qualified Negro lawyers. In 1956 the American Bar Association dropped from its application blanks all questions relating to racial origins of the applicants. Integrated educational and ministerial associations without number are found across the country. The National Press Club elected its first Negro member in 1955.

A frequent reason why Negroes have not been admitted to professional societies—in addition to discrimination because of color—is that their professional training has been inferior to the training of their white associates. Traditionally, the colleges to which Negroes were admitted ranked lower educationally than the other professional schools of the nation. In recent years as Negro students are being admitted to the better graduate and professional schools they are adding their numbers to the top men in their ranks. The medical profession salutes the late Dr. Charles Drew who worked out the method of preserving blood plasma; the legal profession recognizes Thurgood Marshall as one of the leading constitutional lawyers in the United States; military men respect Colonel James H. Robinson for his leadership of fighting forces in North Africa and Italy during World War II, and for his services with the U.S. Eighth Army in Korea; and religious leaders recognize that the Rev. Martin Luther King has given new dimension to Christian practices.

In addition to excellent training there is a social factor that helps determine a man's success in his chosen profession. That factor was discussed by Wesley A. Brown, the first Negro to be graduated from Annapolis Naval Academy, in the *Saturday Evening Post* for June 25, 1949. Soon after his arrival at Annapolis, when roommates were assigned, several of the plebes suggested to Brown that they would like to room with him. "I didn't know if they felt sorry for me or genuinely believed me to be a good prospect." Later, when Brown was thinking back over his days at Dunbar High School in Washington, D.C., he said, "That's a wonderful school, and it certainly helped me intellectually and morally. However, it had the enormous disadvantage of being segregated. Going to school four years with Negroes burdened me, later at Annapolis, with the problem of social adjustment. It's like stepping into a new world. Unless you've had the experience you have no idea what an impediment it is. It often makes you imagine nonexistent troubles and persecutions."

Five years later the Supreme Court expressed Wesley Brown's convictions in different words: "Separate educational facilities are inherently unequal."

With each succeeding year, when the first school bell in the fall calls kindergartners from the playground to their first class, or eighth graders to prepare for their first commencement, or high school students to their restless round of activities, or college students to the new experience of self-discipline, or graduate students to the grueling pressure of professional training, that bell rings more clearly for equality of opportunity for all of America's students.

13.   Fewer Seats for Jim Crow

As a sprightly eighty-year-old minister stepped with a younger companion into an elevator in a hotel in Washington, D.C., he smiled at the occupants as if to let them in on a delightful secret and said to the younger man, "I can remember when I couldn't have done this."

Everyone understood that "this" referred to riding in the same elevator with the white guests, most of whom were attending the convention at which the Negro minister was scheduled to speak that morning. As he continued talking to his friend his voice had a tone of appreciation rather than criticism. "Yes, sir, I came to Washington on an unsegregated train; and I'll return to Iowa on an unsegregated plane; and I'm staying here in an unsegregated hotel. You'll never experience some of the things I remember."

Some of the recollections of this pastor must also have included nights of sitting up in Jim Crow coaches because Pullmans were not available to him; or perhaps at the other extreme of service, he might well recall having been given a compartment—always dubbed

"Lower 13" when used for Negroes holding Pullman tickets—because the railroad company, not wanting to mix Negro and white passengers in the regular section of Pullman berths, had given him a private room for the night. He probably could recall many times when upon crossing a state line he had been asked to move forward from an unsegregated coach into a segregated coach; or when prohibited from entering the dining car, he had eaten a stale box lunch; or later, with dining service opened to him, when he had sat at a table separated from the others by a short curtain to indicate the table was for segregated passengers. For seventy-five years these practices were part of the standard American Way of Life and are remembered by people less than half the age of the "remembering when" minister.

Since the 1954 Supreme Court decision on segregation in the public schools so many references are made to the 1896 Plessy *vs.* Ferguson case that many people have come to associate that court case with school segregation. In reality, Mr. Homer Plessy, who brought the suit into court, was a Negro—although seven-eighths white—who refused to ride in a Jim Crow coach. He based his right to equal service upon an 1873 court decision which had established that to require separate accommodations for Negroes and whites denied the equality of the races.

However, in the intervening years Southern states had passed segregation laws which had, in practice, superseded the earlier Supreme Court decision. So in 1896 when Mr. Plessy's case reached the Supreme Court the pattern of American thinking reflected itself in the new decision that "separate but equal" was acceptable. By logical steps the argument spread that if separate but equal was all right in transportation it was similarly all right in every other aspect of public life. When accusations of unjust discrimination were brought to the attention of the railroads the justification was that if the best of the accommodations for Negroes was equal to the poorest for whites the facilities still maintained the status of separate but equal. The continued practices of segregation on the trains, in the waiting rooms and at lunch counters kept the railroads and the general public in a state of uneasy agitation. The possibility of an unpleasant scene, ranging from angry words to actual bloodshed, was always present. As late as 1947 on two separate occasions a Negro was killed as the result of failure to comply with orders to move into segregated sections.

By 1940, after decades of their total exclusion, Negroes were given limited space on Pullmans, but when the space allotted to Negro passengers had been assigned, no more was available to them even if berths went unused. The classic case that opened general Pullman space was the suit brought by Congressman Arthur W. Mitchell of Illinois who had been denied first-class accommodations when the section set aside for Negroes was sold out. Then in 1941 the Supreme Court decided that travel facilities were for individuals, not for races, and that if a train had space available it had to be given to the person whose ticket entitled him to it.

Two years later the Henderson case opened dining-car service on the same basis. The fact that one table usually took care of the Negro passengers, decided the Court, was no reason to deny service to a Negro because there was not sufficient space at that table to accommodate him.

The decade between 1940–50 not only saw Pullman and dining-car services opened on an unsegregated basis but it also witnessed a change that affected the thousands of rank-and-file citizens who ride the common coaches and the buses.

In 1944, Mrs. Irene Morgan, a Negro, was traveling from Virginia to Maryland on a Greyhound bus. While still in the State of Virginia, with strict segregation laws, the bus driver ordered Mrs. Morgan to move to a rear seat, but Mrs. Morgan refused to move. She was arrested and her case went into the Virginia courts. It finally reached the United States Supreme Court which ruled that to require interstate carriers to observe the regulations of each separate state through which they passed put an undue burden upon the carriers. Therefore, said the Court, interstate passengers did not have to conform to state laws.

During World War II the public became more conscious of the effects of discrimination. There were many stories of "buddies" traveling together only to be separated at state lines, in lunchrooms and waiting rooms. There were stories of Negro soldiers having to wait for a handout of sandwiches until after white service men had been served at tables. In one case the white men sitting at the tables were German prisoners-of-war who were being taken to a prison camp while the Negroes who could not be served were wounded Negro soldiers just back from Europe and on their way to a veterans' hospital.

As Americans became conscious of the injustice of discrimination, as opposed to the mere fact of discrimination, public opinion began to turn in favor of desegregation. So far had it moved by 1948 that when Mr. William Chance, a Negro school principal, was arrested on a charge of disorderly conduct because he refused to move into a segregated coach, the railway company withdrew its charge when the case reached the courts. But Mr. Chance did not withdraw his countercharges and sued the railroad for breach of contract and unlawful arrest. He won his case and a new standard of racial equality was established.

These court decisions and the consequent relaxation of discriminations primarily affected interstate travel. To a great extent, within its own borders each state still remains a law unto itself and many of them require segregation of all travel facilities. This regulation makes possible scenes like the one which took place high in the picturesque Blue Ridge Mountains when a Greyhound bus stopped for its breakfast break and six young men in the uniform of the air force entered the restaurant talking and laughing together. Five of them crowded around one table while the sixth walked by himself over to a corner table, ate his breakfast and sat there alone until the group was reunited as it climbed back onto the bus.

The Pennsylvania Railroad system led the way in actually dropping discriminatory practices, but some of the railroads continue a concealed process of screening Negro passengers out of cars intended for white passengers only. The process is especially easy to effect on coaches that require seat reservations. Ticket agents can assign space in coaches of their own selection as each ticket is purchased; or if an agent discovers a Negro holding a ticket for the "wrong" coach, the agent or at times the conductor can claim some mistake in the reservation and change the assignment. And usually the Negro passenger, rather than face the embarrassment of a public scene, accepts the suggestion that he move.

"It's not a very pleasant experience," said a woman who travels across the continent many times a year, "to be quietly reading and have a conductor stop at your seat and suggest that he will move your bag for you into another coach because through some error you had been assigned the wrong seat. It is possible to argue with him and stay where you are but you feel humiliated in front of all the eyes that are staring at you." In parts of the Deep South fear of physical violence keeps many Negroes from exercising their right to desegregated travel.

In 1952 under the direction of Dr. Herman Long of the department of race relations, Fisk University, a study was made of discrimination in rail travel. For this study Negro men and women offered to travel under ordinary conditions and take whatever discriminations they met. They talked with other passengers, Negro and white; and when possible they interviewed railway employees. One section of the study consisted of interviews with 171 Negro passengers who were traveling in reserved seat coaches either in the South or bound for a Southern destination. A few of the persons interviewed had taken their chances on getting a seat when they arrived at the station and had not tried to make an advance reservation. However, 78 per cent of the passengers had made advance reservations. Of these, one-third reported that they encountered some difficulty; the other two-thirds had obtained their reservations without trouble.

The legality of segregation on local buses remained a matter of state and city ruling until the Montgomery, Alabama, bus boycott brought the question into the Supreme Court. Late on the afternoon of Thursday, December 1, 1955, a thirty-six-seat bus, already carrying twenty-four Negroes and twelve white passengers, stopped in front of the Empire Theater where several white people were waiting to get on. So, according to custom, the driver exercised his right to "equalize facilities" between the races and told four Negro passengers to give their seats to white passengers. Also according to custom, three of the Negroes complied; but Mrs. Rosa Parks, a seamstress in a downtown store, refused—she was just too tired to move. The bus driver called the police and Mrs. Parks was arrested for violating the segregation law, and her trial was set for the following Monday, December 5.

On Saturday, mimeographed circulars prepared by a committee were distributed in the Negro district of the city. The circulars urged Negro passengers to observe Monday as a day of protest and to refrain from riding the buses. Sunday morning many of the Negro ministers referred to the situation, urging restraint on the part of their parishioners. Monday morning came—the day of Mrs. Parks's trial—and 75 per cent of the working force of Montgomery's fifty thousand Negroes stayed off the buses. For the next 381 days Negro taxis and car pools carried workers to their jobs; many white housewives called for their own domestics; but also thousands of shoesoles were worn thin, replaced and worn through again by employees who walked long distances rather than patronize the buses. Negro taxi drivers were intimidated, and Negro motorists harassed. Homes were bombed, including that of the Rev. Martin Luther King who had assumed direction of the boycott. In all, eighty-nine persons were arrested, including twenty-four ministers.

Retail businessmen in Montgomery began to feel the pinch of this pre-Christmas boycott. The bus company felt the financial stranglehold when it lost its Negro patronage which made up three-fourths of its normal riding public. The bus line was willing to settle the dispute and accept desegregation, not because it approved the practice, but because the settlement would put the line again on a paying basis. However, the city served an injunction against the company to prevent its desegregation move.

The boycotting Negroes were not holding out for complete desegregation. They presented three requests. The first was for more considerate treatment on transportation lines. The second was that passengers continue to be seated in the customary manner with white passengers beginning at the front and Negro passengers at the rear, *but* with the added guarantee that no arbitrary division of space be allocated to either race, thus removing the indignity of a Negro passenger's being forced to give up his seat to a white passenger who boarded the bus at a later stop. The third request was for Negro bus drivers on the city routes which served predominantly Negro districts.

During the tense days of the boycott, insults and arrests failed to weaken the determination of the Negroes. Even violence failed to call out retaliatory acts. The Negroes remained calm, persistent and dedicated to their cause. Said one seventy-five-year-old woman midway through the strike, "I've been riding the buses all through the boycott because I'm sick and old, but since they arrested my pastor I'll walk from now on if necessary." Another Negro citizen called out on one occasion, "Ride on, O King! We can walk!"

Four Negro women from among those who had been arrested entered a case in the courts. With almost unprecedented speed it made its way to the Supreme Court which on November 13, 1956, upheld the decision of a lower court that Alabama's requirement of segregation on buses violated the due process and equal protection clauses of the Fourteenth Amendment.

On December 21, 1956, an early bus passenger was the Rev. Martin Luther King who made a trial ride on Montgomery's unsegregated buses. The trial proved good. So again, after a year of by-passing the buses, Negroes waited with white people at the bus stops. But when they entered the buses something new happened. Instead of depositing their coins and then stepping off to re-enter by a back door, the Negro passengers walked into the buses by the front entrances. They took their places on a first-come-first-served-basis with no line of demarcation indicating any section of the buses reserved for either race. A few white passengers chose to sit in the back seats to show their sympathy with the cause of desegregation. A few Negroes sat in seats far front to enjoy their new freedom. But most of the Negroes made no effort to call attention to the justice they were experiencing. Among the first day's passengers was Mrs. Rosa Parks, riding a bus for the first time since the day her last ride had precipitated the boycott.

Although the decision of the Supreme Court that segregation on buses is unconstitutional covers every community of the United States, enforcement of the ruling is a state responsibility. In many states segregation is still practiced, but each year Jim Crow is finding fewer seats reserved for him.

Air travel arrived upon the transportation scene late enough to profit from the experiences of bus and rail carriers. Also as a new type of transportation the air service had to establish itself against the competition of accepted modes. It was important to get passengers, and to give nondiscriminatory service to Negro passengers who could afford to ride in planes meant a ready-made clientele. The airlines also knew that discrimination doubled the cost of all services and they were not in a financial position to carry the extra expense.

However, in some cities service at the airports is segregated. At one landing field two men, one Negro and one white, walked down the ramp together and over to the limousine that would take them into the hotel where they both had accommodations. The driver took the bags of one man but said to the other, "You'll take a taxi in." In this instance, both men picked up their bags and moved over to the taxi. In some cities it would even be necessary to call two taxis because the cab companies are franchised to carry only white or colored passengers.

The persistent efforts of many individuals and organizations have gone into the movement to desegregate trains and buses. Incidents small in themselves have often been large in the measure of comradeship they conveyed. A shared discrimination has frequently removed the sting for a Negro and lessened the embarrassment of a white person who felt as powerless as the Negro in the grip of custom. On one occasion a Negro union official and the white lawyer for the same union traveled together from Chicago to Washington. Because the union member could not have the privilege of Pullman service the young lawyer sat up all night also. Arrived in Washington, when no hotel which catered to white guests would receive the Negro, the lawyer went with him to a hotel for Negro guests.

On another occasion a group of six women were traveling together as delegates to a national convention when the one Negro delegate was asked to move into a different coach; without comment the other five women moved also. Recently two business executives of the same firm, one of them white and the other Negro, stopped at a restaurant in a Southern railway station. When the waitress came to take their orders she said to the Negro, "You move over to the counter." With scarcely a break in their conversation the two men took their places at the counter and ordered lunch together. A few years ago a group of Methodist students were traveling together from St. Paul to attend a youth conference in Texas. Twelve of them were seated in the diner when the steward came to the four Negro students and asked them to go back to their coach. As the other students watched the four start to push back their chairs, they all rose simultaneously and walked out of the car together, the Negro students no more conspicuous than the others.

The impact of hundreds of such experiences has helped to bring about removal of segregation in travel, an accomplishment which many nonwhite citizens put at the top of the list when mentioning the steps in integration which have made life easier for them.

14. On Many Fronts

In 1948 a news story broke across this war-conscious country which even conservative newspapers and magazines recounted in extravagant terms: "incalculable results," "biggest story of the century," "strongest blow to segregation." The news centered around Executive Order 9981, issued by President Harry S. Truman. It reads: "It is hereby declared to be the policy of the President that there shall be equality of treatment and opportunity for all persons in the armed services without regard to race, color, religion or national origin. This policy shall be put into effect as rapidly as possible, having due regard to the time required to effectuate any necessary changes without impairing efficiency or morale."

According to a law of physics, "when an irresistible force meets an immovable body"—something happens. In 1948 segregation in our armed forces was firmly enough entrenched to qualify as an immovable object. The irresistible force was the stream of democracy which had been gathering in strength ever since World War I had been fought on the slogan, "Make the world safe for democracy."

The stream drew from many tributaries as it widened and deepened. World War II was a struggle to block totalitarianism, especially the fascist governments of Germany and Italy. The Korean police action was intended to contain communism, and at the same time it brought the world-wide forces of democracy into closer alignment through the United Nations. Increasingly through this thirty-odd years of conflict of world ideologies the United States had been embarrassed when it tried to explain how it could fight for democracy while at the same time within its fighting forces it practiced one of the most hated tenets of fascism—racial superiority of a chosen people.

World War I ended with conflicting reports on the fighting valor of Negro troops. When the Croix de Guerre was granted en masse to New York's 369th all-Negro Regiment, there were those in this country who resented the fact that Negroes had measured up to such a standard of bravery. In the first phases of World War II Negro troops were kept in the background and assigned to menial tasks rather than to front-line duty. Then as the war continued to go against the Allies and every available man was needed to stem the aggressive push of the enemy at the Battle of the Bulge, General Eisenhower called for volunteers to concentrate in the most dangerous sector. Behind-the-line men, many of them the Negro soldiers whose duties had been restricted to service with the shovel and pickax, rushed to answer the call. The danger over, those Negro troops who had lived through the action were again assigned by the Pentagon to their former duties. However, during the period of their strategic action, psychological studies had been conducted to ascertain the emotional stability of Negro soldiers under fire, the effect of their presence on white troops, and other factors. The studies indicated that there was no reason for keeping troops segregated. However, little publicity was given the findings of this study.

The valor exhibited by other minority groups added to the factual bases of demands for desegregation. The records of the Japanese American fighting units show that the 442nd Regimental Combat Team had the highest individual mental scores of any unit in the infantry; and that it came out of the war the most decorated unit in the nation's history. The American Indians supplied seventeen thousand men for World War I, more than half of them still denied citizenship, and thirteen thousand men for active participation in World War II. One of their race helped raise the flag at Iwo Jima;

and Major General Clarence Tinker, who reorganized the air forces after the attack at Pearl Harbor, claimed membership in the Osage tribe.

In 1943, William H. Hastie, civilian aide to the Secretary of War, graduate of Harvard Law School, former professor and dean of Howard University School of Law, and a Negro, brought into the open the conflict of opinion on discrimination in the armed forces when in protest he resigned his position. None the less, this protest, plus the record of the nonwhite troops, plus insistence on integration by Secretary of the Navy Forrestal and Secretary of the Army Symington—not even the combination of these forces removed segregation of the armed services. When the military remained adamant in their refusal to integrate the troops, on July 26, 1948, President Truman, commander-in-chief of the armed forces, issued Executive Order 9981, introduced with the words: "It is essential that there be maintained in the armed services of the United States the highest standards of democracy, with equality of treatment and opportunity for all who serve in our country's defense."

Opinion as to the wisdom and the probable outcome of such an order varied. Some military men knew integration would never work; others knew it had worked when it had been given a fair trial. Some men in the armed services were angered while others thought their participation in war for the sake of democracy made sense for the first time. The public was likewise divided. However, the world situation was fast moving the United States into a police action in Korea which would test the new policy in action. During the many months of that conflict there were indeed some difficulties, but official investigations showed that most of the trouble arose from the misunderstandings and uncertainties attendant upon partial integration when neither the white nor the Negro soldiers knew the exact status of the latter. As fighting units alternated between all-Negro, partially Negro, and back to segregated units again, the status of the Negro soldier became very confused. However, of two things many of their leaders were convinced: Negroes could fight, and they fought better in integrated units. One Texas colonel who was in command of the most completely integrated battalion in the 2nd Division said he would "fight anyone who even inferred that his troops were not as good as anybody else's." And a white Southern infantryman who served in Korea later affirmed, "If a man can carry a rifle and knows his job, he's my buddy. I don't give a damn what color his skin happens to be." In a moving study, *Breakthrough on the Color Front,* Lee Nichols tells in detail the story of the desegregation of the troops in Korea and the eventual integration of all of the armed services.

With the evidence of the Korean action in favor of desegregation, the various branches of the services speeded their programs of integration so that before the 1954 deadline for desegregation all the armed forces were integrated. There was no fanfare accompanying the accomplishment and the public showed little emotional reaction to it, unless it was to exhibit a general attitude of relief that the step had finally been taken. A young man who was on the campus of the University of Alabama at the time Autherine Lucy tried unsuccessfully to enroll in that school and who later helped to organize the Human Relations Forum expressed the point of view of many ex-G.I.'s when he said, "I was in the Navy and there I learned what I had never had a chance to learn before—namely that Negroes are human beings, just as you and I. I wish everybody in the South could have had the opportunity to get to know Negroes as I did."

A Negro educator recently observed that "once young people have experienced equality they are never the same again." Then he remarked that when he drives through the South he can fairly well tell which filling station attendants have had some experience outside segregationist states, not so much because they do anything different, but because they do the same things differently.

While the armed services were desegregating, government-operated military bases were going through the same process. A few schools for the children of military personnel had started operating on an integrated basis before a government order of 1953 put them all on that basis. The action was questioned in some states where the state laws forbid integrated schools, but the government took the position that federal policies on federal establishments superseded state requirements, and integration went into effect. This step was taken four months before the Supreme Court decision ordered public schools desegregated.

With hundreds of families of all races mixing freely on a military post, the restrictions on their activities in the surrounding communities are coming into sharper focus. One young white mother living in an army trailer camp in Louisiana commented, "It seems so silly. We live together on the post and our youngsters go to school together and play together in the trailer camp playgrounds; but when we go to town, we can't ride together, shop together, or have anything to do with each other. How long can a situation like that go on?"

Sometimes ordinary human reactions help to answer that question. In a small Texas community adjacent to an army base the first of a series of Saturday night informal parties was announced. When the white mothers of the little town learned that the party would be attended by both Negro and white service men, they refused to let their daughters attend. Whereupon the white service men, left without any available "dates," promptly went to nearby towns and imported their girls. The party progressed with no unpleasant incidents, and the proverbial "good time was had by all." So then the town's daughters went to work on the older generation, evidently with unanswerable arguments, because the next month when party time came the local girls were there.

At present there are approximately three million Americans in the armed services. If the number of persons in the families of these men and women were known then it would be possible to compute how many Americans are being directly influenced by Executive Order 9981.

In addition to the direct influence of desegregation of the armed services on the American social structure, there is the indirect effect it has had in creating an atmosphere which makes easier the breakdown of segregation in other contacts. There was a time in most of the Southern states when even a highly educated Negro could not go into the public library and draw out a book. If he wanted the latest treatise on theology or law; if he needed a commentary on the Bible, or a current book on psychology, philosophy or science, a white friend had to get the book for him. In some communities he might find a Negro branch library to which had been relegated the outdated encyclopedias from the main library, along with a few books for children and still fewer for readers above the juvenile level. The luxury for which his educated mind yearned, to sit and browse through the pages of the latest books and the most recent periodicals —these pleasures were denied him because his brain was concealed behind dark skin.

In 1941 Dr. Eliza Atkins Gleason made a survey of library services to nonwhites. She found sixteen Southern communities that served Negroes in any capacity in the main library. Of these libraries, Covington, Kentucky, and El Paso, Pecos and Brady, Texas, allowed full privileges to Negroes; the other twelve offered limited services. Twelve years later the Southern Regional Council conducted a mail survey of Southern communities and found that fifty-nine of them then permitted Negroes free use of the main library. Of these fifty-nine towns, twenty-one were in Kentucky, eighteen in Texas, and six in Virginia; Tennessee, Oklahoma, Florida and Arkansas divided the other fourteen among them. Twenty-four communities allowed Negroes limited use of the main library which might mean separate reading rooms, or no reading room for Negroes; or services only to professional and student clientele; or summer service; or no services for children. Of these twenty-four limited-services communities six were in Florida and Louisiana each; four in North Carolina; and the other eight were scattered through six states. Georgia and Alabama each reported one library with limited services for Negroes, while Mississippi and South Carolina reported no form of integrated library service.

At the present time, although a majority of the main libraries whose entire facilities are open to Negroes are in communities where the proportional Negro population is small, eleven of the localities reporting have a Negro population ranging from 20 per cent to 44 per cent. With the educational level of Negroes steadily rising the demands on Negro branch libraries can no longer be met within any reasonable budget. The problem of financial support is forcing many communities to reconsider their policy of absolute segregation.

In 1951 when Miami built a new public library, the Negroes of that city were becoming politically and economically aware of the proportion of taxes they were carrying. Also, the librarian was a librarian, not a racist. The combination of circumstances made it possible for Miami to open its library on a completely integrated basis. No unhappy situations resulted, and so within a short time all branch libraries in the city were also integrated.

Another amicable settlement was reached in Newport News, Virginia, after an attorney had been refused service at the main library. The case was taken into court but before it came up for trial the question was settled. The city council first contemplated a more adequate Negro branch library, but the council knew that financially such a solution was out of the question, so the main library was opened to the whole community.

Since the 1954 survey, the public libraries of Little Rock, Arkansas; Tulsa, Duncan and Tahlequah, Oklahoma; Greeneville, Tennessee; and San Antonio, Texas, have been opened to everyone. The list is growing month by month as additional communities are adopting integrated policies. In most libraries little fanfare has accompanied integration. Mr. Eugene Cox, a community leader in Mississippi, recounts that one day he was browsing in the stacks of the library at Little Rock which he frequently visited, and not far from him was a Negro looking at some books. "If I thought anything at all about it at the moment it was to assume that he was a janitor," said Mr. Cox. But later when he stopped at the check-out desk the person immediately preceding him was the same man who had been up in the stacks. Mr. Cox added, "That's the way many changes are taking place in this part of the South; one group after another just moves out on a different principle from those on which it had formerly operated."

In the field of press reporting changes are taking place which suggest a new sense of responsibility on the part of editors and also indicate that the public has moved in the direction of integrating Negro life into community life. A community counselor in Virginia, in commenting upon the changed attitude of white people toward the Negro minority, cited the use of courtesy titles for Negroes as one of the important changes of recent years. For example, in 1948 a list of the names of all the women who were to help in a welfare drive was sent to the local newspaper, the names of white and Negro women listed together alphabetically; but before publication the newspaper struck out the Miss or Mrs. before the name of each Negro woman. In this group was the name of one of the city's best-trained social workers, a Negro woman loved by members of both races. Six years later she died and the same newspaper carried a front page tribute to her, and it was to Mrs. ———. "That's a significant change," said the counselor.

During the past decade many newspapers in the South have moved even further and have changed their policies of handling material relative to the Negro population. Sometimes this new approach has been the result of pressure brought against a paper by Negro subscribers, as was the case in Memphis in 1957 when Negro subscribers of that city and of northern Mississippi boycotted one of the papers. While debating the action a group of Negro ministers visited the editor to present a request for the use of courtesy titles, for the inclusion of newsworthy Negro civic events, and for decreased emphasis on Negro crime stories which the paper played up out of proportion to crime stories covering white offenders. At that time the newspaper refused to recognize the validity of the requests, so a committee of businessmen waited upon the editor but got no further than had the first committee. Negro subscribers then canceled their subscriptions and within a few weeks the editor invited them to send representatives to his office and granted every one of the original requests.

Much more frequently the newspapers are voluntarily revamping their methods of news coverage. In addition to correcting the usual abuses as listed by the Memphis subscribers, many large dailies are using Negro reporters; and some of the smaller papers would be willing to employ them, but in many communities editors cannot find a competent Negro reporter. When, because the reporter resigned, a Texas weekly suspended its news column covering Negro activities it received more complaints from white subscribers than from Negro. The practice of putting all stories of Negro happenings on a separate page is being discontinued by some editors on the theory that news segregation is as discriminating as overt segregation.

In December, 1957, the Kansas City *Times* carried a picture of Mrs. L. C. Bates, state president of the Arkansas NAACP, with Mr. Carl Johnson, a Kansas City municipal court judge. This picture was one of the first in the newspaper to present Negroes in a serious role; previously they had been pictured only as entertainers, sports participants or in some subservient capacity.

The question of how best to promote good race relations through the media of mass communications has concerned many people for a number of years. When magazines such as *Ebony,* slanted to a particular racial group, first started publication the problem of advertisements came up. Large firms made up their advertising layouts for magazines circulating to white subscribers, but these advertisements seemed strangely out of place in a publication for Negro circulation, simply because advertisements are supposed to make the reader unconsciously identify himself with the person in the advertisement. Negro publications moved ahead a long step when advertisers were willing to provide them with advertisements which appealed to their readers.

Actually, however, that step was merely an intermediate step. In some way desegregation of advertising has to evolve. Perhaps television has indicated the way this change can be accomplished. On a telecast there is seldom any mention of the race to which an individual belongs—he is presented because he has something to contribute to the discussion or the program. Of all forms of mass communications television has achieved the largest degree of integration.

While desegregation was taking place in the armed services, in industry, travel and in the use of public cultural facilities it was inevitable that it would also have to be considered in recreation. Around the turn of the century a popular song described a little Negro girl who hoped that when she got to heaven there would be a place for "Little Black Me." Highly sentimental, that song nevertheless carried an accurate representation of the exclusion of Negro youngsters from the carefree world of play which white children enjoyed. Sometimes segregation of recreational facilities has been the result of laws or ordinances; sometimes the result of common consent as binding as law. In fact, in Mississippi common consent is stronger than law; the state statutes contain a law passed in early post-Civil War days which makes segregation in public recreation illegal, but strict segregation is currently enforced.

Many people are as fearful of the consequences of desegregation of recreational facilities as they are of desegregation of the public schools. In Washington, federal recreation grounds were opened to Negroes in 1933, but when in 1950 the city took steps to open other facilities, including indoor swimming pools, there was considerable opposition. In April of that year the *Washington Post* wrote editorially:

The Interior Department could not keep the pools closed all summer without producing a justified explosion in the community. Nor could it operate all of them on a non-segregated basis without provoking new racial tension and risking worse disorders than occurred last year. Better race relations are not fostered by dictation . . . nor by the sudden enforcement of rules that are certain to incite interracial animosities.

Therefore the *Post* urged a gradual and more "realistic" policy in moving into nonsegregation. Notwithstanding this kind of opposition, the city held to its announced policy and during the spring months carried on a program of education of the public and of intensive training for the police, the park personnel and all other people who would have any responsibility for the operation of the pools. Then they were opened to the general public and operated unsegregated for the entire summer.

In September the *Washington Post* printed another editorial in which it summarized the record of the six pools during the summer months: of 236,000 swimmers, 90,000 had been colored and 146,000 white; and not one disturbance had been recorded during the entire season. The newspaper then went on to praise the work of the Metropolitan police force, concluding:

> The lesson of last summer's experience, in our judgment, is that non-segregated swimming is here to stay; that it can be conducted safely and harmoniously under level-headed leadership; and that along these lines increased swimming facilities should be made available for use next summer. . . . The outcome is all the more gratifying to *The Washington Post* because last spring we shared the widespread fear that the community was not yet ready to accept nonsegregated swimming without a recurrence of violence.

In 1955 Kentucky opened all its recreational areas to everyone; but even before that action Louisville, the largest city in the state, had started easing its restriction and had eighty-two "tot lots" where Negro and white children played together. In other states golf courses, beaches, sand-lot baseball diamonds—practically every phase of recreation has been letting down color bars. Between 1954 and 1956 sixteen Southern states opened some phase of their recreation programs on an unsegregated basis.

In the opinions of many people sports have done more to ease the public into accepting racial integration than has any other one activity. Back in 1935 Mr. Jesse Owens, a young Ohio State University track man, started sport fans talking when he broke three world records in one afternoon—the broad jump, the 220-yard dash, and the 220-yard low hurdles. He also broke the color line, for Mr. Owens was the first Negro to compete for high athletic honors. The following year he added new laurels to his crown when he participated in the Olympics in Germany and before a crowd of 120,000 people, including Adolf Hitler, won in the broad jump over Luz Long, his German competitor. Actually Long had won for distance but was disqualified because his toe fouled the line. The Olympic crowd took Jesse Owens to its heart, but Hitler failed to call him to his box to offer congratulations. A Negro winner did not tally with Nordic supremacy.

The history of boxing, football and basketball could not be written without the names of Negroes. But it was baseball, America's number one sport, that first firmly established Negroes among America's number one athletes when back in the 1940's Branch Rickey needed some new players to build up his Brooklyn Dodgers and one of his talent scouts out in California turned up a Negro named Jackie Robinson. Here was a young fellow who had made more of a name for himself in football than in baseball but he looked good, and Rickey took him for one important reason—he needed good players and he knew that there was no reason to believe that all good baseball players came in white packages.

Rickey also knew that any Negro who blazed the trail in big league baseball had to be more than a good ball player, but he gambled on Robinson's assets—education, experience in competitive sports, and the intangible personal qualifications that indicated he could "take it." And for a time Robinson had plenty to take. Frequently he had to eat at a table separate from the other members of his club; or stay at a hotel by himself; and at times travel in a separate coach. He suffered insults from opposing teams, the prejudice of umpires and in his early years the antagonism of unsympathetic baseball fans as well.

Even harder to take than discriminatory treatment was the one rule that Branch Rickey had laid down—Robinson was never to talk back or fight back. Robinson promised, and kept his promise. During one session of particularly abusive talk and treatment from the Philadelphia ball club, one of Robinson's teammates rose to his defense, walked over to the Phillies' bench and exploded, "Why don't you ride someone who can talk back?" From then on everyone knew that Jackie Robinson was "in."

With each baseball season Negro players continue to make baseball history. When the Milwaukee Braves walked off with the 1957 championship, little Hank Aaron, right fielder, was feted and filmed, idolized and televised along with Milwaukee's winning pitcher, big Lew Burdette. A few weeks later Aaron was voted the National League's most valuable player of the year.

From many points of view, America's one great moment in sports came in September, 1957, when tall, smash-serving Miss Althea Gibson, following her Wimbledon championship in July, won the women's singles in tennis at Forest Hills. Miss Gibson was the first Negro ever to take a title in tennis. The crowd gave her one of the longest ovations in many years. A Negro sport fan made the remark, "I watched the match on a television set in Shreveport, Louisiana, a state which will have nothing but segregated sports; but over practically every TV set in that state people, black and white, were watching this same sport event. When Althea was acclaimed the winner, for one brief moment this Negro girl was America and the United States bowed to her. That moment will do more to advance good race relations than all the segregation laws will do to retard them."

Not alone in sports do Negroes hold the attention of the nation. They stand out in equally bold relief in the fine arts. A small sampling of their contributions, drawn from many areas, finds poets James Weldon Johnson, Countee Cullen, Langston Hughes and Arna Bontemps holding their places in the anthologies along with Paul Lawrence Dunbar who some years earlier struggled against poverty and prejudice but established Negro poetry as literature worthy of recognition. Then novelists Frank Yerby, Richard Wright, Gardner Smith and juvenile story writer Ellen Tarry widened the scope of Negro contributions to literature.

In music there are Marian Anderson, contralto; Roland Hayes, tenor; Duke Ellington and his jazz orchestra; Harry T. Burleigh, arranger; Louis Armstrong, trumpet player; Camilla Williams in the opera *Madame Butterfly;* and Robert McFarrin in various Metropolitan roles.

The theater, passing beyond minstrelsy and vaudeville, produced serious actors; first in all-Negro casts in such plays as *Porgy and Bess* and *Green Pastures;* then in Negro and white casts in *Lulu Belle, All God's Chillun Got Wings* and *Deep Are the Roots.*

In art Negroes became equally well established with the work of such men as Aaron Douglas, William H. Johnson, illustrator E. Simms Campbell and sculptor Richmond Barthé.

As the decade of the 1960's draws near nobody questions that Negroes have made contributions in all areas of the fine arts. Still, two steps remain to be taken before complete honor is given where honor is due. The first step is removal of discriminations which make it difficult for Negroes to receive the education and experience necessary to develop their abilities to the highest degree. The second step is to remove from creative work all racial tabs, just as reputable newspapers are omitting unnecessary reference to racial origins of people who figure in the news. No longer is a creative Negro an isolated phenomenon in American life so that there is any need to call special attention to his accomplishments as a Negro. Rather, the number of Negro writers, artists, musicians, actors and entertainers has become so large and so diverse that they are an integral part of American life and thought.

15.   *Churches Accept Responsibility*

It happened in a comfortable Florida town, one not overrun with tourists nor yet so remote in the hinterland as to be isolated. The women had their bridge clubs, their art and music study clubs; the men had two service clubs. And the community had its churches; six Protestant churches, four for white worshipers and two for colored; and one Catholic church where all members worshiped in the same sanctuary, but observed a definite line of demarcation in seating. The Negroes "knew where they belonged" and everything went smoothly at St. Theresa.

At least everything went smoothly until a new priest came to serve the church. Father Michael was Irish and seemed not to understand that there were certain customs which if observed made life much easier for everyone concerned. In spite of the fact that he had been told several times that it was better to leave the Negroes in the back of the church where they were more comfortable—even having been told by Mrs. Allan Clark who could usually explain everything in such a way as to gain her point—in spite of all the counseling, one

162

Sunday Father Michael announced to his parish that beginning immediately the Negro parishioners could sit any place they pleased to sit when they came to Mass. The announcement did not please many of the white parishioners, including Mrs. Allan Clark.

Thus was the situation described by one of the members of the church. "Of course," she added seriously, "Catholics who are true to the teaching of the Church could never practice racial discrimination. The heart of the Mass is the Presence of Christ and no one can be barred from that Presence because of his color. But occasionally some of us do put our social status above our spiritual status."

Before many weeks a new church was being built on the outskirts of this Florida town. There were rumors that it was being constructed for a Holy Roller congregation but as the little frame building took shape it became evident that the church was traditionally Catholic in style. However, when the parishioners asked Father Michael about it he gave them little satisfaction. No one had the temerity to question the bishop, and the less curious agreed that time would tell. Although rumors and conjectures continued, other interests in the community came to overshadow the little church on the edge of town until the January morning when Father Michael surprised many of his congregation by announcing the dedication service that afternoon for the new Negro Church of St. Florian.

A good representation of St. Theresa's white members—either out of good will or curiosity—attended the service. The bishop himself was there to consecrate the building and celebrate the Mass. During the first part of the service there was much turning of heads till each person was convinced that his eyes were not deceiving him—there was not one Negro in attendance. After the service there was considerable comment, for no one could explain a Negro church without Negroes.

The regular hour for High Mass at St. Florian was set for eleven o'clock, so the Sunday after dedication many people from St. Theresa drove past the new church to see how many Negroes were arriving. Not one was observed. However, Mrs. Allan Clark and a dozen or more of her friends, all of whom had been absent that morning from the service they customarily attended at St. Theresa, arrived at St. Florian in their Buicks and Cadillacs. According to the latest report no Negroes have ever set foot in the new church. They continue to come to hear Father Michael and sit where they please in his church, while St. Florian is regularly attended by a few former members of St. Theresa.

In southern Illinois a Protestant woman newly arrived in a community where there was a small Negro population remarked to one of the "old-timers" that she had not seen any Negroes in church and asked where the Negro church was located. "There's one about ten miles from here," replied the older resident. "But the Negroes are welcome in our churches—if they keep their place, of course."

"And where is their place?" asked the newcomer.

The long-time resident looked at the newer arrival with a shade of amazement as she answered, "Why, on the back seat, of course."

Details will differ but stories of similar attitudes can be duplicated in thousands of churches across the country; stories of church members who consciously or unconsciously carry their feeling of racial superiority into all their social relations including their relationship with God. Such members help to perpetuate a pattern of segregation which once seemed a necessary framework for American life, but which today has become a high wall of exclusion.

In post-Civil War days the establishment of separate churches for Negroes was another expression of the zeal which prompted the founding of schools for the freed slaves and their children. In addition to being places of worship and channels for religious expression, the churches became gathering places for social events, and this combination of services made them a strong cohesive force for an illiterate, emotional, but deeply religious people.

Throughout all their days of slavery the Negroes had readily identified themselves with the people and events described in the Bible. As slaves they become one with the children of Israel; when they read—or heard—how Moses was sent by God to tell old Pharaoh, "Let my people go," they told themselves that a modern Moses would also be called forth to liberate them. Daniel, Ezekiel, Jacob—with each of the Bible heroes they suffered in defeat and exulted in victory while they waited for their own day of rejoicing to come.

But if the Bible furnished their inspiration it also supplied them with a rule of life, a rule not to be tampered with or adjusted to their own convenience. The Bible was truly and literally the Word of God. No less was the minister the man of God and as such was usually the most highly respected member of the Negro community.

Many of these concepts and habits remain in the Negro churches today. So when discrimination and violence make interracial contacts difficult, the Negroes naturally turn to their churches as meeting places and to their preachers for moral leadership. Because of this church-centeredness the question of integration is more than a matter of white churches' opening their doors to nonwhite members. Integration also involves co-ordinating the interests, traditions and leadership of groups which have ties and loyalties to patterns of long standing. Through the years many denominations have developed a parallel structure of organization for the two races and when these are united there are superfluous presidents, vice-presidents and committee chairmen. Even when adjustment of officers is readily effected there still remains the necessity for finding ways to continue a broad base of responsibility so that leadership training and active participation will continue for as many individuals as possible.

Although the present trend is to bring all churches of a given denomination into one national organization and to accomplish local integration as fast as possible, there are factors outside the church which militate against the accomplishment of the goal. Segregated housing is the most rigid barrier. A church which is located in a one-race neighborhood and whose program is geared to serve its immediate parish is apt to be a one-race church, not from choice but from location. There are many parishes in which immediate integration would be a contrived or forced process. The first question facing the church is not *must* all churches be interracial, but *may* all churches be interracial.

Indelibly written across the movement for interracial churches is the name of Dr. Howard Thurman, Negro educator, minister, and now dean of the chapel at Boston University. The San Francisco Church for the Fellowship of All Peoples stands as a monument to his work and that of his co-workers. In 1943 the population of San Francisco included forty-eight ethnic groups who reflected the uneasiness which the war situation was developing in California where the Japanese were being forced into "concentration camps" and Negro laborers were pouring in at unprecedented rates to replace them, especially at the unskilled labor level. In an effort to bridge the widening gulf between the races an interracial group of thirty men and women began weekly meetings for worship and study under the guidance of Dr. Alfred Fisk, a Presbyterian clergyman and professor of philosophy at San Francisco State College. This nucleus then organized as a mission church under Presbyterian support and continued its interracial program.

Two years later, as the young church began to feel the spiritual power generated by their fellowship they realized that they needed to move out on broader lines of work which would demand the services of a full-time minister, a man with both experience and creative vision. But where could they find a minister with these qualifications who would accept the leadership of so small a group, weak in financial support and with no map for the uncharted regions of interracial fellowship which they hoped to explore?

One of many letters of inquiry for such a man fell into the hands of Dr. Howard Thurman, then dean of the chapel and professor of systematic theology at Howard University, Washington, D.C., one of the country's oldest and largest universities for Negro students. Dr. Thurman knew no one to suggest for the work in San Francisco unless—unless he offered himself. As he and his wife considered the question they sensed something providential in the opening on the West Coast. Nearly a decade earlier they had traveled together over much of Asia on a Pilgrimage of Friendship for the World Student Christian Federation. While in India they had spent three hours with Gandhi, Hindu mystic, prophet, political leader, and had left his presence deeply disturbed; Gandhi had shared with them his conviction that Christianity as an institution was blocking the path of Jesus as a Way of Life. Some days later, at Khyber Pass, high in the Himalayas, the Thurmans rededicated themselves to the task of making the teachings of Jesus a reality in all human relationships. For the Thurmans, that reality could best be achieved in a religious fellowship that recognized no racial barriers.

Because of this conviction the Thurmans went to San Francisco. Under their leadership the church grew in membership so that three times it had to move into larger quarters; it became nondenominational, and financially independent. This outward growth was the visible expression of a deeper inner growth which resulted from the continued fellowship of many national and racial groups—fellowship in worship, study, music, drama, hobbies and social activities.

Dr. Thurman seems always to be moved by some inner compulsion, a force which has never let him rest on previous accomplishments. In his childhood his slave-born grandmother impressed upon him the necessity for an upward and outward look—and hard work.

During school and college days, even into seminary, he met his share of rebuffs. Looking back, however, he feels that the Church for the Fellowship of All Peoples was in a sense born in Colgate Rochester Seminary where a new view of the universality of spiritual experience and a measure of discernment between temporary and timeless issues were laid upon his heart. Later, when his experience with Gandhi made him rethink the relation of the church and Christ; and his friendship with Dr. Rufus Jones, a Quaker, brought him into consciousness of the inner light and the power of meditation, he was quickened to his task.

Dr. Thurman served the Church for the Fellowship of All Peoples until 1953 when he turned the leadership over to other hands while he entered a new field of service as dean of the chapel at Boston University. When he left San Francisco he could count members-at-large of Fellowship Church in nearly every state in this nation and in many foreign countries. In most cases each individual had become a flame to spark new experiments in interracial fellowship in the community in which he lived.

Removed from Fellowship Church by the breadth of a continent, and facing even more concentrated racial conflicts, is East Harlem Protestant Parish in which eight denominations combine to serve one of New York's most depressed areas. In 1948 a group of Protestant ministers opened the first storefront church in this congested district. Today the Parish has grown to include four churches and six additional parish offices and activity centers served by a staff of five ministers, a lay pastor and translator, four educational directors, one administrative secretary and one nurse; plus the part-time services of a doctor, three lawyers, and a varying number of seminary students whose services are part of their fieldwork schedule.

Through its various activities the Parish program touches the lives of about two thousand people of many ethnic backgrounds. The most recent migration is from Puerto Rico but even the language barrier of these Spanish-speaking people does not isolate them from the other groups. In one of the churches the official board is composed of four Negroes, four Puerto Ricans, and three white members of different nationalities. At one time when the congregation had grown so large that it taxed the capacity of the small church building, the board decided to hold two services, one in English and one in Spanish. Before long the members began to ask for a return to one service.

The board countered, "But when the service has to be conducted in two languages it takes too long. Besides, the church is crowded."

To which argument the people answered, "But we like it better to be together. And who objects to being a little crowded? We're used to that."

"We'll give it a try," conceded the board.

The trial period ended with the people again worshiping in one group. The scripture reading, prayers, announcements, sermon—all are now given in English and translated into Spanish. From choice the congregation sits through the two-hour service.

Attendance is not large in any of the churches in East Harlem. Yet when one of the young ministers was killed by a car the entire community was saddened by the news. Five hundred mourning people crowded the chapel for the funeral. But by no means did all of them attend church the following Sunday.

However, church attendance is only one measure of the effectiveness of religion in East Harlem. The ministry is deeply concerned with helping the people assume responsibility for helping themselves. Although all the racial groups resent discrimination and contend that someone or some organization—the city, the schools, the churches, the courts—should abolish it, when a case of discrimination in housing is in the courts no one wants to go testify. In this attitude the people of East Harlem do not stand alone, as their ministers are the first to realize, and perhaps there is more excuse for them than for most Americans because of the many reprisals against families of men who have had the courage to work with the police or to go to court as witnesses.

In this area where even minor differences can develop into major street fights or race conflicts every effort at co-operation and every attempt to develop self-reliance pays off in bigger dividends than in less agitated communities. For this reason the organization of a credit union in the East Harlem Parish is considered one of the best demonstrations of Christian love in action which has yet been achieved. The first step in the formation of the credit union was the organization of a Christian Economics Group made up of eight interested lay men and women who met weekly to discuss anything and everything that interested them—jobs, children, race prejudice, religion. At each meeting this general discussion was followed by a discussion of specific money problems facing the people gathered for the evening.

Then before they broke up there were refreshments and a general social time.

At the end of the first year the group had grown to sixteen regular members, with others drifting in and out. From all their discussion they had become convinced that many of their daily problems were the result of their having no financial credit. They had to resort to installment buying if they were ever going to buy anything because banks would not loan them money. If sudden sickness took their small savings, as it had for one family when their little girl was rushed to the hospital with pneumonia, then they had to borrow from the loan companies whose exorbitant interest kept a family in debt indefinitely. But if even a small group of people would pool their slim savings they would have a mutual fund to loan at reasonable interest rates when it was needed by a member. More than a year went into study and organizational plans before their application to the Bureau of Federal Credit Unions was approved.

In 1957, after one year of operation, the Parish Credit Union had 101 members, had made 45 loans totaling $2,577.79 and had $1,854.64 in savings. Among those who borrowed money during the initial year was a widow with three children. According to the record:

Sickness prevented her from working and from repaying her debt. When a member of the Board of Directors called on her, he did not go as a loan-collector, but as a friend. When he discovered that she had other debts as well on which she was paying more interest, he showed her how she could take out one new, larger loan from the Credit Union, pay off all her debts with the money, and repay the one loan more slowly at a lower rate of interest. At first she was stunned into silence. For years no one had cared whether or not she made both ends meet. Now she saw hope. She took the chance offered.

Day by day, the Credit Union and its leaders are helping people to solve their own economic problems. It is their conviction that this is in keeping with the teachings of Jesus, who did not use the word "love" in the Lord's prayer, but did show an interest in people's getting enough to eat. Give us this day our daily bread—

Another phase of the ministry of the churches in this district is to have someone on call every hour of the day and night. For this reason the clergymen and their families live in East Harlem. Reported one of the ministers, "One night I got an s.o.s. to come settle a fight that was starting between two teenage gangs of boys. Each gang claimed the prettiest and sauciest girl in the neighborhood as 'their girl.' A knife flashed and trouble was about to break loose. We settled the feud before any serious complications arose, but in a district where interracial tensions are always at the snapping point the church must always be within reach."

In countless communities the Catholic Church is insistent that discrimination and segregation must be eliminated, even in sections where the practices are of long standing. The nation still remembers the consternation that was caused in the New Orleans area about ten years ago when Archbishop Joseph Francis Rummel ordered FOR COLORED ONLY signs removed from pews in Catholic churches.

It was not surprising then in 1955, when anti-integration feeling ran high, to find the archbishop outspoken when one of his Negro priests who had been assigned to hold Mass at St. Cecelia outside New Orleans was prevented from fulfilling his duties by the interference of two police deputies and a handful of parishioners. The archbishop administered stern and speedy admonition to the church and threatened even to close its doors if the sin of racial exclusiveness continued. At the same time in Erath, another little town under his jurisdiction, other trouble was brewing. Two white women beat a third woman because she was teaching the catechism to white and Negro children together. The bishop of the area stopped with nothing less than excommunication for the two women and a threat to close the church if any other violence developed. The ban of excommunication was later lifted but Catholics in the New Orleans area were made aware that their church was taking a definite stand to carry out the principles of brotherhood which it professed.

In other parts of the South the Catholic Church is also vocal. Immediately following the Supreme Court decision on integration in the public schools, Bishop Vincent Waters, of Raleigh, North Carolina, ordered integration of the parochial schools in his diocese. He went further and ordered Catholic hospitals to open their facilities to Catholic Negroes and where facilities permitted to non-Catholic Negroes. St. Louis and Louisville both give credit to the parochial schools in their cities for easing the process of desegregation of the public schools.

The position of the Catholic Church on segregation of its members was stated by Bishop A. L. Fletcher of Little Rock: ". . . persons of every race, creed and nation should be made to feel at home in every Catholic church. Every Catholic church is God's house, not only because it is dedicated to Him; not only because we pray and sing there in His honor; not even because we hear His gospel preached there. Every Catholic church is God's house in a more personal way—it is where He dwells, body and soul, in the Blessed Sacrament. . . ."

This emphasis on the presence of God brings definite spiritual pressure on the communicants to observe Christ's teaching in His presence; to bar no one from worship because of race. The Catholic Church has a second strength which makes it effective when direct action is needed. It can speak with authority which is recognized by all communicants from the highest officials to the lowliest parishioners. An influential businessman in Mississippi unconsciously reflected this power when in a conversation he said, "Twenty years from now we'll not know segregation as we know it now. It has to go. The Church has made up its mind."

Sometimes a church which because of its location is insulated against racial contacts assumes that if it is not involved in race tensions it need not be concerned with them. A Minneapolis woman commented, "We don't have to be agitated about race relations in our church because we're so far from the Negro district that none of the Negroes want to come to our church."

Another Minneapolis church, Hennepin Avenue Methodist, held a different point of view. Located in a wealthy, all-white section of the city, the church had no Negro members; but it did have a standing committee to counsel with the small congregation of the Negro Border Methodist Church. Then came a day when Border Church was in great distress. To make room for a superhighway the church building, along with other buildings in that section of the city, was to be razed. The city would relocate the dispossessed families, but relocating the church was a different matter. Moreover, the amount the city would pay for the property was not enough to build another church; and besides, after relocation the membership would be scattered throughout the city. It seemed to be the end of Border Church. Then the committee of Hennepin Church suggested that the membership of Border be invited to join the big-sister church.

At this point the question of procedure became important, for if the union of memberships became a debatable issue animosities could develop which, even if the vote were favorable, might live on for years. There was also another reason for not putting the proposition to the vote of the entire membership—such action would be singling out the members of Border Church for a special process of uniting with the church whose fellowship was open to anyone who wanted to join by confession of faith or letter of transfer. If individual members of Border Church wanted to transfer their memberships to Hennepin Avenue there seemed to be no reason for altering the usual method of receiving new members. Approximately three-fourths of the Border membership, or about eighty people, transferred to Hennepin Avenue.

A few months later when one of the officials was asked if there had not been some open opposition to the move, he answered carefully, "Not exactly opposition; but that doesn't mean that everyone was happy about the move. Of course, many of the people were pleased while others accepted the action of the church as placidly as they accept any other action of the group. A few members were unhappy, but their dissatisfaction has not prevented a very high degree of integration of the membership of the two churches. Within a few Sundays the Hennepin deacons and ushers suggested that the former Border deacons and ushers serve in their usual capacities and other organizations have extended like invitations to the new members." The women's organizations made the slowest progress doubtless because—one member of the church hesitantly ventured—"because many of them meet in private homes."

The addition of so small a group of new members hardly created the need for an additional minister on the staff of Hennepin Avenue, and the pastor of the Border Church, Dr. Charles M. Sexton, was soon called to an all-white church in Champlin, Minnesota. "We think he is a wonderful leader," says the church chairman.

Unlike the Hennepin Avenue Church which reached out to fulfill its ideal of brotherhood, other churches, rapidly increasing in number, find their problem pushing in upon them. These churches are in areas of transition, districts from which the former white residents are moving and into which nonwhite people are coming. The church in this kind of neighborhood faces a dilemma—shall it move out with its white members, or shall it remain and become racially integrated in membership to better serve its existing parish?

In Chicago, a church referred to as "that fine old Baptist Church" is the Woodlawn Baptist located a few blocks from the University of Chicago. For many years the official board had been composed predominantly of men connected with large corporations and old established businesses. "These men believe the Bible, all right," said one of their fellow church members, "and they're dedicated to the church; but it's got to be the kind of church that suits their brand of individual salvation. They're really wonderful men, but they just don't know that the church has a social gospel."

Within the last five years this church has found itself the center of the area in Chicago most rapidly becoming a Negro residential section. For several years, little Negro girls in their starched white dresses and little boys in their blue nylon slacks had streamed into Sunday School—but they could never set foot inside the sanctuary, nor could their parents. In 1955 the minister retired and many members of the church realized the time had come to break with their former exclusive practices.

The church invited the Rev. Hampton E. Price, a South Carolinian serving a church in Utah, to accept its pulpit. Before making his decision Mr. Price came to Chicago to look over the field. He talked with the board and with members of the church; but he also walked the streets of that part of Chicago, watched the children at play, noticed the racial groupings of high school students, visited the schools and the playgrounds; and talked with other ministers and with the businessmen of the community. Some months later he took up the work at Woodlawn Baptist.

When he called his first official board meeting, all the members were ready to accept almost any program he proposed. One of the deaconesses later confessed, "We were excited to hear his plans for the church. We'd been without a minister for more than a year—long enough to appreciate having someone else assume leadership." But instead of presenting a program to the officers the new minister placed before them a large blackboard and suggested that together they would write their corporate creed, the foundation for their mutual task.

"We'll write on the blackboard," said Mr. Price, "only those statements which we all agree upon to the extent that we can each say, 'I believe and I will die for—'" In that creed was a statement on interracial fellowship.

"The Negroes didn't flood in as some of the old-timers feared they would," reported the deaconess. "It was ten months ago that we started on the interracial membership and I think we have about twelve Negroes who are actually members of the church. One of them is our choir director and his wife is a soloist. Both of them have master's degrees in music. Then we have a Chinese graduate student who is a deacon; his wife is a chemist. We have a Filipino seminary student whose wife is a registered nurse. Also among the active members of the church is an American Indian family, a Mexican, some Japanese and one or two Koreans. We're really just started on an interracial fellowship, but the whole church seems changed since we began it."

In close proximity to Woodlawn Baptist Church is the First Presbyterian Church with one thousand members and a history of 124 years. In 1938 this church, then an all-white congregation, erected a new building ample for its traditional program. Just ten years later it found that program outdated, for by 1948 the church was in the heart of a changed community which had become three-fourths Negro. After much deliberation the officials decided the church would remain in its location and open its doors on an interracial basis.

How many members would object to the policy? The answer was never sought. Operating on the principle that any person who applied for admission into the church would be received according to its prescribed policy, the session of First Presbyterian could see no reason for raising the question as to whether Negro communicants were different from others. People, they reasoned, join a church as individuals, not as representatives of a race. When the membership was first opened to Negroes, none asked to come into the church. The children continued to swell the Sunday School, and Negro adults participated in some areas of the church work but it was five years before the first Negro members were taken into fellowship. At the end of the next two years, seventy Negroes were members of First Church and many had found their places in the choir, in young people's work, as Sunday School teachers and as members of the session. In 1957 the church was working as harmoniously as it had worked in any period of its long history, and the average pledge to the church had increased almost nine dollars since the beginning of its integrated membership.

The year 1957 also brought the retirement of Dr. Harold L. Bowman who had led the church in this venture in fellowship. In his place the church called two co-pastors, the Rev. Ulysses B. Blakely, a Negro minister from Philadelphia, and the Rev. Charles T. Leber, Jr., a white minister from Detroit.

The experiences of Woodlawn Baptist and First Presbyterian are not unique in the transition areas of Chicago. A Negro leader in the NAACP commented that there were at least two hundred churches of mixed membership in the city where she and her friends would feel welcome. However, most of the churches are finding that opening their doors is not enough; nonwhites are generally reticent in accepting the invitation to join and the church has to make a special effort to assure them that it is in earnest in integrating its membership in mutual comradeship as well as in name.

For a time this reluctance baffled the Augustana Lutheran Church in Washington, D.C. Located in a downtown area fast becoming a Negro community, the church faced the possibility that when it opened its doors to these new parishioners they would throng through its portals faster than they could be integrated into the former membership and program of the church. But at the end of three years of wholehearted cordiality exactly two Negro families had become members.

Then during 1956 the Rev. Clarence T. Nelson and the church officials worked out a strategy to accomplish the integration they had hoped for. The first step was a survey which revealed that among the twenty thousand people living within a one-mile radius of the church, eighty-one were members of Augustana Lutheran. The church roll listed seven hundred members. Where were they living? As had been surmised most of them had moved, with much of white Washington, into the suburbs. The survey also showed that 50 per cent of the neighborhood was colored.

Then the church went into action. Members canvassed one-third of the homes in a small area near the church, extending to each family a personal invitation to make Augustana their church home. This personal canvass brought several families into the church. The visitation was followed with a mailing campaign during which six thousand pieces of literature, illustrated with actual pictures of Negroes participating in the life of Augustana—choir, Scouts, Sunday School and other groups—were distributed. This invitation was followed by personal visits into every home within a radius of one mile, the phase of the campaign which gives the undertaking its name—Operation One Mile.

Now Negro residents in the area are gradually finding their way into Augustana, and Mr. Nelson reports that less than 1 per cent of the former white congregation has withdrawn from the church because of the new interracial program. The minister's advice to other church groups who come to him for counsel is, "Don't talk about it—do something. The actual experience of interracial worship quickly removes people's fears and misgivings. Since we undertook Operation One Mile, there has been a noticeable deepening of the spiritual life of the church."

In addition to interracial churches in the District of Columbia, the border and Southern states of Oklahoma, Maryland, Missouri, Texas, Arkansas, West Virginia and Virginia each have one or more local churches which include both Negro and white members. Other Southern communities have opened various phases of their church work to both races, perhaps a vacation church school, summer youth camp or adult discussion groups. Others have made a beginning at interracial co-operation by exchanging ministers, choirs or programs of various kinds.

A special problem is faced by churches located in one-race communities, and for these churches there is often no possibility of attaining an integrated congregation. For this reason many of them, ranging in location from tiny hamlets to metropolitan centers, are achieving interracial fellowship by bringing in leadership representing a minority group.

In Old Mystic, Connecticut, the Rev. Simon Peter Montgomery is the Negro pastor of an otherwise white church membership. Mr. Montgomery is also chaplain of the 318-year-old state legislature, the only Negro to hold such a position. A Waltham, Massachusetts, church invited a Negro onto its staff to teach a men's class and at times assist in the morning worship service. Two small Maine churches called a young Negro pastor from Madison, Wisconsin, to serve their combined parishes. A San Francisco all-white church appointed a Negro director of athletics for its weekday program with young people; and an Oakland church named a Negro woman to be director of children's work. A church in Mumford, New York, employed a Negro student pastor; and an all-white congregation in New York City engaged a Negro seminary student to work with its youth group. A 325-year-old Dutch Reformed church called a Negro pastor; and many other churches have added Negro staff members serving in many different capacities.

The same interchange of staff members is taking place in once all-Negro churches, and many are opening their church rolls to white members. Church integration has noticeably become a two-way traffic.

To say that integration of a church's membership is always easy would be to gloss over some stubborn facts. In the history of integration churches have been bombed, ministers have been threatened and have suffered violence, members have been denounced and local congregations divided; yet most of the churches which have moved in the direction of integration agree that the process was easier than they had expected it would be. Their common experience is that the few dissenting members on any issue move along with the more venturesome in the congregation. The acceptance of an interracial membership apparently is no exception to this attitude as was indicated by a 1951 nation-wide survey conducted by three denominations. In the 1,331 churches with some degree of integration, twenty-six members were known to have left their churches because non-white members had been admitted into the fellowship.

Sometimes news releases on the reaction of a congregation are misleading, even though the statistics may be accurate. A report of the integration of the Normandie Avenue Methodist Church of Los Angeles stated that most of the all-white congregation resigned when the Rev. Nelson B. Higgins, Jr., a young Negro minister, was appointed by the Southern California-Arizona Conference to serve this church.

Behind this appointment lay the fact that for twenty-five years the membership which once stood at 253 had been dwindling so that in 1957 there were only forty church members left. Population shifts had changed the community in which the church was located from an all-white area to an interracial district and the Methodist Conference felt that the church should meet the needs of the changing community. Although between twenty and thirty members did resign on the Sunday that Mr. Higgins preached his first sermon as the new pastor at Normandie Avenue, twelve people took membership in the church and a crowd of approximately one thousand gathered to welcome him—a crowd composed of Negro and white church members, high church officials and lowly worshipers who by their presence wanted to express their approval of the stand the church had taken.

At times, the initiative in opening the doors of a church is taken by the minister. His congregation may follow him gladly, or they may rebel, as did the members of a small Iowa church who asked the resignation of their young preacher when he insisted on making the membership interracial. But within a few days they reconsidered their action and asked him to remain, because, as they explained, "We realized that any preacher as good as this one would have the same kind of ideas."

Or, as in the case of a large church in Cincinnati, the minister may fail in his leadership and the people themselves take the responsibility for action. The minister of this particular church had the reputation for being a strong social actionist; in his sermons he consistently pointed up social issues and the church had an active social action committee. But when the committee made a survey of their parish and recommended a reorganization of the church along interracial lines the minister became silent on social issues, delayed in giving his support of the recommendation of the committee, and by his inactivity almost blocked the way to action. However, the church members moved ahead and finally brought Negroes into full participation in the church.

Whoever takes the initiative or carries the responsibility for opening the doors of a church does it because he has heard the same voice that spoke to eight-year-old Della Toby in a small Missouri church. Della was one of a dozen children who attended the otherwise white Sunday School, and because she had a good child's voice she usually sang a solo on the church school programs which were always held in its activities room.

"No one realized that the sanctuary was virtually out-of-bounds for our Negro youngsters," confessed the Sunday School superintendent after his experience with Della. "Several times on Sunday morning when I arrived at the church a little early," he continued, "I found Della standing against the closed door between the hall and the sanctuary. I know now that she was listening to the organist doing her last-minute run-overs for the church service." Then one Sunday morning the superintendent found Della just inside the partly opened door, her eyes intent upon the stained-glass window on the opposite wall where the sunlight was streaming through the presentation of Christ Knocking at the Door. The superintendent stood there quietly too for a few seconds until Della realized his presence and turned around.

She said shyly, "I guess I hadn't oughtta come in, but when I opened the door and peeked through the crack I saw the picture and I thought I heard him say, 'Come on in, Della.'"

16. Motivating Power of Religion

In American life the line between the secular and the religious is not always clearly drawn. Education, once predominantly the function of the church, has been progressively passed over to government, from local to federal levels; yet every church body retains some educational institutions. Hospitals, once services of the church, have tended to become the responsibility of other private or government agencies, although the number of church-related hospitals is still large. Religious organizations have been inclined to pioneer in serving the unmet needs of people, whether directly in church institutions or by focusing public attention upon the deficiencies in public institutions. The precedent set by desegregation of the parochial schools in Louisville, St. Louis and Washington was acclaimed in each city as helping to pave the way for desegregation of the public schools.

Although the number of Negro Jews is negligible, the work of Jewish organizations in combating discrimination against Negroes has contributed to the breakup of segregation. In St. Louis, after

World War II, when pressure for desegregation was growing, Temple Israel was one of the first pulpits into which members of other races were invited. The work of the American Jewish Committee and of the Anti-Defamation League of B'nai B'rith have contributed notably to lessening discrimination against all minorities. The latter organization carries on a program of research, counseling and publication which has included many phases of Negro-white relationships. Its recent study, *The St. Louis Story,* which describes the desegregation of the schools in that city, has been translated into forty languages by the Translation Branch of the United States Information Agency for distribution in other countries.

When in 1952 some of the residents of Kansas City, Missouri, felt impelled to do something about hospital accommodations for the Negro population—nearly 20 per cent of the total—it was a leading Jewish citizen who approached the Catholic bishop with the suggestion that St. Vincent's Hospital be made a Negro hospital. The bishop replied that he would not be interested in working for a Negro hospital, but that he would wholeheartedly support plans for a nonsegregated hospital. As a result, Jewish, Catholic and Protestant forces combined to establish Queen of the World Hospital, a fifty-two-bed institution. Although operated by the Maryknoll Sisters of St. Dominic, the hospital is nonsectarian and interracial in its board of directors, general staff, nursing corps and patients. Dr. Howard A. Rusk described the first Easter morning in the hospital.

"A Negro woman of Baptist faith," he wrote in the *New York Times,* "lies quietly listening to the high Roman Catholic Day of Resurrection mass from the radio of the white woman in an adjoining bed. Last Monday at sundown she heard a Seder service marking the beginning of Passover over the same radio, but then it was on the bedside table of a Jewish woman occupying the bed on her left. Later this morning, the radio will be moved to her bed and the Baptist will hear the Easter services of her own church. Her spiritual strength will not come solely from this service, for it has grown steadily since she was admitted two weeks ago to Kansas City's new interracial nonsectarian Queen of the World Hospital."

In Memphis, when the YMCA for Negroes became antiquated and inadequate, it was a gift of $75,000 from a Jewish businessman which made possible the purchase and enlargement of another building.

"Freedom," says the Anti-Defamation League of B'nai B'rith, "is a dream of a world in which all men, women and children are encouraged to grow to their fullest—physically, mentally, spiritually—so that they may fulfil the great promise of their inner potential." With this statement the dominant religions in the United States are in agreement.

In addition to schools, hospitals and other agencies supported by the church are other movements motivated by religion but not connected with any denomination. Of these groups Koinonia Farm near Americus, Georgia, has come into prominence because of the series of violent attacks made upon it since June, 1956.

The sixty individuals who comprise Koinonia were true to the original meaning of the name—community—and lived in an interracial religious-economic fellowship. The 1,000-acre farm which they had developed since 1942 had become a thriving industry. The sale of produce and eggs, the farm's specialty, at a roadside market five miles from the main buildings brought an adequate income so that the land could be further developed and the families could live in simple comfort. Each family lived in a separate home unit but all the members worked for the benefit of the colony without individual wages or compensation. People in the surrounding area were not slow to admit that the Koinonia folk were industrious—and peculiar. They had no set church services but tried to live "constant in prayer"; they advocated and practiced nonviolent Christianity based upon the power of love. Furthermore, their concept of love made them accept Negroes into their fellowship. It was this practice which became the cause of violence. Had the members of Koinonia merely hired Negro farm hands, had they merely treated the Negro laborers with kindness and consideration, the white portions of Sumter County would not have disapproved. But when Negroes were accepted as part of the Koinonia Farm community on the same basis as white people, some of the residents of the county decided the Farm needed a lesson to teach it to fit its social order into Georgia's concept of proper American life.

In June, 1956, a shot from a heavy caliber pistol was fired into the roadside stand; the next month the stand was wrecked by an explosion. Some months later gunfire from passing cars wrecked the new refrigerator meat case and the electric fuel pump. In January another explosion and fire completely demolished the roadside market. Within the next two months buildings were burned, fence wires cut, and bullets from passing cars whirred within inches of several members of the community. As a result of the disturbances loans were denied, supplies refused, and insurance policies canceled—even Lloyds of London rejected a request for insurance coverage.

In April, 1957, Norman R. Long, thirty-two-year-old president of Koinonia Farm, reported that he was unable to get butane gas to heat the homes. But the trouble had not yet come to an end. The following month a blast of dynamite, intended to ruin the business of a feed store which had offered to serve Koinonia, not only seriously damaged the store, but also tore up the street in front of it and damaged nearby places of business.

Under the pressure and the conflict a few of the members of the Farm, both Negro and white, left their community. But during this same period a new center was developed in New Jersey called Koinonia Communities in order to provide a market outlet for the farm products and also to afford a place of retreat for families showing signs of "battle fatigue" at the Georgia Farm where, as the trouble progressed, it became impossible to get even day laborers because they feared the violence that had come to others. The situation became so desperate that many people took it for granted the Farm would close. But it did not.

Members of the little community admit to deep soul-searching to decide the course they should follow. Their decision to remain was based upon their philosophy that they are themselves responsible for the fear and hatred which has gripped the people in the surrounding communities; therefore they have a responsibility to stay and demonstrate the power of love to break through the barriers of hate.

Many religious organizations have come out in bold statements disapproving the actions of the people of Sumter County and commending Koinonia for its practice of interracial community living. Representative of such statements is one prepared by the executive committee of the United Church Women of Georgia: "Our constitutional rights have meaning only when they are used. Unpopular groups have the same rights as popular groups; the Constitution comes to life most forcefully when the rights of the unpopular are secured. We, as Georgians . . . share in the responsibility to create a public opinion that will make it possible for citizens and law enforcement officers to act to end the violence against Koinonia."

Also to the aid of Koinonia have come personal letters of commendation from all sections of the country, and two thousand individuals have each pledged $50 toward a Christian Brotherhood Plan to compensate for the cancellation of the Farm's insurance policies. So Koinonia continues in its attempt to demonstrate brotherly love even in the midst of unbrotherly surroundings.

In less dramatic circumstances other groups in countless towns and cities are attempting to translate into action their convictions that helpful interracial contacts are possible.

In Virginia members of the United Church Women visited the newly opened branch stores in Arlington to remonstrate the WHITE ONLY signs in the rest rooms. The store managers said that they had assumed that white women in Virginia would want segregation, but when the women themselves protested, the managers removed the signs. A similar council in Barberton, Ohio, after working together for several years to establish a feeling of mutual confidence between the women of the two races finally felt strong enough to work together to remove some of the racial barriers in the community beginning with the two moving picture theaters which Negroes were not allowed to attend. The women felt that this discrimination was particularly hard on the young people, and so the council appointed a committee to talk to the manager of the theaters. However, efforts to arrange a conference with him met with no success. Phone calls, registered letters and telegrams all went unacknowledged. After several months of waiting the committee reported its seeming failure to the council. Then one of the Negro mothers assured them that if the manager had paid no heed, God had; because for several weeks their children had been allowed in the theater. There had been no announcement; word just "got around" that they could come in.

Through their national organizations some denominations have taken steps to alleviate the distress resulting from reprisals against Negroes. In many places an effective method of keeping Negroes under the domination of the whites has been for stores, both retail and wholesale, to cut off credit; or for banks to refuse loans to Negro business concerns, thus ruining their businesses. To help Negroes get loans otherwise denied them, a number of religious and civic organizations and many individuals have deposited sums of money in Southern banks which were willing to serve Negro patrons.

In many communities in the South where desegregation is especially difficult an example has frequently been set by the Ministerial Association. Although for many years there has been a growing tendency for Negro and white associations to unite, the Supreme Court decision on integration of the schools gave impetus to the movement. In the first two years following the Court ruling twenty ministerial groups in Southern cities integrated their memberships. With an equal sense of urgency interdenominational councils of churches have worked toward integration, accomplishing their objectives in communities in Florida, Kentucky, Georgia, North Carolina and Tennessee. In November, 1957, the Maryland-Delaware council went further than mere union of membership and elected a Negro minister, the Rev. Arthur J. Payne, an able and experienced leader, president of the council. It was Mr. Payne who, in 1948, seconded the nomination of Thomas E. Dewey for President, and in 1952 served as chaplain of the Republican National Convention.

A few years ago the Congregational Christian State Conference of Missouri extended membership to the only Negro Congregational church in all Arkansas. Located at Little Rock, the church has a membership under a hundred, but is reputed to have more members holding master's degrees than any other church in the state. The Arkansas churchmen attend all meetings of the Missouri general conference, are entertained in homes of the members as are other delegates and, according to the minister, the Rev. Charles C. Walker, the union has brought new strength and outreach to the members of his Little Rock church. "Also, I will always be grateful," said the gaunt, mild-voiced minister, "that it was in our church that the ministers of Little Rock, white and colored, met every morning at ten for a period of prayer during the trouble centering around admission of Negro students to our high school."

Religiously motivated organizations having still a different relationship to the church are such groups as the Catholic Knights of Columbus and the Young Women's and Young Men's Christian Associations. The trend in all these organizations is toward integration. Some have achieved this end, but across the country can be found examples of all the intermediate stages—as well as complete segregation. An example of the process of integration is found in the record of the YMCA at Bridgeport, Connecticut. When this organization first considered integration it faced most of the problems which any such group would encounter. Much of the credit for their

final solution is given locally to the executive secretary, Mr. Howard
L. Haag. An actionist, but not a driver, Mr. Haag proved that he
had the ability to steer a straight course without being sidetracked
by diverting problems.

It was during the war year 1942–43, when manufacturing plants
for helicopters and other aircraft sprang up almost overnight, that
Bridgeport found itself the center of a sudden influx of twelve thousand Negroes. The entire city experienced the disruption which
accompanies rapid change-over to war production.

"That year," Mr. Haag said later, "the demands on all the service
organizations were so heavy that we almost despaired of meeting
them. All the social agencies were baffled, and our Negro Branch
of the Y was no exception. For a while those of us who carried
responsibility for organization programs looked hopelessly at each
other and asked, 'What can be done?' One answer was squarely to
face our problem. So the night came when our board met to discuss
our future plans."

As the board looked into various possibilities the first suggestion
was to enlarge the Negro Branch, a suggestion which started questions popping. Could it be enlarged enough to accommodate all who
might want to join? After the war, what would happen when such
a large Negro Y was no longer needed? What about the main building? Could it not be used interracially? Would such use be legal?

At this point one of the board members, a lawyer, asked for the
constitution. He went into a huddle with the document while spec-
ulation on what would happen if the main Y were integrated buzzed
all around him. In a few minutes he announced, "According to the
constitution, non-whites have never been ruled out; how can we
debate ruling them in?"

The board decided it should call a meeting of the entire YMCA
membership and present to them some plan of action. Some time
went into threshing out various plans for using the main building,
and also the complications that might arise from such a decision.
Then a public hearing of all the members of the Association was
called. About seventy-five men attended that meeting and the discussion centered around the feasibility of complete integration. The
men who were present favored the move, but they did not know
about the attitudes of the other members. At that point the presiding
officer asked Mr. Haag's opinion.

"I realized that this was the hour when we needed to face every possible eventuality," stated Mr. Haag in review, "so that no man could say later, 'Well, I never expected it to come to this!' whatever the 'this' might be. So I reviewed for the larger group every step of the argument which the board had advanced. Then I told them that the final action was up to this group and that they should realize what might be involved. Integrated use of the building meant interracial use of the eating facilities; it meant Negro and white men living together in the dormitory which was home for 195 men; it meant common use of the locker room and the swimming pool. I went into some detail to try to make the situation very vivid—just as vivid as it would be for these same men the first time they ran into the actual result of their decision. When I finished it was up to the membership to vote."

The vote missed being unanimous by one ballot. A young man, recently arrived from Mississippi and living in the dormitory, said he knew that logically the action was right but he couldn't take it— not quite yet. He moved out of the dormitory, but he was the only one.

To facilitate the new program the board closed the Negro Branch and integrated the staff at the main YMCA. The greatest obstacle to general approval of integration was the fear that if the minority group obtained a toehold they would take over the organization. This fear never materialized and before long the YMCA felt it had not only desegregated but had actually integrated—become one in spirit.

Simultaneous with the efforts at integration on the part of the YMCA, the YWCA was working on the same kind of project and soon closed its Phyllis Wheatley Branch for Negro girls. By that time other community movements were under way. Because of the shortage of nurses, Negro nurses were accepted into the Bridgeport Nursing Association; then Negro teachers were introduced into the school system. Today a principal of one of the high schools is a Negro.

In a final evaluation of their combined efforts Mr. Haag concluded, "The whole city has been moving toward integration and the other night I think I saw the indication that proves we have pretty well succeeded. The bi-racial board of the YMCA had dinner together at one of the most exclusive country clubs. Lots of secretaries from other Y's ask me, 'How did you do this or that';—whatever it is they fear in their own case. And the only answer is, 'We just did it.' "

The church is often accused of moving slowly in aligning its practices of brotherhood with its teaching of the Fatherhood of God. It has been criticized for wasting its energy in pious talk and un-pious action. But discussions and resolutions have their place. Many a lone preacher or small band of church members would be voices crying in the wilderness were it not for the resounding "thus saith the church" which speaks on their side.

In 1955 the little town of Tchula, Mississippi, became the center of heated race hatred when trumped-up charges were brought against Dr. David Minter and Mr. Eugene Cox who with their families were carrying on a co-operative experiment in brotherhood at Providence Farms. Many years previously Dr. Sherwood Eddy had organized a co-operative venture for sharecroppers and Negroes on the site of the present Providence Farms. Although because of a changing economic situation the Eddy venture had been discontinued, the spirit of the project had been continued by the Minters and the Coxes. Then stories told by a young Negro boy—stories of interracial swimming groups and other social mixing—were picked up by a few White Council citizens, never investigated or corroborated, but made the basis for a trial by public opinion for the Minters and the Coxes. With an assembled crowd worked into emotional tension, the accusers made it plain that the Minters and Coxes would be happier in some other locality; that the country would be better off without their irregular racial contacts; and that more colored people would stay alive longer if everyone observed "proper relations."

However, some of the townspeople recalled kindly deeds of the Coxes, their quiet but sustained leadership in the small local church; and the unselfish way the doctor had given himself in service to the community. But their remembering was too little and too late to stem the upsurge of racial hatred, and the two white families had to leave Tchula. The little Southern Presbyterian Church to which both families belonged was also the church of the leader of the White Citizens Council. The lone person in the church with the temerity to speak out for the two banished families was the blacksmith.

In nearby Durant, one other voice was raised in their behalf. A young minister considered the proceedings on the night of the public community trial both undemocratic and unchristian, and he said so.

For his stand he was asked to resign and when he was a little slow in complying, he was fired.

Two years later the 97th General Assembly of the Presbyterian Church, U. S., frequently called the Southern Presbyterian Church, met in Birmingham, Alabama, the city so recently rent by interracial strife. Although the delegates observed the lawful restrictions of segregation in the community they integrated much of their fellowship during the assembly periods. Among the resolutions passed by this group, representing a membership of nearly 833,000 Southerners, was one which called attention to the fact that the Christian faith had never countenanced racial discrimination and that the supreme law of the land required that it no longer be practiced in the public schools. Further, stated the resolution, "it is unthinkable that a Christian should join himself to a klan or council whose purpose is to gain its point by intimidation . . . or that he should lift no voice of protest against those who appeal to prejudice and spread fear."

Simultaneously with this meeting of Southern Presbyterians a Conference on Christian Faith and Human Relations was holding its sessions in Nashville, Tennessee. In this conference three hundred Southern religious leaders, meeting as individuals with a common problem rather than as elected representatives of any denominations, faced the issues involved in the present race tensions. Speaking for his race Dr. Benjamin Mays, president of Morehouse College, an Atlanta school for Negro students, said, "The tragedy of the South is the lack of conviction to action. . . . I am not pleading for Negroes. It doesn't matter what happens to Negroes. Certainly it doesn't matter what happens to me. What does matter is this: can Christianity and democracy function effectively in an area of racial discrimination?" He then added his conviction that if the race relations issue cannot be solved in America, it cannot be solved anywhere. But Dr. Mays had faith that America would meet the test.

Four months later, in partial fulfillment of that faith, a group of eighty Atlanta ministers spoke unitedly on six issues which they believed essential to the preservation of the integrity of both races: freedom of speech must be assured; the law must be obeyed; the public school systems must not be destroyed; hatred and scorn for those of different color or opinion cannot be justified; communication between the leaders of the races must be maintained; human strength and wisdom alone will not solve the difficulties.

Thousands of other voices have been added to those who have carried the solo parts. People of all races and all creeds are falling in step as they swell the marching chorus—some perhaps off key and others dragging their feet—but still more and more unitedly mingling their voices in the strains of "Forward through the Ages—"

Not alone we conquer,
Not alone we fall;
In each loss or triumph
Lose or triumph all.

17. *Assessing Interracial Marriage*

A discussion of race relations, regardless of the point at which it starts, seldom gets far without someone's asking, "What about intermarriage?" The question may be analytical, or a request for information, but more frequently it represents an emotional roadblock which stops all objective consideration.

In New York a vivacious woman, active in an interracial housing project and also the mother of two married children, commented, "I get so tired of having every conversation rush to the question, 'Would you want one of your children to marry a Negro?' that the other day I said to a woman, 'I'd be mighty proud to be the mother-in-law of Ralph Bunche or Marian Anderson.'"

In contrast, a father in Missouri explained why he was sending his daughter to a Southern girls' school. "I'm going to make sure that she never comes in contact with any young man who's not of good white American stock. I'd rather see her dead than to see her marry a Negro."

Just before his graduation a college senior in a Midwest school was facing the problem of his approaching marriage. His mother adamantly refused to meet his fiancée, a classmate whose home was in New Jersey where her father owned an importing business. The girl was of Irish, Scotch, French and Chinese ancestry, but the boy's mother refused to recognize anything but the Chinese, which happened to be less than the Gaelic. "If Mother would only meet Edith," said the young man, "I know they'd like each other; but over and over Mother says she can't bring herself to see her son marry a Chinese."

Expressing the point of view of another part of the world was the diminutive and aristocratic Indonesian lady who had been sent to this country by her government to study textile mills. One night she was a dinner guest in the home of the dean of a Nebraska university and in the course of their conversation she remarked that her son, who would be ready for college in two years, hoped eventually to come to the United States for special work in nuclear physics.

"Fine!" replied the dean. "Send him to us and we'll personally supervise his first year or two, get him acquainted with the country and see that he meets the men who can be of help to him." Then he added, "We'll even try to fix him up with a beautiful wife."

The hand of the Indonesian guest shook as she laid her fork on her plate. "Dean Wilson," she said, "I don't think I could ever face a mixed marriage in my family!"

It may be that an individual's attitude toward intermarriage is based on the mores of his social order; or it may be the rationalization of a prejudice. But just as frequently his attitude is the result of noticing that mixed marriages often go on the rocks. A young Negro lawyer in Chicago, commenting on his legal experience, said, "Because I'm interested in the NAACP I probably get more than my share of Negro-white couples who think they want a divorce. Sometimes I become quite impatient because no matter what may be the real reason of their trouble these couples always put the blame on their racial differences. In a majority of cases the causes of the broken marriage lie within the individuals, not in their color. At times external circumstances contribute to their friction, but most of these people would not have been any more successful in marriage to members of their own race. Take the case of the Harrises that I closed about six months ago—"

Ed Harris, a mulatto, had been an accountant when he married

Martha, a white stenographer in the office. For three years, during which time they had two children, the Harrises were happy. Then in a series of financial reverses they lost the home they were buying, and Martha took a job; and just when the young couple thought they were on their way out of the woods a long illness kept Ed out of work for six months. Finally it seemed that the only thing they could do was to move in with one of their families. However, neither family had been happy about the marriage in the first place, and both were cool to the suggestion that the Harrises come home for a while. Finally Ed's family made room for them. Before the end of the year Ed and Martha were in the divorce court, certain that an interracial marriage could not work.

"When they first called on me," said their lawyer, "their nerves were so frayed that it seemed nothing could ever reconcile these two people. But after several visits to my office they began to see that their real problems were finances, health, and more especially the usual hazards that come when three generations of a family live in one small house. The Harrises agreed to postpone any divorce action for six months, and in the meantime they moved into a rather inadequate apartment, but at least it was their own. The last I heard from them they said they had found happiness again."

However, all troubles are not so well resolved. While Frederick Stock was still conductor of the Chicago Symphony Orchestra he auditioned Mr. William Dolman, a young Negro violinist from St. Louis, and would have been willing to engage him for the orchestra—if only the young man had been white. Indeed, he remarked that he would expect Mr. Dolman eventually to become first violinist. But at that time Bill could not even sit on the main floor of Orchestra Hall. Later Bill married his accompanist, a white girl, and together they did concert work and traveled rather extensively with a small orchestra. But constant discriminations in hotels, on trains, in apartment hunting—the steady stream of society's interracial discord continued to wear thin the ties that held the couple together and their marriage was ended.

That interracial marriages need not end disastrously is also proved by the experiences of other couples. Mrs. Robert Breen, herself the white member of an interracial marriage, is convinced that a mixed marriage can be a happy one, but that both partners have to be more dedicated to happiness than do the husband and wife who do not face social discriminations. Bob and Edna met while both were on the staff of the same college. The other faculty members, white and Negro, were divided as to the wisdom of an interracial marriage but they all accepted this engagement with good grace. Before their wedding Bob took his fiancée to meet his family who lived in Montgomery, Alabama. Their first evening together was an easy and a pleasant one, but after they retired anonymous telephone calls disturbed the household. After several of these calls Bob knocked at Edna's door and told her to dress quickly, go out the back door, take the car and drive straight to the main YWCA where he had arranged for her to have a room, and to wait there until she heard from him again. The following afternoon he telephoned her that she would have to drive north alone into Tennessee where he would meet her two days later.

After their marriage Edna's family all but disowned her. She was welcome to come home, but not to bring her husband with her. Even the birth of their daughter, now an exuberant nine-year-old youngster, did not ease the family resentment. Only within the last two years have any members of Edna's family stopped to see her when passing through the city where she lives.

In summing up her feeling about an interracial marriage Mrs. Breen said, "I think it has been harder on Bob than on me because he not only feels the personal discrimination but he also feels that he is responsible for the ostracism which I am subjected to at times. Actually, the treatment is no worse than I expected it to be. We knew we would face difficulties, but every marriage runs into some troubles. It's true that ours has the added difficulties of an undercurrent of hostility from society in general, but perhaps that makes us appreciate our friends more. Bob and I feel that our marriage was our personal choice and that we are achieving happiness. Sometimes people ask me if I recommend interracial marriages. The only answer is that a happy marriage is based upon mutual respect, mutual helpfulness, mutual interests, and love. If two people have these things in common it doesn't matter so much if they are the same size, age, nationality or color."

Frequently there is no rational basis for an individual's evaluation of mixed marriages. A prevalent evaluation is found in the words of the woman who said, "I just *feel* they're wrong and that's enough." In other words, emotional reactions become the standard of morality, social acceptance and religious sanction. If one could hold his emotions in check long enough to listen to religion, science and national experience, he might or might not change his mind, but at least he would have a firm foundation for his point of view.

The position of the Catholic Church on intermarriage is clearly stated. "In the name of the dignity of the human person, we reject every discrimination based on race. . . . Marriage and procreation are faculties attaching to the very nature of the human person; they are part of his physical and moral nature and constitute rights. The exercise of these rights, as well as of all those inherent in man's nature, are dependent on the judgment of his reason, of his conscience, of his prudence."

In 1948 two Roman Catholics of different races were married in California in defiance of a state law which banned mixed marriages. The validity of the marriage was tested in court where the decision was in favor of the young couple on the basis that the two people were exercising a right granted them by their church and that the state could not nullify this right. Subsequently the state law banning mixed marriages was repealed.

On another occasion Msgr. John A. Ryan wrote: "A Catholic Negro and a Catholic white person, who are otherwise qualified . . . have a canonical right to demand that their parish priest officiate at a ceremony which makes them man and wife. I rejoice that this is the situation, even though I believe that the general question of intermarriage between whites and blacks is irrelevant, unrealistic, and outside the realm of matters that anyone should bother his head about."

The Protestant church has no united word on intermarriage. In 1932 the Federal Council of Churches, predecessor to the present National Council of Churches, representing the leading Protestant denominations, went on record: "Where intolerable conditions are imposed . . . persons contemplating a mixed marriage should be advised not to enter into it." However, mixed marriages as such were not condemned. Some denominations and sects, and some ministers oppose mixed marriages; others do not consider that racial difference is a ground for refusing to marry two people.

Because of discrimination practiced in many Christian churches, a sizable group of Negroes are finding their way into Baha'ism, for this faith not only teaches ecumenicity but practices it. In recognition of the fact that all the great religions are paths to God, the Baha'i temple at Evanston, Illinois, center of Baha'ism in this country, has nine doors, symbolizing divergent paths to God but unity in his presence. "The earth is one country," teaches this faith, "and mankind is its citizens." To the Baha'ist mixed marriages are acceptable because they help move all peoples into a cosmic race.

If within the predominant religious groups in this country there is little official outlawing of interracial marriage, then condemnation must be found in some other authority. Perhaps science? For science is said to look objectively at a question and to assess it on the basis of available facts.

The geneticist, who explores the science of heredity, is always puzzled when he hears someone argue in favor of keeping the white race pure. "Pure—as of what date?" he asks. Most persons answer, "Like we are today." And the geneticist shakes his head at such naïveté. In a conversation between a half dozen adults of German, English, Norwegian and Irish ancestry, someone made the offhand comment that perhaps in the so-called white race there was not a person but had some drop of other racial blood in his veins. "Imagine suggesting that any of us Scandinavians aren't all white!" scoffed a tall, even-featured blonde of Norwegian ancestry.

But some place in her history book this young lady had missed the section which described the intermingling of the Mongols, the Lapps and the Finns, and the later conquest of the Finns by the Swedes. Subsequently the Finns intermarried with the Scandinavians and today an occasional slight indication of a "slanting eye" in a "pure" Scandinavian face is accounted for by this incident of history. Although it does not follow that every Scandinavian has Mongol ancestry in some remote generation, the fact is inescapable that *racially* genes from the Mongols are mixed with genes of Caucasians from the north European countries, so that Scandinavians as an ethnic group are not 100 per cent Caucasian.

In addition, the invasion of Spain by the Moors, the political tie-up of France with North Africa, the movement of the British into the West Indies—all of these interrelations have resulted in something less than the perpetuation of pure Caucasian blood. Thus the historian records the facts of the movements of peoples and the physical anthropologist studies the results of these migrations in terms of what has happened biologically to resulting generations.

When these scientists look at the United States they point out several facts. One is that in addition to whatever mixed blood may have been brought to our shores before 1619, since that time the mixing of the Negro and white races has gone on for three-and-a-half centuries. So widespread and continuous has been this process that scientists often speak of the American Negro as a biological type separate from the Negroid race. A Southern educator suggested, "Take a position on the busiest street corner in any of our Southern cities and try to discover a truly African Negro. You'll have to stand there several days before you locate even one."

Many generations of chattel slavery permitted extramarital relations between white men and slave women with the result that at the outbreak of the Civil War there were approximately 600,000 mulattoes among the 4,500,000 Negroes, a ratio of more than one to seven. Many of today's light-skinned, sharp-featured Negroes are the result of the race crossing of that period. Mrs. Perryman, for instance, is the granddaughter of a man of white skin said to have been born in slavery, who later became professor of Greek and Latin in a college for white students. Then the rumor spread that he was part Negro and he was asked to leave the school after which he took a position teaching Hebrew in a Jewish synagogue. This grandfather was very fair, with blue eyes, softly waving blond hair, and light skin; and throughout his entire life he tried to discover if he were really white, as many people thought, or if he had some colored blood as his family connection would indicate. Whether he was the child of a slave woman and one of the white men of the master's household or the illegitimate child of a daughter in the Big House and had been given at birth to one of the slave women to raise as her own, no one knew. His mother—or was she?—would never talk about his birth and to the day of his death he had no proof of his real identity.

As a young professor he had a very pretty Spanish girl in one of his Latin classes. He courted her in traditional Spanish style, never seeing her alone until the day they were married. The Spanish bride became Mrs. Perryman's grandmother.

This grandfather also had two sisters, one tall, dark skinned and homely, but her very unattractiveness was an asset; because of it she was never ordered to come to the Big House at night. In contrast her younger sister was light skinned, pretty, and very attractive to the men in the Big House. The whole family feared for the younger sister because she always said that if she had an illegitimate baby she would kill it. Finally one night, she was ordered to the Big House and the visit left her pregnant. One evening months later, about time for the baby to be born, the girl left the kitchen where she was working with the excuse that she was going to the outhouse. When she did not return to her work her mother went to find her and discovered that the baby had been born and left in the outbuilding and that its young mother had disappeared. The girl's mother took the new baby into the house, added it to her family, and even though the young mother later returned home the child became one more mulatto to be added to the thousands whose origins were not discussed.

The war and the freeing of the slaves slowed down the rate of Negro-white unions but they have never stopped. Many of the descendants of these mixed unions have continued to marry part-white or all-white mates with the result that there are a large number of people in the United States who have some known Negro ancestry but who are themselves so white that they "pass" for white. Estimates on the annual number of Negroes who disown their bi-racial heritage range from 25,000 to 300,000. If the latter number is accepted it doubtless includes many individuals who pass temporarily in order to get or to hold a good job, a good place to live, or other social advantages, then eventually find that their family ties, or the emotional strain which results from the fear of being discovered, pulls them back to their former racial groups. But the majority of those who pass move into the white race and become part and parcel of "ordinary" Americans.

In discussing a limited housing survey in Minneapolis the secretary of the Urban League commented, "In that area of the twenty families of known Negro stock, we counted only sixteen as Negro because we feel sure that the other four are far along in the process of passing."

"Maybe there is this passing, but what you don't know won't hurt you," is the attitude of many Americans, "still there's no reason to continue to weaken the white race by intermarriage with the darker races." And in many parts of the world the darker races are equally concerned about watering down their stock through intermarriage with white peoples. The almost universal concept of superiority held by every race is nowhere more apparent than in attitudes toward mixed marriages.

Scientific findings, however, have proved many of man's fears about the mixing of races to be unfounded. For generations a favorite argument against intermarriage with Negroes has been that the Negro had a smaller cranial capacity than the Caucasian; therefore he had a smaller brain; therefore he was less intelligent; therefore the races should not mix. But after lengthy investigations and analyses of scientific data, Ashley Montagu, anthropologist, concludes, "In point of fact, a difference of 40 to 50 cc. is so small, falling within the normal range of variation in white cranial capacities, that it can hardly be regarded as significant from any but a statistical point of view." However, if one still wants to believe that the size of the white man's skull makes him superior to the Negro he will need to juggle certain other facts—American Indians, two African tribes, the Japanese, Eskimos and Polynesians have brains averaging larger than the white man's average.

In tests which do not rely on language skills American children of Japanese ancestry have proved equal in intelligence to children of white parents. Indian children have proved to be equal to white children where other cultural factors are consistent. One group which comprised children of six Indian tribes showed great variation within the group but the score coincided with the norm for white children. In one California school test scores indicated that five hundred Negro children ranked higher in intelligence than the white children with whom they were competing.

It is true that test results have also been published which indicate a lower intelligence quotient for Negro students than for white, but when the large number of studies made over recent years are assembled, analyzed and interpreted the cumulative weight of their evidence is that all races have approximately equal innate capacity for learning, and also that mixing of the races does not produce offspring of inferior ability.

In their textbook, *Differential Psychology*, Anastasi and Foley devote several chapters to a consideration of race as a basis for physical, social and mental differences. The authors are deliberate in pointing out the uncertain basis upon which many tests have been made and the tendency to interpret test scores without taking into consideration all contributing factors. Their conclusions are couched in well-guarded phrases. However, commenting on intelligence of children with IQ's of 125 or higher but varying in the amount of Negro ancestry from all-black to predominantly white, they conclude: "One fact which is clearly brought out, however, is that high intelligence is not *precluded* by any degree of Negro blood. Individual cases of highly gifted children can be found among Negroes of any degree of racial mixture or purity."

The same authors, summing up other research, state: "In no case has a consistent physical inferiority of a hybrid been reliably established." Yet in this country we have been prone to consider the offspring of mixed marriages as less desirable than children of parents of the same race. The expressions *half-breed* and *half-caste* are used when one wants to stigmatize children of interracial marriages, and commonly suggest that a mixed racial heritage is undesirable. But social psychologists point out that when children of mixed marriages are below standard intellectually, physically or morally, their level has been determined by the same processes which determine the level of any other children: poor inheritance or poor social environment. The fact of mixed racial parentage does not appear to be a determining factor in the child's heritage.

Among the peoples who have practiced intermarriage over many generations, two countries easily observed are Brazil and the Hawaiian Islands. In Brazil the crossing has been over a period of four hundred years. It is apparent that Brazilians have not become stunted in size nor mentality during the process. To the contrary, social scientists find the present-day Brazilian of mixed ancestry biologically and socially of fine caliber.

Turning to the Hawaiian Islands, the record is plain that the original native Hawaiians were Polynesians, a composite rather than a pure racial stock, and that they have married freely with Japanese, Filipinos, Chinese, Koreans and others. Many studies of physical vigor, mental alertness and productivity indicate that the resulting population is in many ways superior to both its Hawaiian and non-Hawaiian ancestry. Thus when the findings of science are assembled they point to the fact that race depletion is not the end result of intermarriage.

In America, state laws have traditionally opposed interracial marriages, but these restrictions are being relaxed. In 1957, twenty-three states had no restrictive laws; twenty-five still had legal restraints. A test case involving the marriage of a Chinese man and a Caucasian woman has reached the Supreme Court but the decision has not yet been handed down. The case is testing the validity of the marriage of a young couple whose wedding took place in North Carolina but who went immediately to Virginia to live. Fifteen months later the State of Virginia, which prohibits mixed marriages, declared the marriage invalid and annulled it. Pending the decision of the Supreme Court the action of the lower court has been vacated. The final outcome of this case will influence the legal restrictions on mixed marriages in the next several years.

If religion, science and cultures with approved mixed racial populations do not condemn interracial marriages, from what does the persistent dread of mixed marriages stem? It may be that the answer lies in personal emotional reactions. Members of the white race have been socially conditioned to think that other races are inferior and that mixed marriages are therefore morally wrong. Unconsciously they react against them just as they react against other evils which they have been taught to abhor.

Another reason for emotional rejection of mixed marriages lies in fear—often an honest and unselfish fear. All parents know that marriage at its best entails many problems of adjustment and they would like to spare their children as many troubles as possible. They fear the extra hazards which a mixed marriage introduces. Also parents fear for the children of a mixed marriage. They know that these children will have an additional difficulty in social adjustment not because they are lacking in personable characteristics but because they do not fit the accepted pattern of American society.

Since the 1954 Supreme Court decision, anti-integration propagandists constantly link integrated schools with "mongrelization of the white race." In this usage *mongrelization* is intended to suggest contamination, while in its correct usage *mongrelization* merely means race mixture. In its propaganda use the word is intended to infuse in people a fear of speedy assimilation of the races. Assimilation could ultimately take place as it has with other groups of people at different times in the history of the world. Broom and Selznick, in *Sociology*, present a tentative time table for possible assimilation of various national, cultural and racial groups in the United States. For English-speaking non-Christians they estimate one to six generations; for Protestant Armenians and other dark-skinned Protestants, six generations or more; the same time for the Portuguese. To small groups of Spanish Americans in the Southwest, they assign "very long"; for most American-born Chinese, Japanese and Negroes they extend the time to "very long to indefinitely long"; and for others in the same group the time schedule is "indefinitely long."

When considering race relations, the interjection of *mongrelization* or even *assimilation* in place of *integration* befogs the issue; the former words suggest fusion of races; while *integration* means the co-ordination of parts into a harmonious whole.

Exact statistics for the number of interracial marriages taking place every year are impossible to obtain because of the growing practice of omitting racial origins from marriage licenses. The conclusions of scholars and organizations working in the field of race relations offer the most reliable information on the trend in such marriages.

In 1942 Gunnar Myrdal in his substantial study, *An American Dilemma*, attempted to establish the amount of race mixing in the United States between Negroes and whites. Because of the lack of mathematical and scientific data on the subject Myrdal could only state that the evidence seemed to point to the fact that about 70 per cent of American Negroes had some white blood, and that intermarriage between the races was "believed to be on the decrease."

In 1945, *Black Metropolis*, by Drake and Cayton, was accepted as one of the best-documented studies on the Negro in Chicago. This book refers to a study made by Robert Roberts in 1938 based upon the 188 mixed families that could be located in Chicago; but Roberts was of the opinion that there were perhaps several other mixed couples living in common-law marriage. The co-authors use the phrases, "In spite of the fact that intermarriages are relatively infrequent," and "in all probability the rate has been decreasing since the beginning of the century." According to Drake and Cayton, the largest number of mixed marriages come from the lower economic and cultural classes of both races; and the second largest number are found among people who enjoy a Bohemian life; the middle class of both races prefers its own color when it comes to marriage.

In his 1956 book, *Black Bourgeoisie,* E. Franklin Frazier, chairman of the department of sociology at Howard University, traces the status which possession of a light skin has always given to Negroes. This white heritage has presumably made them superior to the darker members of their race. In slave days this concept of superiority was indicated by the more kindly treatment accorded mulatto slaves—frequently the children of the white male members of the plantation family—in being assigned the easier and more pleasant tasks, and in being more likely to receive some education.

Although pride of light skin has been carried over into today's Negro society, the prestige which it gives an individual is no longer a main cause of interracial marriages. For one thing, the Negro upper economic class is coming to possess advantages which at one time came only through marriage with white persons: wealth, education, and social status within Negro society. Also, among the "black bourgeoisie" Dr. Frazier finds that the idea persists that the Negro man who marries a white woman will become the inferior member in the partnership; or that because the man is Negro he can marry only an inferior white woman. And further, Negro women have a deep-seated jealousy of white women and resent their excursions into the Negro race for husbands who are usually among the most eligible Negro men. From any angle, middle and upper class Negroes are not encouraging or entering into mixed marriages to any great degree.

In a small book, *Epistle to White Christians,* Dr. Fred D. Wentzel, president of the board of directors of Fellowship House in Philadelphia, says, "When colored and white persons have the opportunity to associate normally, marriage between the races is rare." Then he cites the experience of Philadelphia Interracial Fellowship where for seventeen years hundreds of young people of various races have worked together, in churches, in one another's homes, in the choir of Fellowship Church and in other groups. Not one interracial marriage has resulted from this fellowship. Three or four couples have considered marriage but in each case they decided that the odds against their happiness were too great.

The *Interracial Review,* a Catholic periodical, August, 1956, states, "As to marriage, it is an established fact that in general Negroes want to marry members of their own race, and white people members of theirs. When all racial prejudices have been cleared away (100 years from now) an occasional interracial marriage will disturb nobody."

In an article in the *Atlantic Monthly* for November, 1956, Dr. Oscar Handlin, professor of history at Harvard University, supports the position that as nonwhites have been given dignified status in their own rights there has been, and will continue to be, less desire on their part to become identified with white people either through marriage or extramarital relations. Accepting the present number of mixed marriages and the fact that such marriages will continue, Professor Handlin thinks it is still unrealistic to expect that school integration will suddenly increase the number. In schools where integration has existed for generations, and in schools recently integrated, there appears to be no reason to think that such integration is unduly responsible for any possible increase in intermarriage.

The Southern Regional Council, an organization of Southerners to work toward better race relations in the South, says that the question of intermarriage is "the most common argument advanced against integrated schools—just as it was advanced against Negro voting in the Democratic primary, integration in higher education, and the other gains in race relations during the last 25 years. Yet there is little evidence to sustain such an argument. Even in states where there has never been legal separation, in schools or otherwise, intermarriage is extremely rare."

There is another consideration in the matter of interracial marriages, a very American point of view that two people have the right to select their own mates. Criteria are frequently set up for a good marriage; biological and moral fitness, similarity of interests, relatively equal cultural backgrounds, and love. To this physical and social conditioning have been added desirable personality traits, such as patience, understanding, co-operation, a sense of humor, and willingness to respect the individuality of the other person. If a combination of a reasonable number of these requirements is found in two persons who desire marriage, society usually considers their prospects for a happy life together to be good. All that can be asked when an interracial marriage is under consideration is that society prejudge it on the same bases that it prejudges any other marriage; and that the man and wife be given the same social co-operation to make their marriage work as would be given to any marriage between two people of the same race.

If the exact present status of intermarriage is difficult to ascertain, the future is still more difficult to predict. The increase in the number of interracial marriages at some future date cannot be ruled out. However, while the fear and dread of such marriages prevails the increase will not be great. And when people no longer abhor them, the number will no longer distress them.

For an individual to attempt to understand the problems involved in interracial marriage does not mean that he either advocates or denounces it. If he admits that biologically and morally there is nothing ethically wrong with interracial marriage, this admission does not mean that he is going to set out to marry off his children to members of other races. However, attempts to evaluate such marriages do mean that he is looking objectively instead of emotionally at the question. They mean that without minimizing the integrity of other persons he is willing to allow them a course of action which he may not want to follow himself. He is doing just about all that can be asked of any person—he is thinking with his mind and not with his prejudices.

18. A Climate for Better Relations

The breakdown of any facet of a social order is a tragic experience
to those who believe in the principles upon which the order is built.
The breakdown is inexcusable to those who profit from the old order,
whether they believe in it or not. It is inconvenient to those who
prefer things as they are to the upheaval that accompanies change.
And it is uncomfortable to those who would keep the imperfections
of the known in preference to an uncertain better of the unknown.
Only to the adventurous is change a challenge. For those who find
change an undesirable experience, the 1954 Supreme Court decision was a blast whose debris was expected to block progress in
race relations for at least two generations to come. For those who
find change a challenge the decision was also a blast, but one that
would clear away the debris of past decades and open the way for
greater progress.

Many and varied are the comments on the necessity or justification
of that decision on segregation in the public schools. Dr. William
Stuart Nelson, quiet, scholarly dean of Howard University, Wash-

ington, D.C., expressed his opinion this way: "I think there is a good analogy between our situation in the South and the person who has undergone major surgery. The patient may have looked well to some, may have been going about his business and entering into his normal family and community relationships. But underneath a cancerous condition existed and there was suffering. Finally surgery is indicated as the only remedy and surgery is undertaken with certain serious aftereffects. The patient questions its wisdom and asks why good enough was not left alone, although deep down he realizes that the path to real health lay through the valley of some suffering. Certain parts of our country are suffering from postoperative pain—and it is very real pain. But this is temporary and is the only course to the health of the entire body.

"The analogy goes a little further, I think," said Dean Nelson. "There is no disposition on the part of the friends of the patient to accuse him in his illness. What they desire is to help him to his feet again that they may walk arm in arm with him as befits the citizens of one nation."

Conceding Dr. Nelson's point that the 1954 judicial operation was necessary to remove a cancerous race relations condition and that the country should not only recover but be stronger after the ordeal, then the nation's urgent business is to provide an environment in which the improving relations may thrive. There are many indications that this environment already exists and other indications that the time is opportune for improving it.

One of the elemental rightnesses about America today is that it is made up of average, reasonably decent citizens; people who have a sense of justice and a respect for law. Of course some grumble at times over laws they do not personally like and a few of the 174 million get out of line, but on the whole Americans respect their own laws. Even compliance with the Supreme Court decision on desegregation of the public schools is urged by many men who themselves prefer segregation.

In the statement signed by eighty ministers at Atlanta, Georgia, in November, 1957, the second basic principle is: "As Americans and as Christians we have an obligation to obey the law. This does not mean that all loyal citizens need approve the 1954 decision of the Supreme Court. . . . Those who feel that this decision was in error have every right to work for alteration in the decree. . . .

It does mean that we have no right to defy the constituted authority in the government of our nation. . . ."

A similar statement was published over the names of 173 ministers of greater Houston, Texas: "While we do not believe in the infallibility of our courts, we do firmly believe that our courts are the bulwarks of our society . . . that for an individual or group to defy decisions with which they are not in agreement is to encourage other dangerous elements in our society to follow the same destructive procedures. . . ."

In 1956, one hundred lawyers representing thirty-one states published a statement which includes: "The privilege of criticizing a decision of the Supreme Court carries with it a corresponding obligation—a duty to recognize the decision as the supreme law of the land as long as it remains in force."

Not a member of the school board at Little Rock personally favored integration of the schools in the city, but they were proceeding as citizens to comply with the court orders for desegregation when they ran into difficulty.

"Each of us has to admit that we are citizens of the United States," wrote Ralph McGill, editor of the Atlanta *Constitution*. ". . . we will work out that law as best we can."

Furthermore, Americans are predominantly a people who believe in giving everyone a square deal. At times every person finds it difficult to live up to the ideal, especially when it necessitates championing the rights of a person whose actions or philosophy one deplores or even hates. But many Americans achieve a large degree of fair-mindedness, perhaps none better than a resident of southern Tennessee who at one time had been driven out of his Mississippi home on a trumped-up charge that he was a "nigger lover." In September, 1957, while Frederick John Kasper was in Nashville at the time of the blasting of the Hattie Cotton school because it started integration, he was fined $250 for a traffic violation. Commenting on the action the Tennesseean said, "I hate everything that Kasper stands for, and I think he should be behind bars. He is a social menace, but he is also a citizen of the United States and as such he has rights that must be respected. We have to be on the alert that our emotions don't run away with our judgment; that we mete out punishment commensurate with the offense."

The second indication of a climate for developing better race relations is to be found in the fact that many Americans are beginning to think of people in terms of their "peopleness" rather than of their color. In the opinion of Margaret Madden, director, Migration Services, Mayor's Committee on New Residents in Chicago, this is the area of human relations which needs special emphasis today. She illustrates her point by the experience of Fred K. Hoehler, consultant to Mayor Richard J. Daley.

One morning an irate woman living on the Gold Coast, that stretch of expensive apartment buildings along the shore of Lake Michigan north of downtown Chicago, called Hoehler's office and ordered him to send out a policeman—right now! "I won't put up with this any longer," she fairly shouted over the telephone.

The woman probably paid a thousand dollars a month for her apartment; nevertheless, one of the city's worst tenement districts begins right at her back door. Hoehler and a police officer answered her summons and found the woman furious because "those awful people"—the Puerto Ricans newly arrived from the islands who were crowding into the tenements—were dumping their garbage into the street, creating an unpleasant sight and an unsavory odor.

Having listened to the woman's demand that they "do something about it immediately" the men went over to the Puerto Rican neighborhood to try to make these newcomers understand that Chicago did not keep pigs to rout through the streets and dispose of the garbage; therefore all the people would have to put their garbage into garbage cans—and put the lids on the cans. Such a procedure seemed utterly ridiculous to the Puerto Ricans. But, while they had the officer and Hoehler conveniently at hand they decided to make their complaint, which was that the Indians who lived in the next tenement section made "terrible noise."

Upon investigation the men found that there was a small factory nearby with a vacant second floor which city-lonely Indians rented at times for a good powwow. "Awful noise" to the Puerto Ricans. The policeman tried to explain to the Indians that war whoops and tom-toms were not customary in Chicago. But the Indians said they only had a powwow once in several moons. But the Filipinos down the street! Every night they gathered in front of some house—grandmothers, aunts, uncles, kids, everybody, with a half dozen guitars—and they sang till the moon went down in the morning.

"There you have much of the problem of race relation," concluded

Mrs. Madden. "Instead of helping people be themselves—within reason—too many of us want to make them like ourselves, whatever we happen to be."

However, there are daily illustrations of individuals being appraised as good businessmen, good lawyers, good mothers, or good citizens who happen also to be Negro or Oriental or Indian in their racial origins. A young college graduate who had been director of recreation at a Colorado army base in which Mexicans, Caucasians, Negroes and American Indians received their training, returned to his alma mater for graduate work. He was asked by a former classmate, "Well, how did it feel to work with those Jigaboos?" Momentarily nonplussed the director finally answered, "To tell the truth, I never thought about their being Jigaboos. When you get to working together, you're all just men."

This same attitude of mutual respect was expressed one afternoon on a commuters' train out of New York City. Two men, one a white college professor and the other a Negro chef, sharing a seat fell into easy conversation which turned to the improvements in race relations as each had experienced them. The chef concluded, "I think we're moving fast, but we might find a shorter road in the future. There have always been people looking for a better way, lots of people. Way back in slave days there were folks who held slaves but wouldn't ever sell them. There've always been people a little farther out in front than the rest of us. If we keep trying we can push the pace a little."

For a moment he watched the scenery out the window then added thoughtfully, "Sometimes we walk a slower road than we should." The chef's station was called and he rose with others to leave the train. But first he extended his hand. "It's been a pleasure, sir, to talk to you," he said. The two men shook hands and the professor replied, "It's been equally helpful to me, sir." In these two men is to be found one basis for better race relations—they have become equally helpful to each other.

Further, just as people are coming to be thought of in terms of people, not races, so are social problems being analyzed in terms of the issues involved instead of merely the races involved. In the days when strikes were generally broken by imported strike breakers called "scabs," many were the scenes of violence between them and the strikers. But if these scabs were Negroes the incident was immediately tagged not a labor problem, but a race problem; and the fighting was a race riot.

Lower East Side Manhattan, whose tenements are shared by Negroes, Puerto Ricans and many older nationality groups, faces constant teenage gang warfare. Some of the gangs are all-Negro, or all-Italian, or all-Puerto Rican; others are mixed racial gangs whose hatred for other mixed gangs is as strong as the hatreds of racial groups for each other—a fact which suggests that gang animosities may be more basic than race antagonisms.

The concern of social workers in Lower Manhattan is not so much with race as with the conditions that breed juvenile delinquency. One of these conditions is overcrowded schools and the resulting truancy. Out of the last forty-four cases of juvenile delinquency which one agency had helped through the courts forty-two had started with truancy. Many of these boys, although technically in high school, were too illiterate to read delivery directions well enough to be hired as messenger boys. And the overcrowded schools, pressed with problems within their own walls, had little time to follow up truants outside with more than a postal card to their parents.

Another angle to the problem in this part of New York City is that the city's elaborate park system contributes more to the beauty of the area than to the needs of tenement children. An attorney who had tried fruitlessly for an entire summer to obtain the use of a school gymnasium or a corner of a park for a group of boys he had volunteered to help, summed up the situation, "It almost takes an act of Congress to get the use of any of these public facilities."

Complicating the entire situation is the attitude of many of the police. Less than half of them appear to have any sympathy for "the kids," and even fewer have any special training in working with young people. Stories of false accusations and distressing treatment at the hands of the police are exchanged on every street corner.

"Schools, police, parks, living conditions, frustrated young people —these are our real problems," concluded the director of one of the neighborhood houses, "but when trouble breaks out the newspapers headline it with RACE as if that factor were the most important consideration."

Another element in the improved health of the nation is the general realization that race relations are not a sectional problem. Because the Chinese settled first along the Pacific coast, for a long time an attitude of "let the West take care of them" prevailed in other parts of the country. But by 1940 Chicago had more Chinese than Portland or Seattle; and Boston had more than Chicago. New York had nearly two and a half times as many as Los Angeles; while San Francisco was the only city with a Chinese population larger than New York's. As the Chinese became scattered throughout the entire United States discriminations against them began to fade.

Similarly, for the first two centuries of our national history slavery was considered a problem of the South. But when Civil War came the tragedy was national. Many decades later, in the 1930's, when continued one-crop farming in the South had depleted the soil, the economic problem that resulted was felt by the entire country. Also, as high factory wages in the North lured Southern Negroes into Northern industrial cities the entire nation felt the restless movement of populations. By 1950 the South, which had 90 per cent of the Negro population in 1900, had only 62 per cent of the Negroes. This movement of the Negroes in large numbers out of the South and across the continent indicates the degree to which race relations have become a national instead of a regional concern. Also, the new movement of industry into the South carried with it the seeds of integration which were planted in Southern soil with the turning of the first earth for Southern factories. Soon young shoots poked their heads above the ground, and the Supreme Court decision was merely a hormone injection which speeded their growth.

Politically, also, there is no longer a solid North or South. The Republican party has broken the solid Democratic South and the Democratic party has claimed its share of the traditionally Republican vote of Northern Negroes. Thus the crossing and crisscrossing of many currents are breaking up once sectional problems.

A fourth factor contributing to the development of healthy race relations is the growing acquaintance of the average person with scientific data. Time was, and not too far back, when the common man distrusted experts; at times even scoffed at them. A statistician? Merely a fellow who could juggle figures to prove whatever he wanted to prove. The sociologist? A pseudo scientist who trained his social microscope on the bugs in society, and if he could not find enough of them he was not above injecting a few. The psychologist? A charlatan who turned people's minds inside out, revealed their hidden hungers and justified the process as adjusting to reality.

But paradoxically, this same common man claimed to worship at the altar of science, that magic word of the twentieth century. Astute writers and editors in such popular magazines as *Time, Life, Collier's, Saturday Evening Post,* the women's periodicals and the digests, discarded scientific jargon and acquainted average Americans with the facts of the world in which they lived.

Doubtless at times everybody rebels against those findings of science which do not fit their preconceived ideas. In 1944 Representative Andrew J. May of Kentucky, chairman of the House Military Affairs Committee, refused to release for circulation to the men in the armed services the pamphlet, *The Races of Mankind,* prepared by anthropologists Benedict and Weltfish. The pamphlet had been ordered by the army and fifty-five thousand copies were in a warehouse ready for distribution. After reviewing the contents of the pamphlet Representative May objected to some of the findings of the study, especially to the one which indicated that Negroes in some Northern states were found to have intelligence equal to that of white men in some Southern states.

General reluctance to accept unwelcome scientific findings has often proved a hindrance to the national well-being. This fact was illustrated in the early days of blood banks when during World War II the Red Cross bowed to public opinion and segregated the blood of white and Negro donors. Finally, unwilling longer to be a partner to the perpetuation of the myth of "racial blood" the Red Cross discontinued the segregation practice. Science has established that all human blood is essentially the same excepting for two factors, its agglutinating properties and its Rh factor. These two properties differ in individuals of all races. The blood of a Caucasian, a Mongolian and a Negro may be identical in nature, or it may differ on exactly the same basis as the blood of two Caucasian brothers may differ. And since, according to geneticists, the blood stream carries no hereditary characteristics, the introduction of the blood of an individual of one race into the blood stream of an individual of another race in no way affects the constitutional pattern of the recipient; nor does it affect his offspring. Thus, the terms *half blood* and *quarter blood* are misnomers carried forward from the days when the nature of heredity and the blood stream were shrouded in superstition and the nature of the genes as carriers of hereditary factors was not understood.

Science has not only contributed facts which should help the present generation to relinquish its prejudices, but it has also furnished valuable insights into the nature of prejudice itself. Psychologists report that although some degree of race prejudice is found almost universally, only about 10 per cent of all people have any basic personality distortion which demands a hate outlet. Such a distortion may be the result of immature mental development, of a sense of insecurity resulting from a lack of social acceptance, from the absence of family love and cohesion, or other circumstances which make the individual constantly seek an outlet for the release of his pent-up emotions. For the other 90 per cent of people their prejudices are acquired from the social environment in which they live.

Many parents have been as baffled to know where their children acquired some of their prejudicial ideas as was Mrs. George, counselor to foreign students on a university campus and also mother of nine-year-old Clara. Out riding one afternoon Mrs. George had three little girls in the back seat of the car—her daughter, the child who lived next door, and the daughter of a Jewish friend a few houses down the street. Mrs. George's attention was turned to the conversation between the girls when she heard the neighbor's child say, "I hear we're going to have a new family in our block."

"I hope they aren't Catholics," spoke up the Jewish child.

"Well, you're a Jew!" retorted the young daughter.

"I was so dumbfounded to hear that remark from *my* daughter that I could hardly believe my own ears," reported the mother. "So before anything else worse could be said I got into the conversation as unemotionally as I could. 'I don't see where people's religion makes any difference in their neighborliness,' I said. 'There are kind and unkind people of all religions. The important thing is to decide which kind of person you're going to be.' Now, where do you suppose those children got such prejudiced ideas?"

Doubtless from the same sources they got measles, mumps and chickenpox—"caught" from someone, somewhere. However, just as consistent programs of inoculation have nearly eradicated many contagious diseases, so similar programs of immunization against prejudice have been effective. Many parents have started their children at a young age in play groups with children of other races. And further, the parents have made friends with families of other races in order that the children might "catch" the spirit of interracial friendliness. Schools, churches and clubs have purposefully brought racial groups together around common interests—music, art, child care, clinics, adult study groups, pageants. Formal teaching has its place in preventing prejudice, but participation in interracial groups is the most normal way for people, children or adults, to develop easy relations with one another. All too frequently the ideal situation does not present itself, so there has to be purposeful planning on the part of someone to create a situation which offers easy interracial friendship.

A young mother in New Jersey, finding no way to get her three-year-old daughter into an interracial play group, frequently invited her Negro cleaning woman to bring her four-year-old daughter with her for an afternoon. Always on those days the two women sat down together with their cups of coffee while the little girls had their tea party.

When a small town in Michigan put its first Negro music teacher into one of the elementary schools the local music club ignored her. Then one of the members invited the young teacher to sing on a club program, but her inclusion in the group stopped there. Not yet discouraged, the same woman appeared on several programs in town as the accompanist for the Negro teacher. Soon the teacher was included in a ladies' trio, the other two members being white teachers from the same school in which she taught. Before the end of the year the music teacher was an active member of the music club.

Mrs. Day lived in New Haven, Connecticut, and although white, she had experienced firsthand some of the prejudices displayed in various parts of the country when as the wife of an army doctor she had followed her husband through thirteen states. Finally returning to her own New England she organized the New Haven Neighborhood Project, composed of parents who wanted their children to have an opportunity to know children of other races and faiths. On an interracial, interfaith basis the parents opened a playground, then a nursery school and a summer play school.

These people who are walking out to meet race relations more than halfway are one of the best guarantees that a healthy climate for better relations is developing. Normally people fear experiences which they dread to meet, and for many people race contacts are such experiences. But when they walk out voluntarily to make interracial contacts, or accept them when they present themselves, individuals usually find that such contacts prove to be only human relations, and better human relations are everybody's concern.

19. *Perhaps So! But How?*

Nearly everyone in the United States thinks that something should be done about race relations; but what, or how, or when—there is the rub. Many are willing to admit that perhaps there is no one answer to the present difficulties; and a few would admit further that even they may not have the right answer. Frequently the problems and their solutions are found to revolve around the question of proper strategy.

One of the decisive questions of strategy arises from a consideration of timing. How fast shall change take place? One Atlanta minister, advocating an extreme gradualism, said, "I do not believe we should invite Negroes into our church membership at present. Let them come as visitors if they care to. I think it's better that we continue to preach kindliness, the love of God and the brotherhood of man, and eventually we will work toward an adjustment of relations between the races. We've been making progress in the South ever since the Civil War; there's no reason to force it now. Let the established trend take its own course."

But many people ask how long it will take for a let-nature-take-its-course gradualism to accomplish actual freedom and equality for minority groups. Since each new generation receives its standards of conduct and morality and its pattern of social organization from the older generation, these ideas and patterns are perpetuated indeterminately unless something happens to challenge the standards or disturb the pattern.

Lillian Smith, Georgia author of the novels *Strange Fruit* and *Killers of the Dream,* speaks to the gradualists from her own experience when in a recent book, *Now Is the Time,* she says:

> During the early decades of the twentieth century, our parents taught my generation in the South to observe segregation . . . along with our lessons of brotherhood and democracy. We learned them well; but of the three, we knew that segregation came first.
>
> There were ideals we must value also: truth and tenderness, courtesy, and good will and hospitality. But segregation came first. Outside the home, it also came first: in church it came before brotherhood; in schools, before knowledge. . . . We lived in a democracy, whether we thought about it or not. And we loved it. We were proud of our Bill of Rights and our Constitution, even though some of us had never read them. It was good to be free. . . .

Then Miss Smith shows the questions that kept pushing themselves into the minds of her generation of young people, questions suggested by reading, travel, war.

> And we changed. So secretly, so slowly. But we changed. How many? . . . I do not know. For though we changed . . . and had begun to feel a concern for the whole world we still meekly obeyed the segregation laws we despised and knew were un-Christian and un-American.
>
> And we remained silent. Silence was our gift to the demagogue. Year after year we gave him this large present . . . each year we underwrote his activities with our silence.
>
> Each, in his loneliness, feeling too weak to speak out. Each thinking he was the only one who did not like segregation.

But, *now is the time,* insists Miss Smith, to say and to do those things which will hasten integration.

Then there is the strategy of the fanatics who would travel only in high gear, regardless of the conditions of the social roadbed or the obstacles in the way. In their frantic effort to reach the end of the journey they push the wheels so fast that the gears cannot mesh.

These speeders see no reason for the "all deliberate speed" phrase in the Supreme Court order. Their attitude is, "Let integration be accomplished by a certain date—and that date not too far distant—OR ELSE."

Between the gradualists and the fanatics are the moderates. A moderate may feel the same urgency for action that the fanatic feels, but he knows that radical changes depend for their success upon both foresighted and courageous leaders and an adequate following to move forward with them. It is difficult to be a moderate for often he is reviled by the fanatics and repudiated by the gradualists, and all the while he feels the urge to move faster than his judgment tells him is feasible.

Thus society operates with a three-speed engine, while the obstructionists—those people who would not change at all—act as a dragging brake. The best speed to be used at any time is a matter of strategy.

It is within this framework of moderation that the Southern Regional Council plans its strategy. "It would be completely unrealistic," said one of its spokesmen, "to expect Louisiana to move into integration at the same speed with which Kentucky moves." The border states are moving with relative ease as Missouri, Oklahoma and Kentucky are demonstrating. Before too long the border of integration will have moved farther south and areas in which segregation now is deeply entrenched will begin to feel their resistance easing.

On occasion, expediency may dictate the timing schedule, a strategy which postpones consideration of the ultimate solution of a problem. In the fall of 1958 several students came from Nigeria, Africa, to Georgetown College, a Baptist school in Georgetown, Kentucky. Having accepted Christianity through the work of Baptist missionaries in Africa the students assumed that they would be part of the fellowship of their parent church when they came to the United States to college. But before long they discovered that the members of the white Georgetown church were not pleased to have Africans in the congregation. Some of the church members, hoping to ease the situation, suggested that the students be asked to attend church in their native garb; but to many of the other church members clothing did not change the fact of race. The students themselves, aware of the situation, resolved the tension by withdrawing from the church and attending a Negro church instead. But the paradox of bringing

Christian students to a Christian college and then refusing them membership in the church fellowship pricked the conscience of the white congregation. The question was put to a vote which resulted in 237-to-29 in favor of receiving the Nigerian students. The vote settled the immediate question but the time may not be far distant when American Negro Christians will ask in what way they differ from Nigerian Negro Christians.

Another question of strategy arises in connection with publicity. A few years ago an organization of girls in a Southern college had the practice of exchanging discussion and music programs with girls in a Negro college in the same community. One day a newspaper reporter heard of this interchange and with the greatest good will he wrote up and published the story. A tempest resulted and the contacts were cut short. No one doubted the reporter's good intentions but they regretted his strategy.

One national organization for girls prefers to have no word of publicity about its interracial policies. "No one knows how many little girls of one race would be kept home from camp by parents who fear the little girls of another race," commented one of its directors.

Early in 1957 segregated seating on the buses of Nashville was discontinued. There was no announcement of the move; the bus drivers were simply told by the company to discontinue requiring Negroes to sit in the back of the buses. One pressure group insisted, "The bus company should announce its new policy. Many people don't even know the change has been made. The officials are afraid to stick their necks out."

Others cautioned, "The state legislature is in session. If a lot of hullabaloo is made about desegregation, the publicity could easily aggravate the school situation and influence the lawmakers to break out with a rash of legislation that would set everything a long, long way back."

To the questions of time schedule and publicity must be added another problem of strategy. At what level or in what areas should change begin? Since the court order desegregation of the public schools has been initiated at various levels in different communities. Mr. Blair Hunt, a Negro school principal in Memphis, in discussing the dynamiting of the Hattie Cotton school in Nashville where desegregation was begun at the first grade level, remarked, "Most people think it is wise to start desegregation in the first grade.

They're right in thinking that little children don't have as well developed prejudices as do older children. But they overlook the fact that parents are more emotionally tied to first grade children than to older ones and it's playing on emotions of parents that makes race riots possible." Asked where he would start desegregation the principal said that in a Southern community where there was deep-seated antagonism to desegregation he would begin in the community, not in the schools. He would first open libraries, museums and art galleries, for it is at the higher cultural levels, he felt, that people most easily accept other people for what they are and not for what color they are. Then he would open colleges, vocational schools and other institutions which people attend for such specific reasons that they are willing to accept desegregation rather than forfeit the special opportunities offered. From there he would move to high schools and elementary schools in that order, or simultaneously if the community was ready to accept the change on both levels.

There are times when an individual may have decided that now is the time, and here is the place to start better relations between the races; but he is still faced with the problem of how to proceed. At this point it is frequently difficult to anticipate the complications which may be involved in even the most simple situation, as Mrs. Jackson discovered. Living in a college town in Missouri, Mrs. Jackson was the outstanding musician in her part of the state. In frequent demand for concerts, she also sang in many churches, including a Negro church where she was pleased to appear as soloist at their choir concerts; their choir in turn coming to her church to sing for special occasions. As time went on she became convinced that the contacts between her and the Negro singers could move a step beyond the relation of soloist and chorus. After long deliberation as to the best approach she finally decided that she would entertain the women's organization of the Negro church in her own home. Then hoping to keep the occasion free from any class distinction she let her colored maid go for the afternoon.

Mrs. Jackson was in an upstairs bedroom when the first of her guests came up the walk to the house. Hearing their voices she looked out the window and saw that a group of about eight women had stopped to discuss something on which there seemed to be a difference of opinion. When she got downstairs to welcome her guests she realized what the discussion had been about, for half of them were arriving at the front door and the other half were coming up the walk to the side entrance.

"At that moment I knew that with all my good intentions I had put some of these women in an embarrassing position, and one which I had not anticipated," the hostess later reflected.

The afternoon business meeting and program moved along smoothly. Then it was time to serve the ladies.

"When I started to the kitchen I could feel a tension in the air and I realized that again my guests were uncomfortable. Many of them actually could not bring themselves to sit in the parlor while I waited on them. I had what I hoped was a happy inspiration for I turned around and said, 'I trust you don't mind coming with me and each taking your own plate. Then we can come back and have more time to talk together.' That did it. They all followed me to the kitchen and we had an easy time serving our refreshments."

But when the guests were ready to leave there was the same uncertainty in the minds of the women. Which door should they use? Some of them started for the front door then changed their minds and used the side door. A few of them left by the front door just as they had come.

In trying to assess the experience Mrs. Jackson said, "I knew that some of my white friends did not approve my action but I was willing to risk their censure. But I hadn't thought of the embarrassment it might cause some of my guests. I'm still wondering if I did the right thing."

In this country the most recent problem in the field of strategy is related to an assumption of long standing that minority groups are childish peoples, immature in their thinking and unable to carry their share of the responsibility for social adjustments. But this theory is rapidly crumbling before the impact of facts, and white people are faced with finding some means of gracefully accepting shared leadership in politics, education, religious organizations and other relationships. In every field Negroes are supplying responsible thinkers and leaders. The late Dr. Charles Johnson, president of Fisk University, editor, author, and at various times a representative of the United States to UNESCO, walked during his lifetime in the vanguard of American educators. Sociologist E. Franklin Frazier of Howard University speaks today with authority in his field, and Dr. Ernest Just moved with the foremost zoologists.

In Memphis, almost any week day finds Dr. Joseph E. Walker, a slightly stooped elderly Negro executive behind his broad mahogany desk in an office in the Universal Life Insurance building. Dr. Walker, president of the board of this company, has helped to make more than a half century of Southern history. On the walls of his office are a dozen narrow-framed awards and certificates of honor which have been given to him at various times for his work in encouraging better practices in medicine, agriculture, industry and business as they relate to the welfare of his own race. One award was presented by President Franklin D. Roosevelt for Dr. Walker's contribution to the war effort. And on the doctor's desk is a small bronze plate mounted on walnut which reads: "State Fair of Texas. Third annual award. To Joseph Edison Walker for outstanding achievement in the field of human relations in these United States."

This award is presented annually to the Negro who, in the opinion of the award committee, has made the greatest contribution to the well-being of his country. The first recognition was given to Dr. Ralph Bunche for his mediation in Palestine; the second went to Mrs. Mary McLeod Bethune for her lifetime of Christian service. And the third to Dr. Walker.

Among the Negroes who have arrested the attention of the nation none stands out more clearly than the Rev. Martin Luther King, Jr., minister of the Dexter Avenue Baptist Church in Montgomery, Alabama. Dr. King has not won pre-eminence by championing a popular cause but by epitomizing the concept of nonviolence as a way of life. For three decades the people of the United States had watched Gandhi in India as he preached to the millions of all castes that love is stronger than hate; that nonviolent resistance is more effective than resistance by force. Americans watched him go to prison for his beliefs; they followed him through the days and weeks of two hunger strikes; they saw him come out of prison each time weaker in body but stronger in his influence and conviction. And people in America said: Maybe love is stronger than force in India— but not in America. This is no homespun civilization like India's; this is a country of steel and iron. You can't pit love against an army of tanks and atomic weapons. You have to meet force with greater physical force—or be crushed.

Then on December 1, 1955, nonviolence came to Montgomery, a Southern city of more than 100,000 people, 40 per cent of them

Negroes. It came in the person of a young preacher. A Negro. It came on the day that a boycott was called against the Montgomery bus company. By any normal standards a race riot should have resulted, but it didn't. Dr. King, who assumed the leadership of the boycott, urged the Negroes of Montgomery and vicinity to refrain from violence. "We believe in law and order," he said. "Don't get out your weapons for the greatest weapon is love." It was conceivable that a minister might be dedicated to such principles, but that he should induce fifty thousand others to follow that principle was inconceivable.

Nevertheless he did persuade them, and the Negro population pooled their cars or walked to work, answering threats with silence.

Night after night hundreds of Negroes met in local churches to strengthen each other in the face of increasing violence against their people. Their leader urged them, "Never retaliate with hate." And in response to shootings and bombings fifty thousand Negroes held their peace.

"We must be sure our methods are rooted in Christian faith," said King, and fifty thousand Negroes guarded their methods that they should not exhibit hate.

"Pray that we who stand amid violence in the South will never retaliate with violence." And as fifty thousand Negroes prayed, all over the land other people of different colors joined in their prayers.

"Our failure to follow the command of Jesus would lead only to a long night of bitterness." And finally, "We can inject a new spiritual dimension into our nation," affirmed this young man, and a growing number of people across the country began to wonder about the truth in the frequently discounted statement that a real Christian is the most dangerous person in the world.

Whatever one's personal feelings may be about Dr. King's philosophy, about the use of boycotts, about the new social recognitions being won by Negroes, the fact of their mature leadership in many sectors of American life is established.

Marion A. Wright, retired president of the Southern Regional Council, speaking recently in Charlotte, North Carolina, said, "As a society we have not permitted the Negro to pull his share of the load. . . . The waste of Negro potential places extra burdens upon the whites. If there is actually a 'white man's burden' it is a burden of his own creation."

A final problem in strategy is pressing upon the United States: What is going to be her position in relation to the total world situation resulting from the shifting relations between majority and minority racial groups?

According to the 1950 census figures, the world population is 2,400,000,000. Of this number 10 per cent are classified as black, or Negroid; 30 per cent as yellow-brown or Mongoloid; and 57 per cent as white, or Caucasoid. But of the total number of people classified as white, 500 million are Hindus, Iranians and Arabs, all of whom are predominantly dark skinned. Further, white peoples of European background account for only 33 per cent of mankind and even some of these are of appreciable Mongoloian and African mixture. So today when racial lines are drawn between colored and white peoples they are usually drawn with two-thirds of the world's population lined up on the colored side, and one-third on the white side. Obviously white-skinned people are a minority group.

Although they have always been a minority, only recently have white people been consistently faced with this minority status. As long as the colored populations of the world could be dominated by the white peoples, numbers mattered little. But today with the once "backward" nations assuming roles of hemispherical leadership numbers have become important.

Since World War II such countries as India, Pakistan, Burma, Indonesia, the Philippines and others have become independent nations, and with this independence has come a strong surge of nationalism and self-respect. The United States has a large stake in the democratic practices of these nations, both because as the leading democratic nation in the world she has long upheld democracy as an ideal, and because she has contributed leadership and financial backing to many of these countries in their struggle for independence.

Similarly the long depressed dark-skinned peoples feel a kinship for the still depressed dark-skinned peoples in every part of the world —including the United States of America. All nonwhites resent personally every affront to a Negro in this country. Americans traveling in Asia are well aware that a race incident in the United States is blown up out of all proportion by the time it has crossed the Pacific. The exclusion of one girl from the University of Alabama became the general treatment meted out to Negro students in American universities; and the blasting of one Nashville elementary school when a few Negro first-graders were accepted symbolized the violence which awaited every Negro first-grader.

At times nonwhite nations express their attitudes in words, such as the statements of the Bandung Conference of African and Asian peoples in 1955 which deplored the racial practices in the United States and South Africa. At other times they express themselves in actions, such as the expulsion of the Dutch from Indonesia in 1958. Although religious and economic factors may have been involved in this issue, the propelling force was the national determination to rid Indonesia of every trace of colonialism—foreign domination and foreign exploitation. Many of the Dutch who were expelled from the country had been born and reared on some of the East Indian Islands which make up the present Republic of Indonesia; and many of the places of business which were confiscated had been in operation for generations. But because the presence of the Dutch on Indonesian soil was a reminder of foreign domination the republic willed that this reminder be obliterated—even if the republic suffered financially, educationally and administratively as a result.

In the Union of South Africa a practice of race relations called *apartheid*, or development by parts, is based upon a theory which seems logical to the dominant white group there. They look upon the three racial groups as representing such extremes of cultural difference as to make impossible any integration. There are the white group of predominantly Dutch descent, the colored people of mixed racial heritage, and the natives, mostly Bantus; and according to *apartheid* each of these racial segments must be developed as a separate unit, progressing educationally, politically and industrially at its own speed. His Excellency John E. Holloway, High Commissioner for the Union of South Africa in London, calls attention to the fact that in the United States the North has perhaps the most ideal conditions in the world for integrating the black and the white races; that the people of both races are relatively equal in their educational, political and industrial potentials; and that they have a large measure of common interests. But, the commissioner points out, even in the North integration is far from an accepted practice, and attempts to foster it frequently result in strife. Therefore it should not be surprising that in South Africa where because of extreme differences there is no reason to believe integration could succeed it is necessary for the good of all three racial groups to try some other policy such as the simultaneous development of the people on three separate levels. Further, Dr. Holloway insists that *apartheid* is merely a plan of operation rather than a national dogma.

Nevertheless, *apartheid* looks to people of other nations as having become more than a working plan. It appears to have the earmarks of a goal toward which the Union is moving, a goal to establish the most tightly segregated society in the world today; a society in which every aspect would be racially segregated with double or even triple facilities for literally everything from telephone booths to schools, with no provision made for eventual equality of the races. Not only are the lines being tightly drawn between them but many individuals are being racially downgraded. The National Population Register which moved into high gear in 1955 is attempting to list and racially grade every individual in the Union. In the process many mulattoes have been classified as natives and some individuals formerly classified as whites have been lowered to the status of mulattoes. Since a person's registration status determines his social, political, educational and economic status downgrading is a tragedy.

In the efforts of the United States to preserve world peace, the strategy which she uses in aligning herself with or against the majority peoples, the nonwhites, may be a deciding factor in accomplishing that peace.

20. *"Things Don't Just Happen"*

An Alabama-born college president sat with a group of friends musing aloud on some of the changes which have taken place in race relations in the last twenty years. Himself a Negro, he spoke from experience of the troubled atmosphere of his own college days, while at present his son is in a state university and his two daughters in privately endowed colleges, all three schools integrated. He spoke of the growing number of Negro voters in many parts of the South and of the promise of more with the passage of the new civil rights legislation. He referred to the breakdown in race barriers in the churches, for he had recently attended a national convention of Negro churches which was working with the white churches of the same communion toward complete integration. He commented on the ease with which he traveled back and forth across the continent many times a year. He also mentioned the tension in Montgomery, his home town, at the time of the bus boycott. At this point he paused a moment before adding, "Dr. King was magnificent in the stand he took; but, you know, men like King don't just happen. They're the result of little known but powerful forces behind them. In Montgomery that force began with the Rev. Vernon Johns."

About ten years ago Mr. Johns, a sixty-year-old Negro and past-president of Virginia Baptist Seminary, was pastor of the Dexter Avenue Baptist Church which Dr. King now serves. An able speaker and possessed of a brilliant mind, he also had strong convictions that the Christian Gospel was a social gospel, even though most of the Negro congregations of his day still leaned toward a theology which stressed individual salvation.

During Mr. Johns's pastorate there occurred an interracial incident in which the police shot and killed a nineteen-year-old Negro boy. A few days later the outdoor bulletin board at Mr. Johns's church posted the sermon topic for the following Sunday: "Policemen Can Kill A Negro Boy in Montgomery, Alabama." Before many hours crowds began to gather and to comment on both the topic and the incident. To prevent trouble a policeman was stationed at the corner by the church. The third day, on Saturday afternoon, Mr. Johns, unrecognized by any of the crowd, mixed with them to pick up their comments.

Many of the white people were incensed, but some indicated appreciation that any man—let alone a Negro—would have the courage to publicize such a topic. Most of the Negroes were pleased that one of their number would take a stand for them, but they were all apprehensive as to what the results might be.

At one time, Mr. Johns turned to the policeman and asked, "Do you suppose this preacher will really tackle a subject like that?"

"Guess so," was the officer's short reply.

The following morning the Baptist church was packed with people, including some white folk, who had come either out of concern for the problem or out of curiosity to see what would happen.

It happened. In the middle of the sermon the police entered, marched to the pulpit and arrested the Rev. Vernon Johns. Although soon released, the action of this minister held a promise that the time for intimidating Negroes was growing short. Johns helped make possible a King a decade later.

Neither does it just happen that the chief legal counsel for the NAACP, Thurgood Marshall, is, in the opinion of many jurists, the best constitutional lawyer in the United States. During the presidency of Dr. Mordecai Johnson at Howard University, the late

Charles Hamilton Houston was made dean of the law school. Houston was a graduate of Harvard Law School and had once been considered by President Franklin Roosevelt as a possibility for the United States Supreme Court. Aware that the coming struggle for the Negroes' civil rights would be a legal battle, Johnson and Houston decided that the greatest contribution Howard University could make would be to prepare lawyers who would be second to none. Said Houston, "In the United States we have many second rate Negro lawyers, doctors, scientists and others, because there is little first rate training available for them. So in the professional fields we have become dependent upon members of the white race. We have no cause to hate them—but we have cause to train our own." Dean Houston and Howard University undertook to train men well. So it did not just happen that in the 1950's as the number of civil rights cases in the courts increased there were brilliant and legally disciplined Negro minds to argue them.

It is not always possible to foresee where complications will arise nor to anticipate emergencies. But even in emergencies, successful solutions do not just happen. Someone or some group has built up enough stability to meet the crisis. In the fall of 1956 when Clinton, Tennessee, attempted to integrate its schools mob violence resulted. In neighboring Kentucky the same epidemic of race hatred broke out in Sturgis and Clay, and threatened also to wreck the three-week-old program of school integration at Henderson. A diary kept by the Rev. C. Sumpter Logan and the Rev. Theodore A. Braun and originally published by the *Christian Century* documents the story of ten days of anxiety in Henderson.

On Thursday, September 18, the White Citizens Council called a mass meeting for the following Saturday night and announced as the main speaker Jerry Waller, a man considered by many in the area to be a rabble rouser. Previous to the meeting the Henderson Ministerial Association met and for two hours discussed its strategy. Representing six denominations and the Salvation Army, the men agreed to attend the mass meeting together and to have their president read a statement of their position and urge parents to abide by the decision of the Supreme Court. During the mass meeting the appointed minister had difficulty in gaining the floor and when he was finally recognized he was drowned out with boos and curses.

The next morning many church members were absent from their

accustomed pews, some because they did not want to get involved in any arguments and others because they resented the action of their minister in supporting the Supreme Court decision on the previous evening. Several of the ministers, to the displeasure of some in their congregations, referred to the crisis in the community; and one church carried out plans of long standing to have a Negro guest minister fill the pulpit. On Monday morning a large number of white parents began the boycott of the public school. Immediately the local ministers, by radio and home visitation, encouraged the parents who were keeping their children in school to remain firm. But Tuesday morning school attendance reached a new low of 206 out of 862 pupils.

The next step of the ministers was to organize a meeting for that evening to which they personally invited every parent who had kept a child in school. Moreover, they secured a promise from the superintendent of schools and the police commissioner to be present. A group of seventy parents gathered, calm but not without apprehension. As some of the more firm-minded of them told why they were keeping their children in school the more timid parents began to strengthen their resolve to hold on a little longer. School and police officials assured the parents that their children would be protected both in and out of school and the meeting adjourned.

Simultaneous with this meeting, the White Citizens Council was holding a mass meeting on the courthouse lawn. Imported ministers harangued God and imported orators exhorted the people to strengthen the boycott. The next morning school attendance picked up a little but for several days fear almost to the point of panic pervaded the town. Under tremendous pressure, even threats of death, certain of the ministers decided it would be wise to slow down their antiboycott campaign; but at the same time they were encouraged to continue as they saw their efforts to keep the schools open resulting in daily increased attendance. On the second Saturday night—a day later than the members of the Citizens Council had originally given themselves to have the the schools closed—the Citizens Council called another community meeting at which another out-of-town speaker urged the mob to take the law in its own hands. At this extreme suggestion two of the local Citizens Council members resigned and the meeting became disorganized.

On Monday morning school attendance approached normal and the strength of the Citizens Council was broken. But their defeat hadn't just happened. The Council conceded that if it had not been for the Ministerial Association they would have closed the integrated school within three days.

It was not by chance that a Vassar graduate, a Negro girl majoring in child psychology, became the first Negro teacher in a New York community. Three years earlier a group of parents had considered the question of Negro teachers in their public schools and decided to do a little quiet investigating. From the superintendent of schools they learned that few qualified Negro teachers had ever applied. Then from teachers in other districts they learned that Negro teachers usually hesitated to apply in a district where they had reason to believe there was prejudice against them.

Next the interested parents got in touch with several colleges and universities and made up a list of prospective Negro teachers who seemed well qualified for the opening in the community and wrote to them, urging them to apply. With both the applicants and the school board aware that a group of white parents was alert on this issue, the way was eased for hiring the first Negro teacher. She is an assistant to an older kindergarten teacher of a class of fifty children, seven of them Negroes. The new teacher, the school staff, the children and the parents are pleased with the appointment.

Not only do communities face a task of making things happen, but frequently organizations within a community face the same problem. Such was the case with a Midwest Branch of the American Association of University Women. For several years some of its members had raised the question of admitting Negro women to its membership. According to the national by-laws any eligible person "shall be entitled to and shall receive admission to membership in the Association. . . ." But since membership in the national organization is not dependent on membership in a local Branch some local Branches, by common consent and established precedent, excluded Negro women from membership. Many of the members of this Midwest Branch thought they ought to receive every eligible member regardless of color, but—.

And that was where the matter stood when Mrs. Grange moved to this city. During her adult life Mrs. Grange had lived in China; she had seen the effect upon the Chinese of their exclusion from the international park along the bund in Shanghai, exclusion marked by signs which read: "DOGS AND CHINESE NOT ALLOWED." She had been in Japan in 1924 when America's Exclusion Act had humiliated the sensitive Japanese and intensified a hatred that less than two decades later triggered a world war. She had been in India after the untouchables had been accepted by the Hindus and she had watched Nehru's government at work integrating the outcastes into the nation's political and economic life. She had lived in Indonesia after World War II and knew from firsthand experience the hatred with which the Indonesians looked upon the Dutch and all other colonial-minded Western nations. Then Mrs. Grange returned to the United States to find many communities in this country practicing tactics that were producing upheavals in other parts of the world. Chief among these practices—racial arrogance.

Soon after moving to this Midwestern town Mrs. Grange was invited to speak at a dinner meeting of the AAUW, and she took with her an Indonesian house guest. Among the many women around the tables this guest was the only nonwhite person.

"It seemed unbelievable to me," later commented Mrs. Grange, "that in this organization made up entirely of college graduates, and heavily weighted with professional women, there was not a single Chinese, Japanese or Negro, when I knew what outstanding women from each race lived right here in the city."

During the dinner she and the women sitting on each side of her discussed the problem and Mrs. Grange discovered that the complications of the *how*, the *why*, and the *what-if* of integration had instilled a lethargy into the leadership.

The following week when Mrs. Grange entertained in honor of her Indonesian guest it was a very interracial group that gathered in her home. "And," said Mrs. Grange joyfully, "I just invited some of the leading AAUW women. Even we adults learn better by doing than by being talked at. Of course they discovered all kinds of interests in common with the Oriental and Negro women and they talked a long time over their teacups. And when people find a meeting of minds they don't stop there."

Since in our material world minds can meet only when people meet, it was the most natural thing in the world that the membership of the AAUW was soon open to women of all races. Mrs. Grange's part in opening the AAUW memberships took some time, some effort, some thought and planning, but it did not entail for her any wrenching of deep-seated prejudices. However, some individuals have to go through an agonizing experience to purge themselves of prejudices which they suddenly discover they have unconsciously been harboring.

Such an experience came to Mrs. Fergus, one of the pillars of her church and of programs of civic merit in the southern Ohio town where she had lived for thirty years. As an officer of the Council of Church Women, an interdenominational organization, Mrs. Fergus became much concerned over the two Council groups in her community, one for white women and one for Negro women.

"Some of our women didn't even realize there was a wall between the two races," explained Mrs. Fergus. "I discovered how unaware we were of our own situation when I was invited to participate in a race relations workshop in one of our local churches." During one session a woman reported with great pride that her denomination had two churches in the city, one for white members and one for colored, and that the women in the churches had wonderfully fine relations. Each year their women took a program of good quality to the women's group in the Negro church, and then every January they invited the Negro women to come to the white church to serve the annual dinner and make some money.

The next fall Mrs. Fergus invited the officers of all church women's organizations to meet at her home. "I decided I was the one to make this move," she said, "because I had absolutely no race consciousness, while I knew some of the other women had. The afternoon went smoothly and from this beginning we gradually moved to an integrated Council of Church Women."

When some of the group to whom she was relating her experience commended Mrs. Fergus, she added hastily, "For that move I deserve no credit. It cost me no effort and my only concern was to avoid giving unnecessary offense to any one." Then she hesitated a moment as if uncertain whether or not to add anything to her story. She decided to go on. "My real test came later."

It was evident that the rest of the experience was not easy for Mrs. Fergus to relate. In the midst of World War II when everyone was being urged to enroll in first-aid courses, Mrs. Fergus had joined a class, an unsegregated group, conducted by the Red Cross. During the second session, following a demonstration of artificial respiration, the members were paired for a practical exercise. One person in each pair was to lie down on the gymnasium floor while her partner worked on her.

Mrs. Fergus found herself paired with Mrs. Blume, a Negro seamstress. Mrs. Blume offered to be the first "victim" and Mrs. Fergus prepared to resuscitate her. As she started to work on Mrs. Blume an unaccountable and uncontrollable wave of nausea swept over Mrs. Fergus.

"I made a hasty and ungraceful exit to the women's rest room," she confessed in a voice hardly more than a whisper, "and lost my food. I stayed there till I felt I could go back and carry through my assignment. But when I returned to the gym and took my place again, the same feeling returned."

A second time Mrs. Fergus hurried to the rest room. Several times she started back to the first-aid class, but each time she found it impossible to return. "Then I learned what it meant to wrestle with the Lord. I doubt if any women's rest room was ever the scene of the kind of spiritual experience that I went through. I who had been so sure that I had no race prejudice—I found that I had been unprejudiced only so far as I was in a position to play a role that was congenial to me. I prayed it out, leaning on the washbowl, and finally I went back to the first-aid class. Don't tell me the grace of God isn't needed to work out good race relations. Our automatic reactions have to be brought in line with our hearts."

There is a rather general assumption that race prejudice exists only between white people and those of another race, and that it is always the white person who exhibits superiority. In reality most people have a feeling that their race is the superior race. At an interdenominational convention of church women someone asked Mrs. Brown, national secretary for a Negro women's fellowship, how it happened she and Mrs. Wu, who held a similar position in China, were such close friends. Mrs. Brown laughed heartily as she said, "It didn't just happen. Even now after five years of friendship when I think back to how it began I'm struck with the humor of the situation. But at that time it was anything but funny. I was a national secretary of a missionary organization. *I* had no race prejudice. *I* was broad-minded. I knew most people were inexcusably biased; but not I!"

Mrs. Brown's story was that she arrived in Buffalo to attend an international conference and when the desk clerk gave her her room assignment she discovered she was to share a room with a Chinese. Indignant, she left her bags just inside the door of her room and went immediately to the manager's office.

"I had to wait a few minutes to see him," and Mrs. Brown tapped her foot to indicate the state of her nerves as she waited, "and my ire grew as the seconds passed."

When the door to the manager's office opened and a Chinese lady came out Mrs. Brown paid no attention to her, except to register an unfavorable reaction. Then she walked into the office and laid her case before the manager, who asked, "What kind of a convention is this?"

Mrs. Brown rattled off the name of the convention group, which unfortunately for her contained the word *Christian*.

"That's what I thought," replied the manager, "and on that basis we never considered any race antagonisms."

Hardly waiting for the thrust to sink in he continued, "Did you see the Chinese lady who just left my office?"

Mrs. Brown nodded.

"Do you know what she wanted?" he asked.

Mrs. Brown shook her head.

"She was in here," said the manager, "to protest having to room with a Negro."

"I know I stumbled out of his office," Mrs. Brown declared, "for I felt as if I had been struck right between the eyes. I went back to my room and when I opened the door I saw tiny Mrs. Wu, the same lady that had come out of the manager's office, sitting on the edge of a large, overstuffed chair, her hands folded in her lap. As I closed the door she stood up and said, 'I am your roommate.' So, you see," concluded Mrs. Brown, "it isn't by chance alone that we are close friends."

It didn't just happen that a Negro porter is characterized by many people as "the most unforgettable man I ever knew." And the qualities that make him unforgettable did not just happen, either. At the age of thirty Ralston Young was bitter because with all of his ambitions to do something fine and worthy he was only Red Cap No. 42, Grand Central Station, New York City.

"That's when I thought that being a porter was menial work," says Mr. Young, "just carrying bags for superior people. But when bitterness went out of my heart, I found that a Red Cap often touches people's lives when they need it most. So many folks who travel are very lonely; maybe they're on a sad journey, or they're suffering from great disappointment, or they're afraid in a big strange city. Sometimes I'm the last one to say 'goodnight' to a person who is dreading the night. But I had to learn all this after I got the bitterness out of my heart—and let God's love come in."

Born nearly fifty years ago, Ralston spent his childhood in Panama. When the boy was thirteen his father died, "and I had to jump into his shoes and take care of my mother, two brothers and two sisters."

Life was neither easy nor happy. Work brought low wages. Sundays, young Ralston attended church, perfunctorily, partly because there was nothing else to do in the days before radio, TV and movies. "My folks weren't pious people, yet you could say I was brought up in the church. But it didn't mean anything to me."

The United States! That seemed the solution to all the needs. "On March 15, 1917, we sold what little we had and came to New York City. But I found I was still dissatisfied. I discovered that everyone was interested in a fine place to live and good clothes to wear. So I wanted these same things. The church went out the window for me —I was going to choose my own course and paddle my own canoe. But the paddling was upstream and mighty difficult. After World War I jobs were scarce and an uneducated young Negro didn't land work that made him rich very fast. Time came when I was lucky to get a job at all."

Then there came a day which changed his life. Young's niece attended church and Sunday School regularly and sometimes a woman from the church would drive the girl home. One Sunday Ralston met this woman, whose dynamic personality fairly radiated joy. She invited Ralston to church and the next Sunday he went. And again the next.

"The third Sunday morning," Mr. Young remembers it well, "the preacher said that God loved *me*. He said it in such a way that I really believed it. This love surged right through me and washed out the bitterness. Now after eighteen years the feeling is just as alive as it was that morning, and the meaning is much deeper. After that Sunday I began to see my job in a new light.

"Soon I realized that I could do more than carry people's bags. I could help carry things they couldn't pack into bags—fears, bewilderments, disappointments. I've loaned money to people I've never seen before and I've telephoned messages to the kinfolks of others. And I discovered that one day a week wasn't enough to give to the Lord's work. I had to live it seven days a week. That's what led to Track 13."

In Grand Central Station "Track 13" has a special meaning among the railroad men. It designates the track on which commuters' coaches stand through the lull period of the day to be cleaned out and made ready for the evening rush. But everyone connected with Grand Central knows that the first empty coach on Track 13 is the place where Red Cap No. 42 holds a meeting at twelve noon on Mondays, Wednesdays and Fridays.

"It's not a prayer meeting," Mr. Young explains, "not in the usual sense. It's a fellowship. It doesn't take the place of church but as we sit there in the dim light—we sit in the light of Spirit instead of a Mazda bulb—we talk about whatever we need help with.

"There may be ten people there, or twenty. You never know who: sometimes women of great wealth who don't find joy in their money; sometimes businessmen who are too rushed or too proud to make a place for God in their weekly schedules; sometimes people who have been helped while passing through this station; sometimes down-and-outs who found they were welcome here when they weren't welcome in fashionable places. We have all kinds of people at twelve noon on Track 13."

It was not by chance that the Harmon Foundation exhibit of portraits of outstanding American Negroes came into being. These thirty-five canvases of such American scientists as George Washington Carver and Charles Drew, diplomat Ralph Bunche, social reformer Mary Church Terrell, sculptor Richmond Barté, Major William Campbell and others are on frequent display across the country. Back of them is the experience of the artist, a quick-moving, white-haired woman now nearing her seventies, a veritable charge of dynamite done up in a firecracker-size package—Betsy Graves Reyneau. Mrs. Reyneau lives in a Brooklyn apartment overlooking the East River. On the walls of her living room are one or two original portraits and several photographic reproductions of others. On an easel there is likely to be a partly finished canvas of the current portrait upon which she is working. For none of these pictures has Mrs. Reyneau ever accepted any money.

For eight years preceding and during World War II Betsy Graves

Reyneau lived in Europe. She was in Italy when Mussolini was hung. She was in England during the blitz and in France during the days of the underground. "Everywhere life was full of terror and horror. Fascism—under whatever name it paraded—was making life valueless. A person was worth nothing. And when people are worthless, what is there of value left in the world?" Mrs. Reyneau became firmly convinced that in a world going to pieces there was no place and no time for dabbling in art. So she packed away her brushes forever—she thought.

Then Mrs. Reyneau came home. Back to the United States. Back to democracy. Back to a Way of Life that a war had just been fought to preserve. And the first place she visited was Coral Gables, Florida. Old friends met her at the railway station. In their excitement at seeing each other again they all stood in the waiting room and talked —all of them at once.

Then the artist looked down at the bench against which she was leaning and right under her hand were the words "FOR WHITES ONLY."

"I pulled my hand away as if it had suddenly been burned," said Mrs. Reyneau, "and I turned on those girls and I said, 'What are you doing about this?'"

The women didn't get the point and asked what she meant.

"Do you mean you don't even see these signs?" she questioned them.

"Oh, that," they replied relieved. "You can't do anything about that."

"Who says you can't?" snapped Mrs. Reyneau. (She probably said, "The hell you can't" because Betsy Graves Reyneau is at times explosive in the face of smugness.)

The next day her friends gave a beautiful tea in Mrs. Reyneau's honor. The literary and social elite were there—beautiful women who talked about equally beautiful subjects, flowers, pictures, books, culture. Then somehow the conversation turned to race relations.

"That was an ugly topic for these women, but I got the feeling it was distasteful conversation rather than awful reality for them. To this day I don't know what I said," and Mrs. Reyneau chuckled at the memory, "but I'm sure it was something about finding in the United States a worse form of fascism than existed in Europe. Suddenly the air was so hot I knew something would soon scorch so I decided I had better get out. Which I did—right out the back door into a lovely garden. And there, sitting on a stone wall at the back of the garden, was the gardener's son. He had a beautiful face, and a look in his eyes—I felt he was trying to see beyond the horizon which shut off part of the world to him. The look went right through me. Suddenly my fingers ached for my brushes and I knew right then that I would have to take up the Battle of the Brush."

Mrs. Reyneau thinks she went back into the house and "acted like a lady" until the guests were gone.

This picture of the gardener's son became the first portrait in the collection. The one which has brought the artist the greatest fame is the portrait of Dr. George Washington Carver, famed for his endless research on peanuts. His picture now hangs in the National Museum in Washington, D.C., Dr. Carver being the only Negro American so honored. It presents the scientist working with the amaryllis, his favorite flower and the object of a large amount of loving experimentation.

"That picture shows Dr. Carver exactly as he looked when he was deep in his research—except for one thing," Mrs. Reyneau corrected. "He made his own aprons out of flour sacks and across the one he was wearing could plainly be seen in faded purple letters, 'Pillsbury's Best.' I just decided the flour was good enough not to need the extra advertising so I left out the printing on the apron."

At one time Mrs. Reyneau had despaired of getting the scientist's permission to paint his portrait. Because the urge to paint Dr. Carver had been growing upon her she had gone to his home to talk to him about the possibility of his sitting for the picture. This visit was just three months before his death and she found him too ill to see her. However, she talked with his secretary who in turn talked to Dr. Carver, but he sent back word that he was too tired, and that he needed what little strength he had to complete some of his experiments. Besides, he sent word to her, he was weary of darkies-at-the-end-of-a-dusty-road pictures and didn't want to help perpetuate that idea.

The artist was disappointed but she respected the scientist's point of view and did not push her request. Then the next day she received word that Dr. Carver wanted to see her so she hurried back to his humble home. There the ailing man was waiting for her.

"Do you know," he said a bit sheepishly, "yesterday as you were leaving I saw you through the crack in the opened door and I was sure you'd never paint a dusty-road picture."

There was no formal posing for the portrait. Mrs. Reyneau painted him as he worked which could be for only very short periods at a time. So the artist turned botanist and studied the amaryllis and painted the flowers in detail. When the portrait was finished Dr. Carver was so pleased with it that he kept it in his home and told several of his friends that it was his favorite picture of himself. After his death it was moved to the National Museum and with elaborate unveiling ceremonies became part of the permanent collection of outstanding Americans.

Over the mantel in her study Mrs. Reyneau has the portrait of Mrs. Mary Church Terrell who worked for more than half a century in Washington trying to improve living conditions for her people and ease the strains of segregation. "There's a woman who knew what trouble you can get into when you live for a cause," said the artist. "It isn't hard to get into trouble; I've been in jail myself four times just because of ideas." And as one looks at this woman waging a Battle with the Brush he knows that her impact on race relations is more powerful than her ninety-pound body might suggest.

After Mrs. Reyneau's portraits had hung for a week in the Milwaukee Vocational School, the largest school of its kind in the world, a Polish boy came to the principal with a request. "Do you think," he asked, "that you could get some pictures of Polish Americans who have contributed something to the United States? There ought to be some that we could be as proud of as we are our Negroes."

All efforts to ease the tensions between races are not as dramatic as the work of Mrs. Reyneau; but whether spectacular or unobtrusive, each action indicates the willingness of some individual or some group to step out and take the initiative. Someone *wills* better race relations.

Index

Aaron, Hank, 159
Abolition societies, 18
Abrams, Charles, 99
Academic standards, integration and, 123–24
Adams, John, 20
Advertising, 72, 156–57
Agriculture, changed methods in, 52
  one-crop farming, 212
Air travel, integrated, 147
Alabama, University of, 131–32, 133, 152
Alcoholic Beverage Control Board, 73
All God's Chillun Got Wings, 160
Amalgamated Clothing Workers, 63
American Airlines, 72
American Association of University Women, 231–32
American Bar Association, 138
American Board of Pediatrics, 138
American Board of Surgeons, 138
American Dilemma, An (Myrdal), 202
American Federation of Labor, 59, 63, 73
American Friends Service Committee, 73, 91
American Indians, citizenship for, 42–43

discrimination against, 8–9, 25–26, 73
franchise extended to, 44
integration of, 78
relocation of, 8
in unskilled labor pool, 51
in World War II, 150–51
American Jewish Committee, 181
American Medical Association, 138
American Missionary Association, 96
American Society of Biological Chemists, 138
Americanization, 77–78
Amherst College, 134
Anastasi and Foley, 199–200
Anderson, Marian, 122, 160
Annapolis Naval Academy, 139
Anti-Defamation League of B'nai B'rith, 181, 182
Antidiscrimination laws, 24, 59–61, 62
Antioch College, 93
Apartheid, 225–26
Apprenticeship training programs, 63
Argo Corn Products plant, 67
Arkansas, integration in education in, 104–7, 115, 130
Armed services, desegregation of, 39, 111, 149–53
Armour and Company, 72
Armstrong, Louis, 160

241

Index

9470 037